CODIFYING CONTRACT LAW

Markets and the Law

Series Editor:
Geraint Howells, University of Manchester, UK

Series Advisory Board:
Stefan Grundmann – Humboldt University of Berlin, Germany, and European University Institute, Italy
Hans Micklitz – Bamberg University, Germany
James P. Nehf – Indiana University, USA
Iain Ramsay – York University, Canada
Charles Rickett – University of Queensland, Australia
Reiner Schulze – Münster University, Germany
Jules Stuyck – Katholieke Universiteit Leuven, Belgium
Stephen Weatherill – University of Oxford, UK
Thomas Wilhelmsson – University of Helsinki, Finland

Markets and the Law is concerned with the way the law interacts with the market through regulation, self-regulation and the impact of private law regimes. It looks at the impact of regional and international organizations (e.g. EC and WTO) and many of the works adopt a comparative approach and/or appeal to an international audience. Examples of subjects covered include trade laws, intellectual property, sales law, insurance, consumer law, banking, financial markets, labour law, environmental law and social regulation affecting the market as well as competition law. The series includes texts covering a broad area, monographs on focused issues, and collections of essays dealing with particular themes.

Other titles in the series

The European Unfair Commercial Practices Directive
Impact, Enforcement Strategies and National Legal Systems
Edited by Willem van Boom, Amandine Garde and Orkun Akseli
ISBN 978 1 4724 2340 5

The Law and Economics of Enforcing European Consumer Law
A Comparative Analysis of Package Travel and Misleading Advertising
Franziska Weber
ISBN 978 1 4 7241 7046

The Organizational Contract
From Exchange to Long-Term Network Cooperation in European Contract Law
Edited by Stefan Grundmann, Fabrizio Cafaggi and Giuseppe Vettori
ISBN 978 1 4724 2124 1

Codifying Contract Law
International and Consumer Law Perspectives

Edited by

MARY KEYES
Griffith University, Australia

THERESE WILSON
Griffith University, Australia

LONDON AND NEW YORK

First published 2014 by Ashgate Publishing

Published 2016 by Routledge
2 Park Square, Milton Park, Abingdon, Oxon OX14 4RN
711 Third Avenue, New York, NY 10017, USA

Routledge is an imprint of the Taylor & Francis Group, an informa business

Copyright © Mary Keyes and Therese Wilson 2014

Mary Keyes and Therese Wilson have asserted their right under the Copyright, Designs and Patents Act, 1988, to be identified as the editors of this work.

All rights reserved. No part of this book may be reprinted or reproduced or utilised in any form or by any electronic, mechanical, or other means, now known or hereafter invented, including photocopying and recording, or in any information storage or retrieval system, without permission in writing from the publishers.

Notice:
Product or corporate names may be trademarks or registered trademarks, and are used only for identification and explanation without intent to infringe.

British Library Cataloguing in Publication Data
A catalogue record for this book is available from the British Library

The Library of Congress has cataloged the printed edition as follows:
Codifying contract law : international and consumer law perspectives / by Mary Keyes and Therese Wilson.
  pages cm.—(Markets and the law)
 Includes bibliographical references and index.
 ISBN 978-1-4724-1561-5 (hardback)
 1. Contracts—Codification. 2. Law--International unification. I. Keyes, Mary, editor. II. Wilson, Therese (Law professor), editor.
 K840.C63 2014
 346.02'2–dc23

2014019350

ISBN 9781472415615 (hbk)

Contents

List of Contributors	vii
Preface	ix

PART I   INTRODUCTION

1 Codifying Contract Law:
   Internationalization Imperatives and Regional Perspectives   3
   Mary Keyes and Therese Wilson

2 The Internationalization of Contract Law   15
   Mary Keyes

PART II   THE INTERNATIONALIZATION IMPERATIVES

3 Regional and Global Unification of Contract Law   39
   Ingeborg Schwenzer

4 The Challenges of Good Faith in Contract Law Codification   57
   Therese Wilson

PART III   REGIONAL PERSPECTIVES

5 Codification Mania and the Changing Nation State:
   A European Perspective   79
   Hans-W. Micklitz

6 Integrating Consumer Law into the Civil Code:
   A Japanese Attempt at Re-codification   107
   Hiroo Sono

7 The Government's Proposed Review of Australia's Contract Law:
   An Interim Positive Response   131
   Luke Nottage

8	The Partial Codification of Contract Law: Lessons from New Zealand *Rick Bigwood*	165
9	Codification and the American Discussion About How Judges Decide Cases *Richard Hyland*	205

Index   *219*

List of Contributors

Mary Keyes is a Professor of Law at Griffith Law School, Griffith University, Brisbane, Australia.

Ingeborg Schwenzer is a Professor of Private Law at the Faculty of Law at the University of Basel, Switzerland.

Therese Wilson is a Senior Lecturer in Law at Griffith Law School, Griffith University, Brisbane, Australia.

Hans-W. Micklitz is a Professor of Law and the Jean Monnet Fellow at the European University Institute, Florence, Italy.

Hiroo Sono is a Professor of Law at Hokkaido University, Japan.

Luke Nottage is a Professor of Law at the University of Sydney, Australia.

Rick Bigwood is a Professor of Law at Bond University, Gold Coast, Australia.

Richard Hyland is Distinguished Professor of Law at the Rutgers University Law School, Camden, New Jersey, USA.

Preface

This book arose out of a symposium held in Bali, Indonesia, in May 2013, at which the authors engaged in lively debate concerning the question of codifying contract law. As reflected in this book, the authors' viewpoints were many and varied, which made for wonderful discussions in Bali and, it is hoped, will provide the impetus for on-going debate and discussion for readers of this book.

We would like to sincerely thank all of the authors, not only for their contributions but also for their excellent company as we enjoyed together the Balinese hospitality of The Mansion, Ubud.

Thanks also to Griffith Law School for generously funding the symposium, and most particularly to the Griffith Law School Dean, Professor William Macneil and Griffith Law School Deputy Head Research, Professor Brad Sherman, for their support. Special thanks is due to the Griffith Law School Manager, Carol Ballard and her assistant, Madonna Adcock, for their hard work in making sure that everything ran smoothly in Bali.

Finally, we would like to say how much we have enjoyed working together on this project, having been friends and colleagues for some years now with the intention of combining efforts at some point, but never really seizing the opportunity until now. It has truly been a pleasure.

Mary Keyes and Therese Wilson

PART I
Introduction

Chapter 1
Codifying Contract Law: Internationalization Imperatives and Regional Perspectives

Mary Keyes and Therese Wilson

1 Introduction

On 22 March 2012 the Australian federal Attorney-General's Department released a discussion paper on reform of Australia's contract law,[1] and invited submissions.[2] This prompted a debate as to whether Australian contract law was in need of reform, as well as to the form which any such modification ought to take.[3] Many submissions considered the possibility of a codification or restatement of Australian contract law, citing such reasons as the need for greater certainty and predictability of Australian contract law, and internationalization of Australian contract law with a view, for example, to attracting international litigation and arbitration to Australia.[4]

---

1 Australian Attorney-General's Department, Improving Australia's Law and Justice Framework: A discussion paper to explore the scope for reforming Australian contract law (2012) ('Discussion Paper').

2 A number of these submissions are referred to in detail in Nottage, Chapter 7 in this collection.

3 There have been several previous proposals to codify Australian contract law. See particularly Joseph G Starke 'A Restatement of the Australian Law of Contract as a First Step Towards an Australian Uniform Contract Code' (1978) Australian Law Journal 234; Victorian Law Reform Commission, An Australian Contract Code, Discussion Paper No 27 (Victorian Law Reform Commission 1992); MP Ellinghaus and EW Wright, Models of Contract Law: An Empirical Evaluation of their Utility (Federation Press 2005). Since the chapters in this collection were completed, three Australian academics who have been enthusiastic proponents of codification have presented the Australian Attorney-General with a 'Draft Australian Law of Contract', in response to the Attorney-General's Discussion Paper. The Draft Australian Law of Contract claims to simplify and modernize the Australian law and to harmonize it with the law of other countries: MP Ellinghaus, D StL Kelly, EW Wright, 'A Draft Australian Law of Contract' (Newcastle Law School, Working Paper No 03.03.14, 2014, available at <http://papers.ssrn.com/sol3/papers.cfm?abstract_id=2403603> accessed 15 July 2014).

4 See generally <http://www.ag.gov.au/Consultations/Documents/Submissionstothe ReviewofAustralianContractLaw> accessed 15 July 2014.

Australia is an interesting case study for this discussion, as it is a common law country whose contract law is to be found primarily in case law alongside a myriad of statutes that might apply to particular categories of contract. The general body of contract law is largely unchanged from the English law inherited by Australia in the nineteenth century. It is almost universally accepted that there is room for clarification, refinement and improvement with respect to many aspects of Australian contract law,[5] and some academics and lawyers believe that the challenge of securing a place for Australian contract law in international trade litigation and arbitration also requires consideration.[6] Is codification an appropriate mechanism for addressing these concerns?

A code has been defined as:

> ... an instrument enacted by the legislature which forms the principal source of law on a particular topic. It aims to codify all leading rules derived from both judge-made and statutory law in a particular field ... it has an organizing and indexing role that an ordinary statute does not share.[7]

Whether such an instrument can function effectively within the context of common law methodology, or without causing law to become unnecessarily and unhelpfully rigid, are questions that have been raised by a number of common law scholars.[8]

Whether codification is a necessary or desirable step towards internationalization is another contested question. Skinner writes that:

---

5 These are comprehensively identified by Bigwood, in this collection, Chapter 8, text accompanying nn 6–15, with references. See also N Seddon, R Bigwood and M Ellinghaus, Cheshire and Fifoot Law of Contract (10th Australian edition, LexisNexis Butterworths 2012), xi; Andrew Stewart, 'What's Wrong With the Australian Law of Contract?' (2012) 29 Journal of Contract Law 74.

6 See, especially, Paul Finn, 'Internationalisation or isolation: The Australian cul de sac? The case of contract' in Elise Bant and Matthew Harding (eds) Exploring Private Law (Cambridge UP 2010), ch 2; Don Robertson, 'The International Harmonisation of Australian Contract Law' (2012) Journal of Contract Law 1. Although as a party to the United Nations Convention on Contracts for the International Sale of Goods ('CISG') Australia already has what might be called a 'partial' international contract law code that applies to contracts involving Australians and nationals from other signatory states, or that will apply where, under private international law rules, Australian law applies to a contract for the international sale of goods: see CISG, Art. 1(1)(a) and (b). The Attorney-General's Discussion Paper (n 1) followed a substantial review of the Australian legislative framework for international commercial arbitration, which led to reforms to the International Arbitration Act 1974 (Cth).

7 Catherine Skinner, 'Codification and the Common Law' (2009) 11(2) European Journal of Law Reform 225, 228.

8 Ibid. See generally discussion at 229–231.

With its disparate nature, the common law may be unfit for export. By failing to explore the possibilities of codification, common law jurisdictions could be missing an opportunity to make meaningful contributions to global legal development.[9]

This is a matter of some concern to a number of Australian lawyers[10] although others might argue that codification itself inhibits any legal development, let alone global legal development, and that the flexibility of the common law remains superior.[11]

Notwithstanding some common law resistance to codification, there are examples of legislation enacted in common law jurisdictions, including Australia, which come close to satisfying the definition of 'code' given above. Some of these statutes have contributed significantly both to improving the certainty and the logical development of an area of law. These statutes are examples of partial or sectoral codification, refining the law in its application to particular issues or sectors.[12] One example is the English Sale of Goods Act 1893, which Atiyah describes as a 'declaratory Act' in the sense of declaring the law on a particular subject matter.[13] While the Act specifically preserves the application of the common law and is in that sense not a code, the comprehensiveness of this legislation is said to have caused judges to focus on the language of the statute and its natural meaning, without applying pre-statute case law, thus breaking with traditional common law statutory interpretation methods.[14]

A more recent example is the UK Arbitration Act 1996 which aimed at being a clear statement of the English law of arbitration, to be interpreted by the courts without reference to pre-statute case law, drawing instead on the legislation's overall purpose.[15] In terms of the internationalization imperative that is often associated with recent codification projects, it has been noted that the UK Arbitration Act 1996 has:

---

9 Ibid, 226. See also Roy Goode, 'Insularity or Leadership? The Role of the United Kingdom in the Harmonisation of Commercial Law' (2001) 50 International and Comparative Law Quarterly 751.

10 See generally <http://www.ag.gov.au/Consultations/Documents/SubmissionstotheReviewofAustralianContractLaw> accessed 15 July 2014.

11 Skinner, 'Codification and the Common Law' (n 7), 228–231.

12 In relation to partial codification, see Bigwood in this collection, Chapter 8. In relation to sectoral codification, see Micklitz in this collection, Chapter 5.

13 Patrick Atiyah, 'Common Law and Statute Law' (1985) 48(1) The Modern Law Review 1, 16. The United Kingdom Sale of Goods Act is the basis of legislation of the same name enacted in all Australian states and territories: for example, Sale of Goods Act 1923 (NSW).

14 Discussed in Skinner, 'Codification and the Common Law' (n 7), 233, citing Lord Herschell in *Vagliano v The Bank of England* [1891] AC 107 at 144.

15 Ibid, 234, citing the House of Lords in *Lesotho Highlands Development Authority v Impregilo Spa and others* [2006] 1 AC 221.

... significantly enhanced London's attractiveness as a centre for national and international arbitration, which was one of its express purposes.[16]

In the United States, the Uniform Commercial Code has been described as a highly successful Code which has provided legal clarity while maintaining flexibility, and led to interpretation based on the purpose of the code and on drawing analogies with the principles on which it is based, rather than interpretation based on case law precedent. This is said to have been made possible by: its comprehensiveness as a Code; the direction contained in Article 1-103[17] to construe the code consistently with its underlying purposes, notwithstanding a preservation of common law and equitable principles where not inconsistent with the provisions of the code; and the extensive commentaries and guidelines that accompany its Articles.[18] This is a model worthy of consideration in any codification project in a common law jurisdiction.

Many of the questions and issues that arise with respect to codification of law are explored in this book. The book commences with a discussion on the internationalization imperative for codification of contract law. It then turns to regional issues, exploring firstly codification attempts in the European Union (EU), in Japan, and then issues relevant to codification in the common law jurisdictions of Australia, New Zealand and the United States. Codification in common law systems brings its own challenges, in the sense that whereas a Code is intended to provide the solution to any legal question related to its content without resort to outside legal sources, in a common law system case law precedent would always have to be relevant to at least the interpretation of the Code's provisions.

---

16   Ibid, 235. A similar purpose was a key motivation for recent amendments to the International Arbitration Act 1974 (Cth): Mr McLelland (Attorney-General), International Arbitration Bill 2010, Second Reading, Commonwealth of Australia, House of Representatives, Hansard, Wednesday 25 November 2009, p 12,790.

17   § 1-103. Construction of [Uniform Commercial Code] to Promote its Purposes and Policies: Applicability of Supplemental Principles of Law.

(a) [The Uniform Commercial Code] must be liberally construed and applied to promote its underlying purposes and policies, which are: (1) to simplify, clarify, and modernize the law governing commercial transactions; (2) to permit the continued expansion of commercial practices through custom, usage, and agreement of the parties; and (3) to make uniform the law among the various jurisdictions.

(b) Unless displaced by the particular provisions of [the Uniform Commercial Code], the principles of law and equity, including the law merchant and the law relative to capacity to contract, principal and agent, estoppel, fraud, misrepresentation, duress, coercion, mistake, bankruptcy, and other validating or invalidating cause supplement its provisions.

18   Atiyah, 'Common Law and Statute Law' (n 13), 27; Skinner, 'Codification and the Common Law' (n 7), 240, 245.

2 The Internationalization Imperative

The first chapter by Mary Keyes, 'The Internationalization of Contract Law', uses Australian contract law as an example of a system in need of internationalization, in the senses of ensuring the suitability and relevance of the law to a context in which many contracts have cross-border elements and particularly taking into account important legal developments which have occurred in response to that context in many other legal systems, including England and several Asian countries. Keyes describes an insularity and parochialism in both Australian contract law and Australian private international law that extends to legal education, which focuses almost exclusively on domestic contract law. Most law schools do not mandate the study of any aspect of internationalization of the law; for example, most curricula neglect the United Nations Convention on Contracts for the International Sale of Goods ('CISG'), to which Australia is party and which therefore forms part of Australia's contract law pertaining to international sale of goods contracts. Private international law is generally treated as a separate area of law from the several areas of private law, including contract. Keyes also describes Australian contract law as uncoordinated, noting in particular the confusing lack of integration between statute and common law, which may be exacerbated in international cases. The tendency of Australian courts to assert jurisdiction in international disputes is said to support the need for a less parochial Australian contract law. The chapter concludes that Australian contract law and private international law are not appropriate to a context in which cross-border transactions are common, and suggests that the reform of Australian law should be informed by recent international developments.

Schwenzer's chapter on 'Regional and Global Unification of Contract Law' takes the internationalization debate more broadly, beyond the Australian case study. It explores the need for a comprehensive, international contract law code for commercial contracts which expands upon the CISG and deals with areas not covered by it, such as contract validity. Schwenzer argues that such internationalization is important for commercial contracts given the significant increase in international trade in recent years. On the other hand, she argues that consumer contracts are best left to regulation by domestic legal systems. This raises an interesting question as to the appropriate scope of any codification project. Should it focus on international and commercial contracts, leaving international consumer contracts, and perhaps other international contracts in which one party is presumed to be more vulnerable than the other,[19] to be dealt with by a domestic contract law system chosen to govern any disputes arising under the contract? Is it not equally important that consumer contract law be clear and accessible across state boundaries? Is it not the case that consumer contracts are often the clearest examples of unequal bargaining power in contractual relationships? This is important because Schwenzer provides as an impetus for a uniform, international

---

19 For example, contracts of employment and insurance contracts.

commercial contract law code the problem of commercial contracts involving parties with unequal bargaining power. As she notes, this disparity in bargaining power might result in the law of the stronger party's jurisdiction being chosen to govern any dispute arising under the contract, often to the detriment of the weaker party.[20] Schwenzer's other concern relates to parties with equal bargaining power who may choose what they perceive to be a 'neutral' third law to govern the contract, not really understanding the nature and content of the law that they are choosing. She suggests that this kind of problem is best addressed by the development of uniform law.

The third chapter focusing on the question of internationalization of contract law is Wilson's 'The Challenges of Good Faith in Contract Law Codification'. Wilson asks whether, if internationalization is an important consideration in any codification project, this should include the incorporation of the good faith doctrine, as derived from civil law systems and subsequently incorporated into many international instruments,[21] into the contract law of a common law system. Wilson argues that part of any internationalization of Australian contract law should be the incorporation of the good faith doctrine, given that this is a doctrine well understood by lawyers in nation states with which Australia engages in international trade, both from civilian systems and other systems the law of which has been influenced by civil law codes. Good faith is a doctrine which many of Australia's trading partners might expect to find in the law governing their contract, to protect against unfair advantage-taking at the pre-contractual negotiation, contract performance and contract termination stages. The chapter seeks to address the concerns of common lawyers regarding the alleged 'uncertainty' of good faith, by noting that the concept is not so far removed from, and is no more or less difficult to clearly articulate than, an obligation to act with good conscience, which is the foundation of equitable doctrines, many of which apply to contracts. The chapter then goes on to note, however, that in seeking to internationalize a domestic body of law or to develop an international code, existing domestic legal systems may be resistant to foreign legal concepts. Those concepts become what Teubner calls 'legal irritants'[22] which will be re-moulded and re-shaped by the host system. The changes will not be a neat 'transplant' but an organic re-shaping through which, in the same way that languages develop, the law can develop to allow for international understandings. While the doctrine of good faith may change in the Australian context and this might also result

---

20 This is regulated in many legal systems, but not explicitly in Australia, by protective principles which limit the effect of choice of law agreements in contracts involving consumers and employees: for example, Rome I Regulation, Art.6 (consumers), Art.7 (insureds), Art.8 (employees).

21 For example, UNIDROIT Principles of International Commercial Contracts 2010, Art 1.7.

22 Gunther Teubner, 'Legal Irritants: Good Faith in British Law or How Unifying Law Ends Up in New Divergences' (1998) 61(1) The Modern Law Review 11.

in changes to the doctrine in other jurisdictions, it is argued that this may have a generally positive effect in the sense of enhancing commonalities in the development of international understandings of contract law.

3 Regional Perspectives on Contract Law Codification

Focusing on the EU and its predominantly civil law context, Micklitz raises concerns regarding the very nature of codification in a 'market state' environment in his chapter: 'Codification Mania and the Changing Nation State: A European Perspective'. Micklitz regards the development of civil codes in Europe as having been part of nineteenth-century nation building strategies, but argues that codification in the context of the new EU market state needs to be approached differently. Referring to the failed European Civil Code project in 2001, Micklitz argues that the project had been too deeply rooted in 'nation state thinking'. It is nation state thinking which focuses on traditional areas of private law such as contract and tort, using concepts such as freedom of contract to build capitalist economies. Developing private law at the EU level requires very different thinking, as the EU is not a nation state. Micklitz questions the very possibility of systematization and rationalization of law through any codification which is intended to operate beyond nation states, given that each state might be viewed as a subsystem governed by particular rationalities. The development of private law through a *market* state such as the EU as opposed to a nation state, should, according to Micklitz, be concerned with the development of law regarding 'economic transactions with a social outlook', with a view to building both an economic and a social order beyond national economies and societies. Micklitz also explores the idea that the systematization of an area of private law such as contract law may be redundant in the market state context and that there needs to be a move away from 'traditional private law' to 'new regulatory private law'. He notes that there are a number of market subsystems requiring their own distinct regulation or systematization, for example in the areas of energy, telecommunications and financial services. He also argues that consumer law should be kept separate from the private law regulation of commercial law, due to the focus of consumer law on the pre- and post-contractual stages, rather than on contract formation, revocability of offers and so forth. Certainly, the chapter calls upon us to consider a more sophisticated and nuanced approach to the codification or systematization of contract law, particularly where the proposed code is an international, 'market state' focused code rather than a national one.

Continuing to explore codification in a civil law, but national, context is Sono's chapter entitled 'Integrating Consumer Law into the Civil Code: A Japanese Attempt at Re-codification.' While Schwenzer and Micklitz oppose the incorporation of consumer law into contract law codes, at least where they are codes of an international nature, Sono considers the possibility of an integration of consumer law into the domestic Japanese Civil Code (JCC). He refers to the on-going reform of the JCC, in particular regarding contract law in Book 3. The impetus for reform is said to be the need for modernization, transparency and global harmonization. In keeping with all of these goals, there was a proposal to integrate the Japanese Consumer Contracts Act (CCA) and case law pertaining to consumer contracts into the JCC. This would serve the purpose of modernization through recognizing the consumer – and most importantly the vulnerable consumer – as a 'person' under the JCC in place of its traditional assumption that contracting parties were strong and rational. It would assist in transparency and clarity as the JCC would serve as a true Code, not needing to be supplemented by Acts such as the CCA or case law; and it would also assist with global harmonization. Sono describes how, under pressure from both business groups and consumer advocates who opposed the integration of consumer law into the JCC (the former due to concerns about paternalism and the latter due to concerns about difficulties in amending law as necessary once it became embedded in the Code) the full integration of the CCA into the JCC was abandoned. The proposal for reform of contract law under the JCC through the incorporation of consumer law principles is now confined to the inclusion of a duty of disclosure on business where silence can amount to 'fraud by silence'; consideration being given to unequal bargaining power in applying good faith provisions; a principle of 'gross disparity', similar to the equitable concept of unconscionability; and rules regarding the incorporation of standard terms that cause excessive disadvantage to one party. Sono concludes by suggesting that while the abandonment of a comprehensive codification of consumer law may be regarded as disappointing by some, it does leave consumer law with the space to develop through targeted legislation and case law, which may be an appropriate outcome for this area of law.

The focus of the book then shifts to the national, common law contexts of Australia, New Zealand and the United States.

Nottage's chapter is entitled 'The Government's Proposed Review of Australia's Contract Law: An Interim Positive Response'. Nottage notes the need for greater certainty, accessibility, harmonization and internationalization of Australian contract law, which he describes as confusing and complex. Contrary to the positions taken by Schwenzer and Micklitz in their chapters, Nottage does advocate for consumer issues to be part of any contract law codification. In the Australian context this is important because of the current confusion and uncertainty surrounding consumer law, not least because of the various and conflicting definitions of 'consumer' incorporated into the Australian Consumer Law.[23] Given the reliance by consumers on what Nottage refers to as 'background contract law for minimum standards of protection', the interests of consumers under consumer contracts would be well served by increasing the clarity and accessibility of consumer contract law. Nottage regards codification as an opportunity to improve, modernize and internationalize Australian contract law. The chapter concludes with suggestions for reform which do involve considerable

---

23 Australian Consumer Law 2010 (Cth).

fragmentation, rather than harmonization, of Australian contract law through distinguishing between international and domestic transactions and between commercial and consumer contracts. The suggestions are for a 'opt-in' Restatement entitled 'Principles of Australian Contract Law' which would apply to domestic commercial contracts; an 'opt-in' to the UNIDROIT Principles of International Commercial Contracts which would apply to international commercial contracts; and an 'opt-in' to the Common European Sales Law model which would apply to international consumer contracts.

Turning to New Zealand, Bigwood in his chapter, 'The Partial Codification of Contract Law: Lessons from New Zealand' provides a very detailed and comprehensive discussion and analysis of the partial codification of New Zealand's contract law, and its interpretation and application by the courts. In doing so, Bigwood focuses on two pieces of legislation which represent a partial codification of New Zealand contract law: the Contractual Mistakes Act 1977 and the Contractual Remedies Act 1979. These Acts confer discretionary powers upon the courts to grant relief and authorize contract variations, as part of what Bigwood describes as a 'piecemeal response' to particular areas of contract law regarded as performing unsatisfactorily in practice. The broad judicial discretion provided by the Acts is said to be an attempt to solve some of the practical problems of codification, that is, the rigidity or inflexibility that might prevent justice being done in individual cases. Accordingly, Bigwood argues, the New Zealand Acts do not actually provide any greater certainty or predictability than previously existed under New Zealand's common law of contracts. Bigwood does note, however, that pursuing a partial codification of contract law focused only on particular issues may be an appropriate model of codification to follow for Australia. He describes the partial codification in New Zealand as generally successful, although he notes that it can add to complexity rather than reduce it, due to a fragmentation of the law. The partial codification he describes, however, will not amount to a comprehensive statement of even the particular issues at hand, as it leaves considerable scope for judicial interpretation and discretion. This might of course be overcome by following the Uniform Commercial Code model whereby judicial discretion is directed towards purposive interpretation and analogizing on the basis of Code provisions, with the benefit of extensive commentary and guidelines.[24] This chapter includes a brief discussion of the British Columbia (BC) Law Institute's 2011 report on Proposals for Unfair Contracts Relief, itself based on an abandoned project of the New Zealand Law Commission. As for the New Zealand partial codes, Bigwood suggests that the BC Law Institute's attempt partially to codify 'fairness-based doctrines of contract law underscores just how difficult it can be to avoid unintended ... consequences' in reforming contract law. Bigwood acknowledges that there are problems with Australian domestic contract law, however he describes perceptions of deficiencies from time to time as 'experiential and perspectival'. He describes current Australian contract law

---

24 Skinner, 'Codification and the Common Law' (n 7), 240, 245.

as 'merely impoverished or deficient in isolated and relatively minor respects'. He is certainly opposed to the 'Herculean task' of codification of Australian contract law, beyond some partial codification, for what in his view is likely to be a minimal return.

The United States' Uniform Commercial Code is considered in Hyland's chapter on 'Codification and the American Discussion About How Judges Decide Cases'. Hyland is clearly in favour of the common law method of gradual development of the law principally by the judiciary, rather than a law imposed through codification or legislation, as the former is a method most likely to 'discover and apply' customary norms developed by people over time, rather than impose laws constructed from 'above'. Hyland draws on legal realism to note that even statutes and codes need to be interpreted by judges, so – like Bigwood – he takes the view that codification will not in any event achieve the goal of predictability and certainty. He asserts that each case will be decided by a judge on its merits, not by strictly applying legal rules to a set of facts. Hyland describes the Uniform Commercial Code as developed by legal realist, Karl Llewellyn, as merely a 'source of new questions for the judge to ask to assist in gathering all relevant considerations before deciding the case'. Hyland does, however, suggest that a well-drafted code such as the Uniform Commercial Code can make a number of positive contributions to an area of law through the guidance that it provides to judicial decision-makers. These include assisting judges to make economically rational decisions and decisions which give deference where it is considered appropriate to such frameworks as legal feminism, critical race theory and political theory. Hyland notes that through the development of the considerations and criteria that are set out in a code, judicial consideration of relevant factors and the elimination of undesirable influences is facilitated. He also points out that while codification attempts are often hindered by concerns about a lack of consensus on the appropriate legal rule, this is not necessarily fatal, identifying examples both from the CISG and the Uniform Commercial Code in which lawmakers incorporated two incompatible principles.

4 Conclusion

This book undoubtedly raises more questions than it answers with regard to the codification of contract law generally, and in the Australian context in particular. These include:

1. Will a codification of contract law lead to a rigidity and inflexibility that will prevent justice being done in given cases?
2. If not, will the judicial discretion that will continue to exist undermine any possible gains in clarity, predictability and accessibility of the law sought to be achieved through the codification process?

3. Is internationalization (alongside modernization) an important aspect of codification, or will attempts to internationalize national laws be met with resistance, the foreign matter acting as a 'legal irritant' which will not be maintained in its current form within the host system?
4. If so, is there a case to be made in any event for greater cross-pollination of legal irritants in an effort to achieve greater international harmonization of contract law?
5. Particularly where codes are intended to have international application, is it inappropriate to seek to systematize a 'traditional private law' area such as contract law, rather than develop new order private regulation which focuses on regulation of particular sectors as part of a 'new regulatory private law'?
6. Should the regulation of both commercial contracts and consumer contracts be provided for within single codes or are the areas so different as to require separate codes?
7. Are consumer contracts capable of being regulated under international codes or are they best regulated under domestic laws or codes? If the latter, how are those laws or codes to be applied in cross-border disputes?
8. Is a partial codification of contract law, focused on particular areas of concern, preferable to a comprehensive codification, notwithstanding that this may increase rather than reduce fragmentation of contract law?

A range of different and contradictory answers to these questions will be found within the pages of this book, hopefully encouraging much fruitful debate and discussion. Although, at the time of writing this chapter, political interest in the reform of Australian contract law appeared to have waned, the debate which was sparked by the Discussion Paper[25] has had the effect of revitalizing interest both from the profession and the academy in the importance of contract law, both domestically and internationally.

---

25 Discussion Paper (n 1).

Chapter 2

The Internationalization of Contract Law

Mary Keyes

1 Introduction

Australian contract and private international law have hardly adapted to the increasing frequency and volume of international transactions. The Australian law applicable to international contracts is outdated, uncoordinated and parochial, and has become isolated from important international developments, including harmonization and the convergence of contract laws. These two bodies of law, independently and in concert, are less effective, fair and coherent than they ought to be. Internationalization and harmonization were among the catalysts identified as indicating the possible need for the reform of Australian contract law.[1] In this chapter, I suggest that both Australian contract and private international law are in need of renovation,[2] particularly taking into account the phenomenon of cross-border agreements.

2 Contract Law

Australian contract law retains a local focus, in which agreements with international elements as well as international developments affecting contracts are largely neglected. It is generally assumed that contracts are localized within Australia, and that contract disputes are resolved exclusively by Australian courts applying Australian law. Of course, this no longer reflects the reality that many Australian consumers, employees and firms regularly engage in international transactions,

---

1 Australian Government, Attorney-General's Department, Improving Australia's Law and Justice Framework: A discussion paper to explore the scope for reforming Australian contract law (Commonwealth of Australia 2012) 6 (referred to as Discussion Paper).

2 In April 2012, the Standing Council on Law and Justice determined to establish a working group to consider whether 'harmonization of jurisdictional, choice of court and choice of law rules would deliver worthwhile micro-economic benefits for the community': Communiqué, 12–13 April 2012. This project was in progress as at July 2014.

and that disputes may never result in litigation.³ Australian contract law has been very slow to recognize these changes.⁴

Australian private law, including contract law, is founded on classical English common law and English cases remain influential in Australia. This is a source of exasperation for some scholars.⁵ The authors of one treatise, itself a local version of a classic English work, declare that 'deference to English decisions continues to be an inhibiting and distorting element in the development of Australian contract law'.⁶ In the late 1980s,⁷ it was suggested that a distinctive Australian version of contract law had begun to emerge.⁸ A small but enthusiastic number of judges and scholars lauded the development of this variant, the features of which were said to include more frequent reference to foreign courts other than those of England,⁹ the development of unconscionability¹⁰ and the enactment of peculiar legislation.¹¹

---

3 Nor does it account for the propensity of Australian parliaments to enact legislation which differs from that of other Australian jurisdictions. This is not a new phenomenon, but it may be becoming more significant, given that cross-border contracting within Australia appears to be increasing.

4 They are referred to repeatedly in the Discussion Paper (n 1).

5 This may not be entirely justified in the case of international contracts. Many studies have shown that English law is commonly chosen in international contracts: Stefan Vogenauer, 'Regulatory Competition through Choice of Contract Law and Choice of Forum in Europe: Theory and Evidence' (2013) 21 European Review of Private Law 13.

6 N Seddon, R Bigwood and M Ellinghaus, Cheshire and Fifoot's Law of Contract (10th Australian ed, LexisNexis Butterworths 2012) 1256, giving as an example 'the now consummated flirtation of Australian law with the thoroughly useless invention of an "intermediate" or "innominate term"' (citing *Koompahtoo Local Aboriginal Land Council v Sanpine Pty Ltd* (2007) 233 CLR 115). See similarly MP Ellinghaus, 'An Australian Contract Law?' (1989) 2 Journal of Contract Law 13, 13–14.

7 The so-called nationalization of Australian law is usually associated with the abolition of appeals to the Privy Council in the Australia Acts 1986. The effect of this was that decisions of the English courts ceased to be binding in Australia: *Cook v Cook* (1986) 162 CLR 376, 390.

8 The character of this Australian species is widely agreed to be influenced by the prevalence of real property disputes in the Australian cases: for example, Seddon et al. (n 6) 1256; Andrew Stewart and John Carter, 'Commerce and Conscience: The High Court's Developing View of Contract' (1993) 23 University of Western Australia Law Review 49, 53. The necessarily local nature of such disputes may have contributed to the sense of contract law having an indigenous quality.

9 It was suggested that Australian courts referred more often to Canadian, New Zealand and United States decisions: Sir Anthony Mason, 'The Break with the Privy Council and the Internationalization of the Common Law', in Peter Cane (ed), Centenary Essays for the High Court of Australia (LexisNexis Butterworths 2004) 80–81.

10 Sir Anthony Mason, 'Australian Contract Law' (1988) 1 Journal of Contract Law 1, M Ellinghaus, 'Towards an Australian Contract Law' (1989) 2 Journal of Contract Law 13. See also Stewart and Carter (n 8) 63.

11 Anthony Mason, 'Future Directions in Australian Law' (1987) 13 Monash Law Review 149, 149. In this chapter, I refer in particular to the prohibition of misleading or

The first and third of these features may have caused Australian law to become less outward-looking. Smyth's study of the decisions of Australian Supreme Courts during the twentieth century shows that while there has been a substantial decrease in the citation of English authorities,[12] there has been no increase in reference to authorities of other foreign countries.[13] The decline in citation of English authorities has therefore led to fewer references to foreign authorities. Similarly, legislation has the unfortunate tendency in common law systems to emphasize the local nature of law,[14] as discussed in further detail below.[15]

The debate about whether there is, and ought to be, an unique Australian version of contract law may be of historical interest,[16] but insularity is hardly a commendable virtue when many agreements have cross-border elements.[17] It seems obvious that 'there is very little in a legal system which could be characterized as a distinctive feature immune against influences coming from outside'.[18] Law-makers should instead consider the benefits of harmonization, modernization and convergence of laws *where that would improve the existing law*. International consensus is already well-established in conventions, model

---

deceptive conduct, first enacted in section 52 of the Trade Practices Act 1974 (Cth), now contained in section 18 of the Australian Consumer Law 2010.

12   He found that citation of British cases in the state Supreme Courts declined from '68.5 per in 1915 to 15.3 per cent in 2005': Russell Smyth, 'Citations of Foreign Decisions in Australian State Supreme Courts Over the Course of the Twentieth Century: An Empirical Analysis' (2008) 22 Temple International and Comparative Law Journal 409, 418.

13   Smyth found that citation of authorities from non-British courts remained throughout the twentieth century 'consistently low ... hovering between 2 and 4 per cent of total citations with no observable upwards or downwards trends': ibid, 418.

14   Christopher Bisping, 'Avoid the Statutist Trap: The International Scope of the Consumer Credit Act' (2012) 1 Journal of Private International Law 35; Mary Keyes, 'Statutes, Choice of Law, and the Role of Forum Choice' (2008) 4 Journal of Private International Law 1. Dietrich makes the same point in the context of tort law: Joachim Dietrich, 'Teaching Torts in the Age of Statutes and Globalisation' (2010) 18 Torts Law Journal 141, 144–146.

15   Text to nn 98–99.

16   See Harold Gutteridge, Comparative Law (Cambridge UP 1949) 157–158. According to Basedow, 'It was widely assumed throughout the 19th and in part of the 20th century that the national law gives expression to national preferences...that it is deeply rooted in the national character.': Jürgen Basedow, 'The gradual emergence of European private law' in Talia Einhorn and Kurt Siehr (eds), Intercontinental Cooperation through Private International Law: Essays in Memory of Peter E Nygh (TMC Asser Press 2004) 4.

17   While other areas of civil obligations such as equity are beyond the scope of this chapter, it has been suggested that Australian law has tended to isolationism in these areas too: M. Kirby, 'Overcoming Equity's Australian Isolationism' (2009) 3 Journal of Equity 1; Paul Finn, 'Internationalization or Isolation: the Australian cul de sac? The case of contract law' in Elise Bant and Matthew Harding (eds), Exploring Private Law (Cambridge UP 2010) 47.

18   Basedow (n 16) 6.

laws and principles, including the United Nations Convention on Contracts for the International Sale of Goods[19] and the UNIDROIT Principles of International Commercial Contracts.[20]

Finn recently observed with regret that the 'influence of the international upon [Australian contract law] is slight'.[21] The majority of Australian scholars, courts, practitioners and legislatures give little attention to internationalization generally and its effect on contracts specifically.[22] The Priestley 11 Prescribed Areas of Knowledge,[23] which must be studied in order to qualify for admission to the Australian legal profession and therefore are highly influential in the design of law school curricula, include contract law but make no mention of international or comparative law. Most works on contract note briefly in their opening chapters that internationalization affects contract law, but otherwise the topic is given little detailed attention.[24] Some books include reference to the contract law of other countries, most of which are common law systems.[25] The value of this is not perfectly obvious. Willmott et al. state that the reason for including references to foreign law is that it is 'increasingly important for the modern lawyer to become at least acquainted with areas of divergence in the law

---

19   Referred to in this chapter as 'the CISG'.

20   Referred to as 'the UNIDROIT Principles'. In this chapter, references are to the 2010 version of the Principles.

21   Finn, 'Internationalization or isolation' (n 17) 65.

22   There are some signs that this is very gradually changing. See, in particular, Finn, ibid; Paul Finn, 'The UNIDROIT Principles: An Australian Perspective' (2010) 17 Australian International Law Journal 193; James Allsop, 'Some Reflections on the Sources of our Law', Address to the Supreme Court of Western Australia Judges' Conference, 18 August 2012; Don Robertson, 'The International Harmonisation of Australian Contract Law' (2012) 29 Journal of Contract Law 1 and Don Robertson, 'Long-Term Relational Contracts and the UNIDROIT Principles of International Commercial Contracts' (2010) 17 Australian International Law Journal 185. Of the Australian contract books, Willmott et al. deserves special recognition for its coverage of international aspects of contract law: Lindy Willmott, Sharon Christensen, Des Butler and Bill Dixon, Contract Law (4th ed, Oxford UP 2013).

23   The 11 Prescribed Areas of Knowledge were determined in 1992 by the Consultative Committee of State and Territory Law Admitting Authorities, chaired by Justice Priestley.

24   Jeannie Paterson, Andrew Robertson and Arlen Duke, Principles of Contract Law (4th ed, Lawbook Co 2012) 36; JW Carter, Elisabeth Peden and GJ Tolhurst, Contract Law in Australia (5th ed, LexisNexis Butterworths 2007) 18–20. Willmott et al. includes a separate chapter on international contracts: (n 22) ch 28.

25   Willmott et al. refer at the end of each chapter to the relevant laws of the United States and in New Zealand: ibid. The first edition of this book also included discussion of comparative Japanese law, but that has not been included in the three subsequent editions: Willmott et al. (n 22). Similarly, Clarke and Clarke include references to Indian and Chinese domestic contract law which is interspersed with their exposition of the Australian law: Philip Clarke and Julie Clarke, Contract Law: Commentaries, Cases and Perspectives (2nd ed, Oxford UP 2012).

of other jurisdictions'.²⁶ Clarke and Clarke's justification is that because India and China are important trading nations 'it will be advantageous for Australian lawyers to have some familiarity with the commercial law of those countries'.²⁷ It would be more practically useful to explain the relevance of foreign laws according to choice of law rules, but this is rarely discussed in contract books in any detail.²⁸ Although there can be no conflict of laws within Australia so far as the common law is concerned,²⁹ there is a diversity in statutory regimes which affect many different aspects of contract law.³⁰ While those differences are often noted, the textbooks scarcely address how those differences are resolved in cross-border cases.

The Australian law applicable to contract is an uncoordinated amalgam of common law contract rules and equitable principles, which overlap to a considerable degree with legislation and other areas of law, including tort and restitution. The inter-relation between these areas is obscure, particularly in an adversarial legal system, and this renders the law complex and uncertain in its effects. In this chapter, I focus on the impact of statute in international litigation; in particular, upon the statutory prohibition of misleading or deceptive conduct, and the state and territory legislation which gives effect to the United Nations Convention on Contracts for the International Sale of Goods. These examples demonstrate the limited integration of statute with the common law of contract,³¹ as well as serious problems in the treatment of cross-border contracts in Australian litigation.

---

26 Willmott et al. (n 22) 12.

27 Clarke and Clarke (n 25) 20. This book notes that the Indian Contract legislation is an attempt to codify contract law, undertaken by English lawyers in the nineteenth century: ibid 21. Its possible value as a model for codifying Australian law seems not to have been considered by the authors.

28 Willmott et al. includes a discussion of private international law: Willmott et al. (n 22) 999–1004. Cases which mainly concern private international law are cited in Australian books in the context of explaining domestic contract law, usually without noting the relevance of international elements of the case. For example, *Brinkibon Ltd v Stahag Stahl und Stahlwarenhandelsgesellschaft mbH* [1983] 2 AC 34 (cited in relation to the application of the postal rule to communications technology), *James Miller & Partners Ltd v Whitworth Estates (Manchester) Ltd* [1970] AC 583 (cited in relation to contractual interpretation) and *Vita Food Products v Unus Shipping* [1939] AC 277 (cited in the context of illegality).

29 *Lange v Australian Broadcasting Corporation* (1997) 189 CLR 520, 563 ('There is but one common law in Australia').

30 For example, legislation in three States modifies the common law rules relevant to the consequences of frustration: Frustrated Contracts Act 1978 (NSW), Frustrated Contracts Act 1988 (SA), Fair Trading Act 1999 (Vic), part 2C.

31 The 'continuing segregation of the common law from statutory influence' has been likened to the lack of integration between common law and equity: Paul Finn, 'Statutes and the common law', in Suzanne Corcoran and Stephen Bottomley, Interpreting Statutes (Federation Press 2005) 62–63.

Misleading or Deceptive Conduct

The most significant Australian legislative innovation affecting contract law is the prohibition of misleading or deceptive conduct in trade or commerce, which is now found in s 18(1) of the Australian Consumer Law.[32] This is usually regarded as a statutory version of misrepresentation, but it has not been integrated in any meaningful way with the common law.[33] Until recently,[34] misleading conduct was considered to be much easier to establish than misrepresentation, and to provide a better range of remedies, and therefore it was pleaded in many commercial cases, either in preference to misrepresentation or as an alternative to it. Although contained within legislation the main purpose of which is consumer protection, this provision has been interpreted as applying also to commercial transactions and most litigation involving claims of misleading conduct is between commercial parties. It is commonly pleaded in international litigation in Australian courts.

The legislative prohibition of misleading conduct was first enacted in 1974, and it has been prominent in international commercial litigation for decades. The legislation in which it was formerly contained did not clearly indicate its

---

32 This provision was originally contained in the Trade Practices Act 1974 (Cth), s 52(1). For constitutional reasons, this provision only applied to the conduct of corporations. It was supplemented by the Fair Trading legislation of the States and Territories, which extended the prohibition to 'persons'. The Australian Consumer Law is intended to operate as uniform national legislation. Subsection 18(1) states that 'A person must not, in trade or commerce, engage in conduct that is misleading or deceptive or is likely to mislead or deceive.' To the extent that the Commonwealth legislation lacks constitutional foundation, legislation of the States and Territories supplements it, by enacting the Australian Consumer Law as part of the law of each jurisdiction: for example, Fair Trading Act 1987 (NSW), s 28(1). The remedies available for a breach of this provision are more generous than the remedies available for misrepresentation: for example, Australian Consumer Law 2010, ss 232 (injunctions), 236 (damages), 237 (compensation).

33 A majority of the High Court of Australia stated that 'tools of analysis drawn from the common law of deceit (misrepresentation and reliance) ... may sometimes be helpful in identifying contravening conduct', but went on to insist that 'References to misrepresentation or reliance must not be permitted to obscure the need to identify...misleading or deceptive conduct': *Campbell v Backoffice Investments Pty Ltd* (2009) 238 CLR 304, 341. In *Google Inc v Australian Competition and Consumer Commission*, Hayne J went further, stating that use 'of the language of misrepresentation' to determine whether there had been a breach of section 52 was 'apt to distract and confuse': (2013) 249 CLR 435, [93].

34 Since 2004, the High Court has significantly limited the application of this prohibition in transactions involving sophisticated parties: see *Butcher v Lachlan Elder Realty Pty Ltd* (2004) 218 CLR 592. Parties of 'equal bargaining power and competence' to the party whose conduct is impugned are required to have regard to their own interests: *Miller & Associates Insurance Broking Pty Ltd v BMW Australia Finance Ltd* (2010) 241 CLR 357, 371.

intended application in international situations.[35] The position under the Australian Consumer Law, enacted in 2010, is no clearer.[36] A lawyer advising a foreign firm could be excused for assuming that legislation with the word 'Consumer' in the title did not apply to commercial transactions, although Australian courts have interpreted it to have such an effect.

The Convention on Contracts for the International Sale of Goods

The United Nations Convention on Contracts for the International Sale of Goods has had limited impact in Australia. Australia acceded to this Convention in 1988, and it is given direct effect by legislation of every State and Territory.[37] Australian resistance to the Convention is infamous. The CISG is infrequently taught in compulsory subjects,[38] and contract texts do not refer to it in detail.[39] It has had little effect on the rules applicable to domestic contracts.[40] Most practitioners are unaware of its provisions; to the extent that they are aware of the existence of the

---

35 The legislation explicitly gave Parts IVA and V of the legislation an extraterritorial effect, in that is stated that those parts applied to conduct outside Australia of Australian citizens and ordinary residents, and Australian companies, although claims for damages against such persons could only be maintained with the written consent of the Minister: Trade Practices Act 1974 (Cth), s 5(1), (3). Subsection 52(1) was in Part V. Misleading conduct was analogized to misrepresentation in this context, in that a statement that was made by a person outside Australia to a person in Australia, where the statement was intended to be, and was, acted upon, was taken to have occurred in Australia: *Sydbank Soenderjylland A/S v Bannerton Holdings Pty Ltd* (1996) 68 FCR 539, applying *Diamond v Bank of London and Montreal Ltd* [1979] 1 QB 333. The application of other parts of the Trade Practices Act was not clear. In *Borch v Answer Products*, Holmes J stated in obiter that 'both from first principles and by inference from the absence of an equivalent provision [to s 5(1)], s 75AD was incapable of having effect outside the jurisdiction': [2000] QSC 379, para 22.

36 The Australian Consumer Law is schedule 2 to the Competition and Consumer Act 2010 (Cth). Section 5 of that Act, which applies to the Australian Consumer Law, is the same as section 5 of the Trade Practices Act 1974 (Cth) (described ibid). The State and Territory legislation which gives the Australian Consumer Law effect in each State and Territory, contains scope provisions which are similar but not identical to section 5: for example, Fair Trading Act 1987 (NSW) s 32.

37 Sale of Goods (Vienna Convention) Act 1986 (NSW), and legislation of the same name in all the Australian States and Territories.

38 Schwenzer and Kee report that this is common in member states of the CISG, the main exception being China, where it is part of the compulsory curriculum: Ingeborg Schwenzer and Christopher Kee, 'International Sales Law – The Actual Practice' (2011) 29 Penn State International Law Review 425, 438–439.

39 Seddon et al. refer to the CISG only once: Seddon et al. (n 6) 124.

40 Carter et al. predicted that the CISG 'may lead to a reconsideration of some aspects of our (domestic) law', but then state that the CISG is beyond the scope of their book: (n 24) 20. For an unusual exception, see Kirby J in *Koompahtoo Local Aboriginal*

Convention, they often expressly exclude its application.⁴¹ The CISG is seldom referred to by courts even in cases in which it is clearly applicable.⁴²

The prospect that the parties will use dispute resolution other than litigation, including arbitration, to resolve contract disputes is rarely addressed in the context of contract law.⁴³ One of the consequences of this is that the development and acceptance of non-state law internationally,⁴⁴ particularly in international arbitration, is hardly acknowledged, although there appears to be a growing awareness of and interest in the UNIDROIT Principles of International Commercial Contracts.⁴⁵

3 Private International Law

Like the law of contract, Australian private international law continues to demonstrate its English heritage,⁴⁶ and has remained unaffected by significant

---

Land Council v Sanpine Pty Ltd (2007) 233 CLR 115, 157 (noting that the CISG, like other sources of contract law, does not recognize the category of intermediate terms).

41   Luke Nottage, 'Who's Afraid of the Vienna Sales Convention (CISG)? A New Zealander's View from Australia and Japan' (2005) 36 Victoria University of Wellington Law Review 815, 816, 817, 836; Lisa Spagnolo, 'The Last Outpost: Automatic CISG Opt Outs, Misapplications and the Costs of Ignoring the Vienna Sales Convention for Australian Lawyers' (2009) 10 Melbourne Journal of International Law 141, 160.

42   Spagnolo, ibid, 159. Peter L Fitzgerald reports a similar lack of familiarity on the part of US lawyers and judges: 'The International Commercial Contracting Practices Survey Project: An Empirical Study of the Value and Utility of the United Nations Convention on the International Sale of Goods (CISG) and the UNIDROIT Principles of International Commercial Contracts to Practitioners, Jurists, and Legal Academics in the United States' (2009) 27 Journal of Law and Commerce 1.

43   The United Nations Convention on the Recognition and Enforcement of Foreign Arbitral Awards 1958 (referred to as the New York Convention) is discussed below, text to nn 70–72. Some texts do not refer to it at all – for example, Seddon et al. (n 6), Clarke and Clarke (n 25). It is referred to very briefly by Willmott et al. (who note, in the penultimate chapter, that it is commonly used in international commercial transactions) (n 24) 1004.

44   Australian contract law generally excludes non-state law as irrelevant, even in the domestic context. Suggestions that the Indigenous law of agreements should be integrated into Australian contract law (MP Ellinghaus, 'An Australian Contract Law?' (1989) 2 Journal of Contract Law 13, 20–28, 31–33) have mainly been ignored, if not dismissed: John Gava, 'An Australian Contract Law? A Reply' (1998) 12 Journal of Contract Law 242.

45   See, in particular, Finn, 'Internationalization or isolation?' (n 17), Finn, 'The UNIDROIT Principles' (n 22) and Robertson, 'Long-Term Relational Contracts' (n 22).

46   Pryles suggested that 'Perhaps in no subject did the Australian rules more closely correspond to the English rules than in private international law': Michael C Pryles, 'Internationalism in Australian Private International Law' (1989) 12 Sydney Law Review 96, 108.

international developments.[47] It is regarded as an aspect of domestic law,[48] and is considered in isolation from substantive areas of private law.[49] Accordingly, there is little direct coordination between contract and private international law. Private international law is compulsory in only one Australian law school,[50] and many Australian lawyers have never studied it.[51] In the context of the private international law relevant to contracts, foreign authorities[52] and international instruments[53] have had limited impact. As for contract law, the law is an uncoordinated amalgam of common law rules modified by statutory provisions, some of which give effect to international conventions. In the following sections, I briefly outline the principles of jurisdiction and choice of law relevant to international contract litigation. Accumulation of actions is permitted in Australian litigation and it is common for claimants to claim not only in contract but also in related areas, particularly tort

---

47 The Australian law has not been static, but the major changes to private international law in the last 25 years relevant to contract are only relevant to intra-Australian litigation and to litigation between Australia and New Zealand. Two are intra-Australian schemes which enlarge the courts' personal and subject matter jurisdiction in intra-Australian litigation: respectively, Service and Execution of Process Act 1992 (Cth), and Jurisdiction of Courts (Cross-vesting) Act 1987 (Cth) (and legislation of the same name enacted in the States and Territories). The third gives effect to a treaty between Australia and New Zealand: Trans-Tasman Proceedings Act 2010 (Cth).

48 This is not entirely true, to the extent that the Australian law gives effect to international conventions, which are especially prominent in the area of family law. As in other common law systems, Australian private international law includes the procedural issues of jurisdiction and judgments, as well as choice of law. The inclusion of procedural issues may have had the effect of emphasizing the domestic nature of private international law, because of the dominant role of the law of the forum in resolving procedural questions.

49 Jurisdiction and recognition of foreign judgments are considered to be part of private international law.

50 The University of Sydney required every student to study private international law as from 2013.

51 The Priestley 11 Prescribed Areas of Knowledge (see n 38) mandates the study of Civil Procedure in order to qualify to apply for admission to practice as a lawyer. One of the topics which the Priestley 11 suggests, but does not require, for coverage in Civil Procedure is service out of the jurisdiction, and choice of court.

52 In comparison, in recent reforms to the tort choice of law rule, the High Court was particularly influenced by Canadian case law: *John Pfeiffer Pty Ltd v Rogerson* (2000) 203 CLR 503.

53 For example, Australia still has not signed or ratified the Hague Convention on Exclusive Choice of Court Agreements 2005, the provisions of which are hardly contentious. In comparison, in the context of international family law, the Australian law incorporates many of the Hague Conventions, including the Conventions on Recognition of Divorces and Legal Separations 1970; on the Law Applicable to Maintenance Obligations 1973; on the Celebration and Recognition of Foreign Validity of Marriages 1978; on Child Abduction 1980; and on Inter-country Adoption 1993.

and statute. In this part, I refer in particular to the confounding impact that a claim for misleading conduct may have in an international commercial contract dispute.

Jurisdiction

As is typical in common law systems, the issues of competency and exercise of jurisdiction are addressed separately. The Australian courts regard themselves as jurisdictionally competent in an unusually wide range of circumstances. The courts' jurisdiction is determined by the ability to serve the defendant, either within the jurisdiction or ex iuris,[54] unless the defendant has submitted to the jurisdiction. In addition to other grounds of jurisdiction which are less controversial,[55] most Australian courts permit service ex iuris where the contract was made within the jurisdiction.[56] In two jurisdictions, service out of the jurisdiction is permitted when the only connection to the forum is that either party to the contract is resident in or carries on business in the forum.[57] The grounds of competency relevant to tort, which probably includes statutory claims for misleading conduct,[58] are even broader. In all but one jurisdiction, the rules of court permit service out of the jurisdiction where the claimant claims to have suffered loss or damage within the forum, even if the tort occurred outside the forum.[59] In most jurisdictions, the claimant can serve process outside Australia

---

54 The rules relating to service out of the jurisdiction are contained in the rules of court in each jurisdiction. These are comprehensively described in Reid Mortensen et al., Private International Law in Australia (2nd ed, LexisNexis 2011) 52–77. In this chapter, I refer by way of example to the rules of the Federal Court and the rules of the New South Wales Supreme Court.

55 For example, if the contract was breached within the forum; and if the contract is governed by forum law: for example, Federal Court Rules 2011 (Cth), r 10.42(2), (3)(c); Uniform Civil Procedure Rules 2005 (NSW), sch 6(b), (c)(iii).

56 For example, Federal Court Rules 2011 (Cth), r 10.42(3)(a); Uniform Civil Procedure Rules 2005 (NSW), sch 6(c)(i). This connection has been criticized as trivial: *Amin Rasheed Shipping Corporation v Kuwait Insurance Co* [1984] AC 50, 62.

57 Court Procedures Rules 2006 (ACT), r 6501(1)(g)(ii); Uniform Civil Procedure Rules 1999 (Qld), r 124(1)(g)(ii).

58 The characterization of claims for breach of the misleading conduct provisions are not really settled in Australia. In *John Pfeiffer Pty Ltd v Rogerson*, the joint judgment of the High Court observed that characterizing actions for breach of s 52 of the Trade Practices Act 1974 (Cth) 'may be difficult and may raise questions whether the private international law rules about tort or some other rules are to be applied': (2000) 203 CLR 503, 539. In the context of jurisdiction, the better view, and the more popular view amongst primary judges, in Australia is that these claims are to be treated as tortious: *Commonwealth Bank of Australia v White* [1999] 2 VR 672; *Borch v Answer Products Inc* [2000] QSC 379.

59 For example, Federal Court Rules 2011 (Cth), r 10.42(5); Uniform Civil Procedure Rules 2005 (NSW), sch 6(e). The Federal Court Rules alone expressly extend this basis of jurisdiction to statutory breaches: ibid, r10.42(13).

without the leave of the court.[60] In short, many of the Australian rules relating to the courts' jurisdictional competence are exorbitant by internal[61] as well as by international standards.

It is characteristic of courts in common law systems that they always retain a discretion whether or not to exercise jurisdiction, even if they are competent according to their own rules. Different principles guide this discretion depending on whether the parties have agreed to litigate abroad.[62] The court should decline jurisdiction in favour of the parties' agreement to litigate in a foreign court unless there are 'strong reasons' for non-enforcement of the agreement.[63] While this is ostensibly similar to the position in many other legal systems, in the leading High Court case, the majority stated that a stay 'may be refused where the foreign jurisdiction clause offends the public policy of the forum whether evinced by statute or declared by judicial decision' and noted that considerations of public policy might '*flow from*, even if not expressly mandated by the terms of, the Constitution or statute in force in the Australian forum.'[64] This parochial attitude to overriding party agreement, expressed in a dispute between legally advised commercial parties in which the choice of court was negotiated,[65] gives the courts much too broad a discretion not to enforce foreign jurisdiction clauses. Until recently, Australian courts had a very patchy record in their enforcement of contractual choices of foreign courts, relying on a range of reasons, including that the clause was non-exclusive, that the clause did not apply to all the claims or to

---

60   Leave is a requirement in the Federal Court, the Supreme Court of the Northern Territory and the Supreme Court of Western Australia.

61   In the sense that if a foreign court asserted jurisdiction on many of the weaker bases that permit service ex iuris under the Australian rules of court, its judgment would not be recognized. This test of exorbitance is referred to by Lord Diplock in *Amin Rasheed Shipping Corporation v Kuwait Insurance Co* as indicating the need for circumspection in deciding whether to grant leave to serve process out of the jurisdiction: [1984] AC 50, 65.

62   Australia is a party to the United Nations Convention on Recognition and Enforcement of Foreign Arbitral Awards, pursuant to which the court is required to stay proceedings brought in breach of an agreement to arbitrate with very limited exceptions: art.II, reflected in International Arbitration Act 1974 (Cth), s 7(2), (5). The Australian courts usually treat jurisdiction and arbitration agreements as cognate: *Global Partners Fund Ltd v Babcock & Brown Ltd* (in liq) (2010) 79 ACSR 383, para 85. However, in *Faxtech Pty Ltd v ITL Optronics Ltd*, concerning an English jurisdiction clause, Middleton J distinguished two cases involving the enforcement of arbitration agreements on the basis that 'this matter does not concern arbitration and the statutory requirements involved when the parties to an agreement have included an arbitration clause': [2011] FCA 1320, para 22.

63   *Huddart Parker Ltd v The Ship 'Mill Hill'* (1950) 81 CLR 502.

64   *Akai Pty Ltd v The People's Insurance Company* (1996) 188 CLR 418, 445, 447 (emphasis added).

65   The insurer's proposal included an express choice of its own law and courts. This was rejected by the insured, which proposed an express choice of its own law and courts, which was rejected by the insurer. The parties then agreed to the express choice of English law and courts: *Akai Pty Ltd v People's Insurance Co Ltd* [1998] 1 Lloyd's Rep 90, 93.

all the parties, and that for public policy reasons the court should always retain jurisdiction for claims under some local legislation, including the misleading conduct provisions.[66] Since 2009, the courts have been more likely to enforce express foreign jurisdiction clauses,[67] but there are still some recent cases in which the courts have refused to enforce such agreements if the claimant has claimed entitlement to relief under forum legislation.[68]

The gradual improvement in enforcement of foreign jurisdiction agreements has been influenced by the regime applicable to arbitration agreements.[69] Australia is a party to the New York Convention and has implemented the UNCITRAL Model Law on International Commercial Arbitration.[70] After a somewhat hesitant start, most Australian courts now strictly enforce international arbitration agreements,[71] which may be seen as growing evidence of a commitment to party autonomy. This has influenced the courts more strictly to enforce foreign jurisdiction agreements, and the relevance of arbitration to private international law is now accepted.[72]

Australia seems unlikely to sign or ratify the Hague Exclusive Choice of Court Agreements Convention 2005, even though its provisions generally replicate those of the New York Convention, to which Australia is a party and which is accepted as effective in Australia. The Hague Exclusive Choice of Court Agreements Convention requires courts to stay proceedings brought in breach of

---

66 Mary Keyes, Jurisdiction in International Litigation (Federation Press 2005) 163–168 (foreign jurisdiction clauses were only enforced in 54 per cent of cases from 1991–2001), Mary Keyes, 'Jurisdiction under the Hague Choice of Courts Convention: Its Likely Impact on Australian Practice' (2009) 5 Journal of Private International Law 181, 198–204 (foreign jurisdiction clauses were only enforced in one of eight cases from 2001–2008).

67 *Global Partners Fund Ltd v Babcock & Brown Ltd (in liq)* (2010) 79 ACSR 383.

68 In *Faxtech Pty Ltd v ITL Optronics Ltd* Middleton J stated that 'there is no doubt that the claim for misleading or deceptive conduct can only be dealt with in this Court, and not by an English court. The relief sought under the Australian Consumer Law can only be obtained in this Court.': [2011] FCA 1320, para 18. In *Australian Commercial Research and Development Ltd v ANZ McCaughan Merchant Bank Ltd*, Browne-Wilkinson VC stated that he had 'considerable doubts whether the English court if called on to adjudicate on this matter would apply the Australian Trade Practices Act 1974 as part of the applicable law', which was the law of Queensland: [1989] 3 All ER 65, 72.

69 Many of the leading authorities involve arbitration rather than jurisdiction agreements: for example, *Huddart Parker v The Ship 'Mill Hill'* (1950) 81 CLR 502.

70 These are given effect in the International Arbitration Act 1974 (Cth).

71 Mary Keyes, 'Jurisdiction Under the Hague Choice of Courts Convention' (n 66) 185–197.

72 The most recent editions of the Australian textbooks include separate chapters on arbitration: Martin Davies, AS Bell and PLG Brereton, Nygh's Conflict of Laws in Australia (8th ed, LexisNexis Butterworths 2010) ch 39 (jurisdiction and arbitration agreements are dealt with together: ch 7); Mortensen et al. (n 54) ch 6.

a foreign jurisdiction agreement, with very limited exceptions.[73] Ratification of this Convention would improve the treatment of foreign jurisdiction agreements in Australian law. The provisions of the Convention influenced the drafting of the Trans-Tasman Proceedings Act, which requires Australian courts to stay proceedings brought in breach of an exclusive choice of New Zealand courts, with very limited exceptions.[74] It may be hoped that this legislation will have an influence in improving the treatment of jurisdiction agreements in other cases.

If there is no express choice of court, proceedings will only be stayed if the defendant can establish that the forum is *clearly* inappropriate,[75] which is very unlikely.[76] This version of the forum non conveniens principle, which is unique to Australia, has been widely condemned as forum-centric and unfair to defendants, but it has been repeatedly endorsed by the High Court. In *Puttick v Tenon*, the High Court unanimously and emphatically rejected the only direct challenge so far made to the Australian version of the forum non conveniens principle.[77] Some of the High Court cases have involved personal injuries,[78] in which particular protective interests arise. Although the Australian principle of forum non conveniens on its face does not distinguish commercial from non-commercial cases, the High Court has stayed proceedings in commercial disputes.[79] Refinement of the principle to reflect this different treatment in practice of commercial and non-commercial disputes would improve the clarity and certainty of the law.

The rules relating to exercise of jurisdiction in combination with the exorbitant bases of jurisdictional competency in the rules of court mean that Australian courts are too likely to take and retain jurisdiction in international cases. This jurisdictional parochialism places stress on the substantive rules and the choice of law rules, making it essential that substantive forum law is cosmopolitan, and that the choice of law rules do not unduly preference forum law. Neither of these conditions holds: I have already suggested that substantive Australian contract law is isolationist in origin and outlook. In the following section, I argue that Australian courts are too ready to apply Australian substantive law in international cases.

---

73 Art.6.

74 The Trans-Tasman Proceedings Act 2010 (Cth): ss 20(1), (2). These provisions do not apply to contracts involving consumers or employees: s 20(3)(b), (c).

75 *Voth v Manildra Flour Mills Pty Ltd* (1990) 171 CLR 538.

76 Keyes, Jurisdiction in International Litigation (n 66) 168 (the court only found itself to be clearly inappropriate in 22.5 per cent of all Australian superior court decisions on forum non conveniens between 1991 and 2011).

77 *Puttick v Tenon Ltd* (2008) 238 CLR 265, 277, 280.

78 *Oceanic Sun Line Special Shipping Co Inc v Fay* (1988) 165 CLR 197; *Regie Nationale des Usines Renault SA v Zhang* (2002) 210 CLR 491; *Puttick v Tenon Ltd* (2008) 238 CLR 265.

79 *Voth v Manildra Flour Mills Pty Ltd* (1990) 171 CLR 538; *CSR Ltd v Cigna Insurance Australia Ltd* (1997) 189 CLR 345.

Choice of Law

The Australian common law choice of law rules for contract have not changed significantly in the last 80 years, although their operation has become less clear due to the intrusion of statutory claims.

Express choice of law, evasion and forum statutes
The High Court of Australia was an early adopter of the rule that is now accepted in most legal systems, allowing the parties expressly to choose the governing law of the contract. This was established in Australian case law in the 1930s,[80] and the rule has repeatedly been confirmed since then.[81] Most other legal systems now also enforce express choices of law, and therefore, this rule ought to promote uniformity of outcome and act as a disincentive to forum shopping. This rule is consistent with Australian domestic contract law, almost all of which is permissive.

This superficially simple rule is undermined by a number of cases in which the parties' express choices have not been applied, either out of a concern that those choices were evasive[82] or because forum legislation is given an overriding effect, or both.[83] Evasion is an ambiguous concept, and the cases provide little definite guidance as to how it can be identified. It tends to be determined by reference to whether the parties have chosen a law other than that with the closest and most real connection to the contract (referred to as the proper law of the contract).[84] There are several problems with this approach. The first is that the proper law rule is uncertain, unpredictable and likely to lead to the application of forum law. The second follows from the first: the perception of an express choice of law as evasive is almost always forum-dependent, so whether a choice will be regarded as offensively evasive depends upon jurisdictional rules and litigation strategy. The effectiveness of a decision that a choice is evasive ultimately depends on the location of the defendant's assets.[85]

---

80 *Barcelo v Electrolytic Zinc Co of Australasia Ltd* (1932) 48 CLR 391; *Merwin Pastoral Co Pty Ltd v Moolpa Pastoral Co Pty Ltd* (1933) 48 CLR 565.

81 Most recently in *Akai Pty Ltd v People's Insurance Co Ltd* (1996) 188 CLR 418.

82 *Kay's Leasing Corporation Pty Ltd v Fletcher* (1964) 116 CLR 124.

83 *Akai Pty Ltd v People's Insurance Co Ltd* (1996) 188 CLR 418.

84 For example, Insurance Contracts Act 1984 (Cth), s 8 (requiring application of that statute if the objective proper law of the contract is that of an Australian State or Territory).

85 *Akai Pty Ltd v People's Insurance Co Ltd* is a classic example. Compare the attitude of the chosen English court (*Akai v The People's Insurance Company* [1998] 1 Lloyd's Rep 90) and the Singaporean court whose law was proposed but rejected (*People's Insurance Company v Akai Pty Ltd* [1998] 1 SLR 206), with that of the Australian court whose law was also proposed but rejected (*Akai Pty Ltd v The People's Insurance Company* (1996) 188 CLR 418). The decision of the High Court that the parties' express choice of English law was evasive was ultimately ineffective because the English court granted an anti-suit injunction, and it seems absolutely certain that the Singaporean courts (where the

The application of forum statutes in international cases is a major problem in common law countries, which routinely apply their own legislation without reference to choice of law.[86] Of course, courts are constitutionally required to do so, if the forum legislation stipulates its scope of application.[87] When forum legislation stipulates its scope of application, this is usually done by an unilateral choice of law rule, which states that the legislation must be applied if particular choice of law criteria are met.[88] Many commentators are highly critical of unilateral choice of law rules as being anti-internationalist and overtly forum-centric.[89] Morris famously and rightly observed that 'Confusion is bound to result unless a clear distinction is maintained between domestic rules and conflict rules; and a statute with a particular choice of law clause is a bastard hybrid.'[90]

International instruments often also include scope of application provisions that are unilateral in that they indicate only the circumstances in which they apply. These may not apply sympathetically with choice of law rules. The CISG exemplifies this problem. It contains two, not necessarily consistent, scope of application provisions. The first is that the Convention applies if the parties' places of business are in different Contracting States, and the second is that the Convention applies if the parties' places of business are in different states and 'the rules of private international law lead to the application of the Convention'.[91] The former was intended to dominate any choice of law analysis,[92] although this is hardly clear from the wording of the provision and does not seem necessarily consistent with the Convention's support of party autonomy. The latter is not necessarily inconsistent with choice of law rules,[93] but it creates the possibility of divergent outcomes depending on forum.[94]

There is still much confusion as to the application of the CISG in Australia, and the uncertain relationship between its scope of application provisions and forum choice of law is likely to exacerbate this confusion. In a recent case, even though

---

defendant's assets were located) would have refused to enforce any Australian judgment that did not give effect to the parties' express choice of English law.

86 Keyes, 'Statutes, Choice of Law and the Role of Forum Choice' (n 14).

87 *Compagnie des Messageries Maritimes v Wilson* (1954) 94 CLR 577, 585.

88 This technique is used in Australia: for example, Insurance Contracts Act 1984 (Cth), s 8; Australian Consumer Law 2010, s 67(a).

89 J Unger, 'Use and Abuse of Statutes in the Conflict of Laws' (1967) 83 LQR 427, 444, 448.

90 JHC Morris, 'The Choice of Law Clause in Statutes' (1946) 62 LQR 170, 172.

91 CISG, art.1(1).

92 Secretariat Commentary on Article 1, CISG, paragraph 6. A choice of law analysis would still be required if there were substantive issues in dispute that were not addressed by the CISG.

93 Under CISG art.95, a Contracting State may declare that it will not be bound by art.1(1)(b).

94 Art.1(1)(b) does not state which legal system's private international law rules are applicable. The Secretariat Commentary refers in several places to the 'rules of private international law of the forum', without addressing the issue of the proper forum (para. 6, 7).

the judge found that the CISG was applicable, and applied it to determine the place of contracting,[95] her Honour concluded that domestic forum law applied as the proper law of the contract, because she stated that 'the Convention does not deal with choice of law'.[96]

If it is applicable according to its own rules of application, the CISG allows the parties contractually to exclude almost all of its provisions,[97] which has the ultimate effect of consistency with the Australian choice of law rule allowing the parties to choose the governing law, albeit via an unattractively circuitous route.

It is more common that legislation is silent as to its application in international cases. In that case, courts in common law countries tend to apply their own legislation without regard to choice of law rules, usually determining as a matter of forum statutory interpretation that this is required.[98] This has the effect of giving all forum legislation mandatory effect in international cases, which is parochial, promotes forum shopping and may be futile. Unless the legislature has specifically stated that forum legislation has international effect, it should only be applied if the forum's law is selected by the choice of law rules. This is how foreign legislation is treated.[99] The differentiation in the treatment of foreign and local legislation is unjustifiable, and is particularly unfortunate given the major flaws of the Australian jurisdictional principles.

There are few other limitations to the parties' ability expressly to choose the governing law. It is not a requirement that the chosen law have any connection to the contract, although as noted above, a choice of an unconnected law may well be treated with suspicion if one party subsequently challenges an express choice of law as being evasive of forum law. A choice of non-state law as the governing law is probably not enforceable in Australian courts.[100]

Actual, unexpressed, choice of law

The High Court in 1996 insisted that if there was no expressed choice of law, the courts must determine whether the parties shared a mutual but unexpressed

---

95 *Castel Electronics Pty Ltd v TCL Airconditioner (Zhongshan) Co Ltd* [2013] VSC 92, para 15–22.

96 *Castel Electronics Pty Ltd v TCL Airconditioner (Zhongshan) Co Ltd* [2013] VSC 92, para 23. It seems clear that the CISG was applicable to all the issues in dispute.

97 CISG, art.s 6, 12, 96. Article 6 states that 'The parties may exclude the application of this Convention or, subject to Article 12, derogate from or vary the effect of any of its provisions.' An express choice of law is taken to have this effect. If the choice of law was of a country which is a contracting state, then this would presumably lead to the application of the CISG.

98 The majority in *Akai Pty Ltd v People's Insurance Co Ltd* stated that 'Where there is no expressed connecting factor [indicating the scope of application of forum legislation], the issue becomes whether there is to be implied any restraint upon the apparently universal application of the law': (1996) 188 CLR 418, 443.

99 *Akai Pty Ltd v People's Insurance Co Ltd* (1996) 188 CLR 418, 442–443.

100 *Engel v Adelaide Hebrew Congregation Inc* (2007) 98 SASR 402.

intention as to governing law.[101] This aspect of the rule has been criticized as unrealistic, uncertain and unpredictable, as well as redundant, in that the parties' mutual unexpressed intentions are determined in the same way as the objective proper law. In practice, the courts usually do not attempt to identify an unexpressed mutual intention.[102]

Objective proper law
In the absence of an agreement as to choice of law, the law of the legal system with the closest and most real connection to the contract is applied. This is done by identifying and weighing the connections the contract has to various legal systems. This rule is uncertain and unpredictable. The High Court has repeatedly refused to allow a proper law exception in the context of tort choice of law for precisely these reasons.[103] The rule has also been criticized on the basis that it is likely to result in the application of forum law.[104] This would be less concerning if the jurisdictional rules were stronger or if forum law was more international in character.

Weaker contracting parties
Australian private international law generally gives little explicit consideration to the position of vulnerable contracting parties.[105] The principles of jurisdiction and choice of law make no specific provision for the protection of consumers, employees or franchisees.[106] International consumer cases are seldom litigated in Australia; in the few cases that have been brought to court, the courts have usually but not always been highly sympathetic to the situation of consumers[107]

---

101   *Akai Pty Ltd v People's Insurance Co Ltd* (1996) 188 CLR 418, 440–443.

102   For example, *Castel Electronics Pty Ltd v TCL Airconditioner (Zhongshan) Co Ltd* [2013] VSC 92, para 23; *Fleming v Marshall* [2011] NSWCA 86; *Thomson Aviation Ltd v Dufresne* [2011] NSWSC 864; *Mendelson-Zeller Co Inc v T & C Providores Pty Ltd* [1981] 1 NSWLR 366, 368–369. This seems to be common in other legal systems: for example, Takahashi Koji, 'A Major Reform of Japanese Private International Law' (2006) 2 Journal of Private International Law 311, 371.

103   *John Pfeiffer Pty Ltd v Rogerson* (2000) 203 CLR 503, 538; *Regie Nationale des Usines Renault SA v Zhang* (2002) 210 CLR 491, 520; *Neilson v Overseas Projects Corporation of Victoria Ltd* (2005) 223 CLR 331, 348, 357, 363, 364.

104   It should therefore be a matter of concern that, where Australian legislation includes a choice of law criterion, this is the criterion most often used. See, for example, Australian Consumer Law 2010, s 67(a), Insurance Contracts Act 1984, s 8.

105   Jonathan Hill made the same observation about the English common law: Cross-border Consumer Contracts (OUP 2008) para 3.03.

106   The provisions of Trans-Tasman Proceedings Act requiring that exclusive choice of court agreements in favour of New Zealand courts be strictly enforced does not apply to contracts involving consumers or employees: s20(3)(b), (c). The legislation does not specify how exclusive choice of court agreements involving those parties should be treated.

107   *Oceanic Sun Line Special Shipping Co Inc v Fay* (1988) 165 CLR 197, *Quinlan v SAFE International Försäkrings AB* (2006) ANZ Ins Cas 61–693.

and employees,[108] although not to franchisees.[109] This often has the effect that foreign jurisdiction and choice of law clauses are not enforced. On the other hand, protective substantive statutes are sometimes applied to the benefit of commercial parties. For example, the remedial provisions of the Insurance Contracts Act 1984 (Cth) have been held to apply for the protection not only of consumer but also of commercial insureds, rendering choice of law agreements involving commercial parties ineffective in Australian litigation,[110] no doubt to the surprise of foreign insurance companies and their lawyers. The misleading conduct provisions are often invoked by, and are still sometimes applied in favour of, commercial parties.

Where legislation is given an internationally mandatory effect explicitly, it is not always clear that this is done mindfully. For example, the consumer guarantees under the Australian Consumer Law are stated to apply with mandatory effect to contracts the objective proper law of which is that of Australian state or territory.[111] The drafters of this provision presumably intended that Australian consumers' rights under the Australian Consumer Law should not be affected by a choice of foreign law, whereas the reference to the proper law rule, if correctly applied, ought to lead to the application of the seller's, not the buyer's, law.[112]

International developments
As for the law of contract, important developments internationally have had little impact on the Australian law. In particular, the European Union Regulations dealing with jurisdiction and judgments and choice of law have been highly influential in many parts of the world. They have significantly changed the English law and have influenced reforms in many countries, including China, Japan and Korea.[113] This has led to a remarkable degree of convergence in choice of law

---

108 *Old UGC Inc v Industrial Relations Commission of NSW in Court Session* (2006) 225 CLR 274. On the other hand, see *Moldauer v Constellation Brands Inc* [2013] SASC 38, in which proceedings brought in Australia by an employee of a US company were stayed, mainly because of cost and convenience to the company, even though Kourakis CJ accepted 'that bringing proceedings in New York would be costly' and noting that 'Unless he [the employee] is a man of unusually wealthy means he will find it difficult to maintain an action in New York': para 20.

109 *Nicola v Ideal Image Development Corporation* (2009) 261 ALR 1; *Timic v Hammock* [2001] FCA 74.

110 Insurance Contracts Act 1984 (Cth), s 8, applied in *Akai Pty Ltd v People's Insurance Co Ltd* (1996) 188 CLR 418.

111 Australian Consumer Law 2010, s 67(a).

112 *Mendelson-Zeller Co Inc v T & C Providores Pty Ltd* [1981] 1 NSWLR 366.

113 China, Japan and Korea are Australia's top three export markets; in 2011 they accounted for 49.3 per cent of Australia's total exports: Australian Government, Department of Foreign Affairs and Trade, Composition of Trade Australia 2011 (Commonwealth of Australia 2012) 31. In 2011, they were Australia's first, second and fourth two-way trading partners, accounting for 37.2 per cent of total two-way trade: ibid.

rules internationally. For example, in relation to choice of law for contract, these legal systems all apply the characteristic performance presumption[114] to determine the law of the cause if there is no express choice, in order to improve certainty. In its 1992 report on *Choice of Law*, the Australian Law Reform Commission recommended that the characteristic performance presumption should be applied,[115] but that recommendation has not been acted upon. Recent legislation in the European Union and in other countries usually includes tailored protections for consumers[116] and employees.[117]

4 Improving the Australian Law

A wholesale, comprehensive and exhaustive codification of either contract or private international law is not necessary in order to achieve even modest improvements in coherence, clarity and certainty. Many instruments are tailored to specific types of contracts, and to particular aspects of private international law. Some private international law legislation focuses on jurisdiction, sometimes also addressing the related question of judgment recognition;[118] or on choice of law, sometimes comprehensively,[119] and sometimes in relation to specific areas of law.[120] Within the European Union, related legislation is designed in order to

---

114 Act of the People's Republic of China on Application of Law in Civil Relationships with Foreign Contacts 2010, art.41; Regulation (EC) No 593/2008 of the European Parliament and of the Council of 17 June 2008 on the law applicable to contractual obligations (Rome I), art.4; Act on the General Rules of Application of Laws (Law No 10 of 1898, as newly titled and amended 21 June 2006) (Japan), art.8; Conflict of Laws Act of the Republic of Korea 2001, art.26(2).

115 Australian Law Reform Commission, Choice of Law (Commonwealth of Australia 1992) Report No 58, para 8.48. The ALRC recommended, as is allowed in other legal systems, that presumption should be displaced if the contract had its closest and most real connection with another legal system: ibid.

116 For example, Law of the People's Republic of China on the Laws Applicable to Foreign-Related Civil Relations 2010, art.42; Rome I Regulation, art.6; Conflict of Laws Act of the Republic of Korea 2001, art.27.

117 For example, Law of the People's Republic of China on the Laws Applicable to Foreign-Related Civil Relations 2010, art.43; Rome I Regulation, art.8; Conflict of Laws Act of the Republic of Korea 2001, art.28.

118 Council Regulation (EC) No 44/2001 of 22 December 2000 on jurisdiction and the recognition of judgments in civil and commercial matters (Brussels I Regulation).

119 The Chinese, Japanese and Korean choice of law statutes address choice of law for most areas of private law.

120 This is the technique used in the European Union: e.g. Rome I Regulation, Regulation (EC) No 864/2007 of the European Parliament and of the Council of 11 July 2007 on the law applicable to non-contractual obligations (Rome II Regulation). See also the Hague Draft Principles on the Choice of Law in International Contracts.

operate harmoniously,[121] and the same could be done in Australia. In particular, attention should be given to improving the integration of contract law and private international law,[122] as well as the inter-relationships between jurisdiction,[123] judgments and choice of law.

My comments for improvement to the Australian law focus on private international law; others, including in this collection, have identified areas for improvement in contract law.[124] I make only two specific points concerning improvements to contract law, in relation to the CISG and the UNIDROIT Principles. The first is to note that these instruments take contradictory positions about the distinction between international and domestic contracts. Each of them, by their titles and other means,[125] assumes that international contracts warrant specific regulation. This is effectively the current Australian position, given that the CISG is not integrated with domestic contract law. On the other hand, each has been proposed as suitable for,[126] and has been used in the context of, the reform of domestic contract law in other countries.[127] Whether international contracts require separate regulation is a possibility that has not been much explored in Australia,[128]

---

121   Rome Convention on the law applicable to contractual obligations 1980 (Rome Convention), preamble; Rome I, preamble, para (7); Rome II, preamble, para (7). See generally Xandra Kramer, Current Gaps and Future Perspectives in European Private International Law: Towards a Code on Private International Law (Directorate General for Internal Policies, European Parliament, 2012).

122   Choice of law rules remain important, even if substantive law is able to be harmonized. Both the CISG and the UNIDROIT Principles refer to private international law rules; the former in its scope of application provisions (art.1(1)(b) and the latter in its provisions about the applicability of mandatory rules (art.1.4).

123   The rules relating to judgment recognition are beyond the scope of the discussion in this chapter. Unless there is a bilateral arrangement in place between Australia and the other country, the common law rules for recognition are limited and are unlikely to facilitate recognition of foreign judgments. On the other hand, arbitral awards are routinely and strictly enforced in Australia under the New York Convention, and this could be used as a stimulus to improve the treatment of foreign judgments.

124   See also Finn, (n 17), Andrew Stewart, 'What's Wrong with the Australian Law of Contract?' (2012) 29 Journal of Contract Law 74.

125   The CISG applies only to international contracts: art.1.1. The Preamble to the UNIDROIT Principles states that the Principles 'set forth general rules for international commercial contracts'.

126   The Preamble to the UNIDROIT Principles also states that the principles 'may be used to interpret or supplement domestic law' and that they may be used as a model for national legislators.

127   Peter Schlechtriem, 'Basic Structures and General Concepts of the CISG as Models for a Harmonisation of the Law of Obligations' (2005) 10 Juridica International 27, 30–31; Xiao Yongping and Long Weidi, 'Selected Topics on the Application of the CISG in China' (2008) 20 Pace International Law Review 61, 62–63.

128   Cf Robertson, 'The International Harmonisation of Australian Contract Law' (n 22) 6–8.

but it demands attention, especially in relation to the application of local statutes to cross-border agreements.

The second point is that, if international and domestic contracts should not be differentiated, then the lack of congruence between the Australian law relevant to international and domestic sales contracts should be addressed. The provisions of the CISG ought to be referred to in any reform of domestic contract law. They might be used, for example, in reviewing the law relevant to good faith,[129] consideration,[130] the requirement of communication of acceptance,[131] and contractual interpretation.[132] The UNIDROIT Principles should also be considered in relation to these and other issues.

In many areas, the Australian principles relevant to private international law require improvement. In this section, I focus on improvements to the law of jurisdiction and choice of law relevant to international contracts. The Australian principles of jurisdiction are far too expansive. The courts assume jurisdiction in cases in which it could not be argued that that court ought to resolve the dispute; and the rules on declining jurisdiction will not always correct this. Even if they did, it is inefficient to permit service out of the jurisdiction with no formal checks, and the jurisdictions which do not require leave to serve out should reinstate this requirement. The rules permitting service out of the jurisdiction on the basis of trivial connections should be repealed, unless there are significant protective concerns, as in the case of personal injuries claimants, consumers, employees and possibly franchisees. The courts should enforce foreign jurisdiction clauses unless there are exceptional circumstances, and this might include contracts including vulnerable parties. Forum public policy should only be applied with an overriding effect if the legislation expressly requires it, and this should be done rarely in commercial situations. Jurisdictional rules should be better coordinated with related choice of law rules and other techniques that lead to the application of forum law.

The contract choice of law rules require improvement in order to achieve greater consistency with international developments, to increase the clarity and certainty of the law, and to minimize the effect that is given to forum law. It is particularly desirable to consider whether expressed choices are to be respected, as the choice of law rule suggests. If so, limitations to actual choices should be exceptional and they should be easily identifiable. If the legislature intends a substantive rule of the forum to have an internationally mandatory effect it should say so clearly,

---

129 CISG, art.7(1), UNIDROIT Principles, art.1.7. For further discussion, see Therese Wilson, 'The Challenges of Unconscionability and Good Faith in Contract Law Codification', in this collection.

130 Consideration is not required under the CISG (by implication; in the case of agreements to modify or terminate the agreement, see art.29(1)) or under the UNIDROIT Principles (art.3.1.2).

131 CISG, art.18(2), UNIDROIT Principles, art.2.1.6(2).

132 CISG, art.8; UNIDROIT Principles, art.4.3.

but this should only be done rarely, particularly in law applicable to commercial transactions. Valid protective interests generally relevant to particular kinds of contracts should be more explicitly indicated in the choice of law rules. The Hague Conference Draft Principles on Choice of Law in International Contracts should be considered in any review of the Australian law.[133]

Finally, it would be wise to reflect on what may be learned from the success of international commercial arbitration in terms of improvements to international litigation in the Australian courts, as well as in the reform of contract and private international law. This might include allowing the parties greater choice in procedure,[134] enforcing choices of non-state law, and improving the recognition of foreign judgments.

5 Conclusion

The principles of Australian contract law and private international law are outdated and inappropriate to an environment in which international transactions are commonplace. It is timely, if not essential, to reconsider both the form and the substance of the law in these areas. In doing so, consideration ought to be given to international developments, including harmonization and modernization of the law, by reference to international instruments including the CISG, the UNIDROIT Principles and the Hague Draft Principles on the Choice of Law in International Contracts, as well as regional agreements and changes in the national laws of Australia's trading partners. The benefits of unification, harmonization and convergence of laws have been accepted in many other legal systems and in Australia in the areas of international commercial arbitration and international family law. They are at least as valuable in the context of international contract law.

---

133 In particular, those Principles permit the choice of 'rules of law' and expressly exclude renvoi: art.3, 8.

134 Justice James Allsop, 'International Commercial Law, Maritime Law and Dispute Resolution: The Place of Australia, New Zealand and the Asia Pacific Region in the Coming Years' (2007) 21 Australian and New Zealand Maritime Law Journal 1, 12 (suggesting that the parties to litigation might be able to choose their judge; to choose not to have the right to appeal, or to limit their right to appeal; and to choose to waive their right to reasons for judgment or choose to receive only truncated reasons).

PART II
The Internationalization Imperatives

Chapter 3
Regional and Global Unification of Contract Law

Ingeborg Schwenzer*

1 Introduction

Before turning to the main subject matter of this chapter, a few words shall be said about the development of international trade: due to globalization, the overall development of international trade over the last half century is startling. Without having regard to 2009's dramatic decrease of world merchandise exports, which in any case was basically equalized in 2010, it may be useful to have a look at the demonstrated trend during the last decades. World Trade Organization (WTO) figures for 2012 indicate that world-wide merchandise export trade amounted to USD 17.850 billion and world-wide merchandise import trade to USD 18.155 billion.[1] These figures are approximately 100 times more than 50 years ago. The average annual export growth from 1992 to 2012 was more than 5 per cent world-wide.[2] No longer is the highest growth found in North America and Europe, but instead it is the transition economies from different points of the globe – particularly Brazil, China, Russia, and some African countries.[3]

These economic developments prompted legal answers in a variety of fields.[4] The focus of this chapter, however, shall be on harmonization and unification of contract law as contract law is at the very heart of international trade.

---

* Dr. iur. (Freiburg, Germany), LL.M. (Berkeley, USA), Professor for Private Law, University of Basel, Switzerland. The author is deeply indebted to Ref. iur Lina Ali for editing the footnotes. All web pages were last accessed on 18 April 2013.

1 World Trade Organization, 'World Trade 2012, Prospects for 2013' (Press Release, PRESS/688, 10 April 2013) 19 <www.wto.org/english/news_e/pres13_e/pr688_e.pdf>.

2 World Trade Organization (n 1) 2 <www.wto.org/english/news_e/pres13_e/pr688_e.pdf >.

3 World Trade Organization, 'International Trade Statistics 2012', 22 <www.wto.org/english/res_e/statis_e/its2012_e/its2012_e.pdf >.

4 See Ingeborg Schwenzer and Claudio Marti Whitebread, 'Legal Answers to Globalization' in Ingeborg Schwenzer, Yesim Atamer and Petra Butler (eds), *Current Issues in the CISG and Arbitration* (Eleven International Publishing, 2014), pp. 1 *et seq*.

2 The Need for a Uniform Contract Law

Contract law and especially commercial contract law has always been at the forefront of harmonization and unification of private law. The reason is that different domestic laws are perceived as an obstacle to international trade.[5] This has always been true and still holds true nowadays as has been proven by many recent field studies around the world.[6] In the nineteenth century this prompted unification at the nation state level all over Europe, in the twentieth century the Uniform Commercial Code in the United States (US) can be mentioned as a prominent example as well as endeavours especially on the European level.[7]

Let me briefly discuss who is in need of a uniform contract law and why. In general, on the international level we may roughly distinguish three different scenarios of contracting parties.

In the first group we find parties from countries where the same language is spoken. In general, these countries also belong to the same legal family with differences between the legal systems being minor if not negligible.[8] This first of all applies to parties from English speaking Common Law countries, like parties from the US and Canada, from Australia and New Zealand, or from India and the United Kingdom (UK). But it also holds true for other scenarios like those of parties from France and Cameroon, from Argentina and Mexico, or from Germany and Austria. First, it is well possible that the parties can agree on one of their respective legal systems. If this is not the case they can be expected to choose the law of a third country with the same language and belonging to the same legal tradition. In any case, the outcome of a possible dispute – be it litigated or arbitrated – will be more or less predictable. In this group which comes close to purely domestic contracts there is hardly any need for a unification of contract law as the parties would still prefer the law that is more familiar to them than any unified law.

---

5 Cf Ewan McKendrick, 'Harmonisation of European Contract Law: The State We Are In' in Stefan Vogenauer and Stephen Weatherill (eds), *The Harmonisation of European Contract Law, Implications for European Private Laws, Business and Legal Practice* (Hart Publishing 2006) 5, 14–15.

6 See Stefan Vogenauer and Stephen Weatherill, 'The European Community's Competence to Pursue the Harmonisation of Contract Law – An Empirical Contribution to the Debate' in Vogenauer and Weatherill (n 5) 105, 125–26.

7 See, for example, the Principles of European Contract Law (PECL) (1999) <http://frontpage.cbs.dk/law/commission_on_european_contract_law/PECL%20engelsk/engelsk_partI_og_II.htm>; for more information on PECL see Ole Lando and Hugh Beale (eds), *Principles of European Contract Law, Parts I and II* (Kluwer Law International 2003) and Ole Lando and others (eds), *Principles on European Contract Law, Part III* (Kluwer Law International 2003).

8 For an overview of the legal families with regard to domestic sales law see Ingeborg Schwenzer, Pascal Hachem and Christopher Kee, *Global Sales and Contract Law* (OUP 2012) paras 2.01–2.135.

In the second group a – most probably western – company with overwhelming bargaining power contracts with an economically weaker party. The powerful company usually will be able to impose anything that it wants on its contract partner. It has sophisticated in-house lawyers who carefully draft the contract preferably with a choice of law clause designating its own domestic law. If this is combined with a forum selection clause designating the domestic courts of the economically stronger party, usually there will be no problems at least not for the powerful party and thus no need for a uniform contract law. The domestic courts apply their domestic law which in general will yield predictable and satisfactory results for the company seated in this country. The picture may immediately change, however, if the other party brings suit in the domestic courts of its own country and there the forum selection clause and/or the choice of law clause are not honoured.[9] But even if these courts accept the choice of law, it is a totally different question how the courts will apply this foreign law. By agreeing on arbitration many of the aforementioned imponderabilities may be circumvented. Still, problems of ascertaining and proving the chosen law – as will be described below – can be encountered.

The third group is probably by far the biggest one. It consists of parties from countries where different languages are spoken, be they parties from a Common Law and a Civil Law country or from two Civil Law countries. If none of the parties has the economic power to impose its own law upon the other party, that is, where the parties are dealing at arm's length with one another, more often than not they will agree on a third law. This might be a law that appears to be closely related to both parties because it influenced the law of both parties' countries in one way or the other, as is true for German law for example in relation to Italian and Korean law.[10] If no such common background exists, more often than not the parties think to solve their problems by resorting to what they believe is a "neutral law" thereby often confusing political neutrality with suitability of the chosen law for international transactions.[11] In particular, this seems to be the case with Swiss law.

In such a case the first hurdle that the parties have to take, at least once it comes to litigation or arbitration, is the language problem. They have to investigate a

---

9 A prominent example is Brazil, where the validity of choice of law and choice of forum clauses is highly controversial. For more information see Dana Stringer, 'Choice of Law and Choice of Forum in Brazilian International Commercial Contracts: Party Autonomy, International Jurisdiction, and the Emerging New Way' (2005–06) 44 Columbia Journal of Transnational Law 959.

10 For German influences on Italian Civil Law see Konrad Zweigert and Hein Kötz, *An Introduction to Comparative Law* (Tony Weir tr, 3rd edn, OUP 1998) 104–06; for German influences in the East Asian region see Schwenzer, Hachem and Kee (n 8) paras 2.123–2.127.

11 cf Christiana Fountoulakis, 'The Parties' Choice of "Neutral Law" in International Sales Contracts' (2005) 7 European Journal of Law Reform 303, 306–07.

foreign law in a foreign language. If the language is not the one of the litigation or arbitration in question all legal materials – statutes, case law and scholarly writings – must be translated into the language of the court or of the arbitration. Legal experts are required to prove the content of the law that is chosen by the parties. In some countries the experts may be appointed by the court, in others as well as generally in arbitration each party will have to come forward with sometimes even several experts.[12] Needless to say the procedures can be very expensive and may be prohibitive for a party who does not have the necessary economic power to invest these monies in the first place. This may even be harsher under a procedural system where each party bears its own costs regardless of the outcome of the proceedings as is especially the case under the so-called "American Rule" as it applies not only in the US but also for example in Japan.[13] However, even if a party is willing to bear all these costs to prove a foreign law in court or arbitration the question as to how this law is interpreted and applied can be highly unpredictable.

Second, the parties will very often be taken by surprise when they realize the true content of the law that they have chosen. One example, that is in my view rather typical for an international contract between two small and medium enterprises (SMEs), would be a sales contract between a Chinese seller and an Italian buyer. As German law has had great influence on both Chinese and Italian law[14] the parties – although none of them speaks German – believe that they have a rough idea of German law and agree on German law to govern their contract. The Chinese seller for its standard form contract copies a form it finds on the internet including a limitation of liability clause. Whereas the clause may well live up to the standards of the United States Uniform Commercial Code (US UCC), it is totally invalid under German law that provides for substantive control of standard terms even in business-to-business (b2b) relationships.[15] This is certainly not what both parties wanted and expected in choosing German law.

Third, the outcome of the case under the law chosen may be highly unpredictable. This especially holds true if the parties choose Swiss law. As Switzerland is such a small country, many central questions of contract law have not yet been decided by the Swiss Supreme Court or if so the decision may have been rendered decades

---

12   cf for court proceedings Michele Taruffo, 'Evidence' (2010) 16 International Encyclopedia of Comparative Law paras 7.65–7.66; cf for arbitration proceedings Gabrielle Kaufmann-Kohler, 'Globalization of Arbitral Procedure' (2003) 36 Vanderbildt Journal of Transnational Law 1313, 1330; Siegfried H Elsing and John M Townsend, 'Bridging the Common Law–Civil Law Divide in Arbitration' (2002) 18 Arbitration International 59, 63–4; see, for example, Art 25(3) ICC Arbitration Rules (2012); Art 27(2) UNCITRAL Arbitration Rules (2010).

13   For a comparative overview as to how litigation costs and attorney fees are allocated between the parties in civil litigation see Mathias Reimann (ed), *Cost and Fee Allocation in Civil Procedure* (Springer 2012).

14   cf Schwenzer, Hachem and Kee (n 8).

15   cf §§ 305–10 BGB (German Civil Code).

ago and is disputed by scholarly writings. This makes the outcome of the case often rather unpredictable; another reason that may well prevent a party from pursuing its rights under the contract.

Furthermore, especially Swiss domestic contract law in core areas is unpredictable and not suitable to international contracts. This can be demonstrated by reference to only two examples. First, the Swiss Supreme Court distinguishes between *peius*, that is, defective goods, and *aliud*, that is, different goods;[16] the latter giving the buyer the right to demand performance for ten years after the conclusion of the contract notwithstanding whether it gave notice of non-performance or not,[17] while the former requires the buyer to give prompt notice of defect according to Art. 201 OR (Swiss Civil Code) to preserve any remedies for breach of contract. Where the line between *peius* and *aliud* will be drawn in a particular case can be extremely difficult to predict.[18] The second example is compensation of consequential losses.[19] Whether there is a claim for damages without fault depends on the number of links in the chain of causation.[20] Extremely short periods for giving notice of defects[21] furthermore militate against domestic Swiss law for the international context. Similar examples could be drawn from many domestic legal systems.

3 Global Instruments on Contract Law

UNCITRAL Endeavours

It was exactly against this background that UNCITRAL started working on the unification of sales law in 1968, culminating in the Convention on Contracts for the International Sale of Goods (CISG) which entered into force on 1 January 1988. The CISG proved to be the most successful international private law convention world-wide. Today there are 79 contracting states with the number continuously increasing.[22] According to WTO trade statistics, nine of the ten largest export

---

16   BGer, 5 December 1995, BGE 121 III 453 (Switzerland).

17   cf Art 127 OR (Swiss Civil Code).

18   See Fountoulakis (n 11) 308–09; for more information on the differentiation between *peius* and *aliud* see Heinrich Honsell in Heinrich Honsell, Nedim Peter Vogt and Wolfgang Wiegand (eds), *Basler Kommentar, Obligationenrecht I* (5th edn, Helbing Lichtenhahn Verlag 2011) Art 206 paras 2–3.

19   Art 208(2) OR (Swiss Civil Code).

20   See BGer, 28 November 2006, BGE 133 III 257, 271 (Switzerland); Honsell (n 18) Art 208 paras 7–8.

21   cf Art 201(1) OR (Swiss Civil Code), according to which the notice must be made immediately ('sofort'); see also BGer, 27 June 1950, BGE 76 II 221, 225 (Switzerland) (notice within four days in time as these included a Sunday).

22   A list of all current contracting states to the CISG is provided by UNCITRAL <www.uncitral.org/uncitral/en/uncitral_texts/sale_goods/1980CISG_status.html>. Recently, Brazil has deposited its instrument of ratification of the CISG. The Convention will come into force

and import nations are contracting states, with the UK being the only exception.[23] It can be assumed that approximately 80 per cent of international sales contracts are potentially governed by the CISG.[24]

Moreover, a truly great success is the strong influence the CISG has exerted at both the domestic and international level. The Uniform Act on General Commercial Law by the Organization for the Harmonization of Business Law in Africa (OHADA) in its sales part is in many respects practically a transcript of the CISG.[25] The UNIDROIT Principles of International Commercial Contracts,[26] the Principles of European Contract Law,[27] the Draft Common Frame of Reference[28] and now the Draft Common European Sales Law[29] are all modelled on the CISG. Furthermore, the EC Consumer Sales Directive heavily draws on the CISG.[30] Similarly, the Sale of Goods Act in the Nordic Countries,[31]

---

on 1 April 2014, making Brazil its 79th contracting state. In Bahrain and Madagascar ratification processes have started. See also Ingeborg Schwenzer and Pascal Hachem, 'The CISG – A Story of Worldwide Success' in Jan Kleineman (ed), *CISG Part II Conference* (Iustus 2009) 119.

23 cf World Trade Organization, 'International Trade Statistics 2011' (n 3) 24.

24 See Peter Schlechtriem and Ingeborg Schwenzer in Ingeborg Schwenzer (ed), *Schlechtriem & Schwenzer, Commentary on the Convention on the International Sale of Goods (CISG)* (3rd edn, OUP 2010) Introduction I.

25 Acte uniforme portant sur le Droit commercial general (AUDCG) (1998, amended 2011) <www.ohada.org/presentation-generale-de-lacte-uniforme/telechargements1.html>; cf Ingeborg Schwenzer, 'Regional and Global Unification of Sales Law' (2011) 13 European Journal of Law Reform 370, 373–76; Ulrich G Schroeter, 'Das einheitliche Kaufrecht der afrikanischen OHADA-Staaten im Vergleich zum UN-Kaufrecht' (2001) Recht in Afrika 163, 166.

26 UNIDROIT Principles of International Commercial Contracts (PICC) (2010) <www.unidroit.org/english/principles/contracts/principles2010/integralversionprinciples2010-e.pdf>; cf Michael Joachim Bonell, 'The CISG, European Contract Law and the Development of a World Contract Law' (2008) 56 American Journal of Comparative Law 1, 16–18.

27 See for more information on PECL n 7; cf Ole Lando, 'CISG and Its Followers: A Proposal to Adopt Some International Principles of Contract Law' (2005) 53 American Journal of Comparative Law 379, 381.

28 Christian von Bar and Eric Clive (eds), *Principles, Definitions and Model Rules of European Private Law, Draft Common Frame of Reference (DCFR)* (Sellier 2009).

29 See Ingeborg Schwenzer, 'The Proposed Common European Sales Law and the Convention on the International Sale of Goods' (2012) 44 Uniform Commercial Code Law Journal 457. The draft forms Annex I of the 'Proposal for a Regulation of the European Parliament and of the Council on a Common European Sales Law' COM (2011) 635 final (11 October 2012) <http://eur-lex.europa.eu/LexUriServ/LexUriServ.do?uri=COM:2011:0 635:FIN:EN:PDF>.

30 Directive 1999/44/EC of the European Parliament and of the Council of 25 May 1999 on certain aspects of the sale of consumer goods and associated guarantees <http://eur-lex.europa.eu/LexUriServ/LexUriServ.do?uri=OJ:L:1999:171:0012:0016:EN:PDF>.

31 cf Kjelland, *Das neue Kaufrecht der nordischen Länder im Vergleich mit dem Wiener Kaufrecht (CISG) und dem deutschen Kaufrecht* (Shaker Verlag 2000).

the modernized German Law of Obligations,[32] the Contract Law of the People's Republic of China and other East Asian codifications,[33] and the majority of the recent post-Soviet codifications in Eastern Europe,[34] Central Asia,[35] and in two of the Baltic States[36] build on the CISG. Likewise, the draft for a new Civil Code in Japan follows the CISG.[37] It is reported that in developing countries the CISG is used to teach traders the structures of contract law so as to improve their level of sophistication.[38]

Despite this notable world-wide success, the CISG is merely a sales law convention that nevertheless covers core areas of General Contract Law. In addition to the obligations of the parties and typical sales law issues such as conformity of the goods and passing of risk, it contains provisions on the formation of contracts and remedies for breach of contract.[39]

The shortcomings of the CISG firstly relate to the areas not at all covered by the Convention, which approximately amounts to 50 per cent of the entire area of General Contract Law. Especially, the CISG does not deal with agency, validity questions such as mistake, fraud, duress, gross disparity, illegality, and control of unfair terms, third party rights, conditions, set-off, assignment of rights, transfer of obligations, assignments of contracts, and plurality of obligors and obligees. Furthermore, many issues that were still highly debated in the 1970s had to be left open in the CISG such as the problem of battle of the forms, specific performance as well as the applicable interest rate.[40] Some areas that are covered by the CISG have in the meantime proven to need more detailed attention, such as the rules on unwinding of contracts. Finally, conventions meant to supplement the CISG, such as the 1974 United Nations Convention on the Limitation Period in the International

---

32 Peter Schlechtriem, 'International Einheitliches Kaufrecht und neues Schuldrecht' in Barbara Dauner-Lieb, Horst Konzen and Karsten Schmidt (eds), *Das neue Schuldrecht in der Praxis* (Heymanns 2003) 71.

33 cf Gary F Bell, 'Harmonisation of Contract Law in Asia – Harmonising Regionally or Adopting Global Harmonisations – The Example of the CISG' (2005) Singapore Journal of Legal Studies 362, 365–6.

34 Rolf Knieper, 'Celebrating Success by Accession to CISG' (2005) 25 Journal of Law and Commerce 477, 478.

35 ibid.

36 cf Martin Käerdi, 'Die Neukodifikation des Privatrechts der baltischen Staaten in vergleichender Sicht' in Helmut Heiss (ed), *Zivilrechtsreform im Baltikum* (Mohr Siebeck 2006) 19.

37 See for the English version of the Draft Proposal <www.shojihomu.or.jp/saikenhou/English/index_e.html>.

38 Schwenzer, Hachem and Kee (n 8) para 3.21.

39 The formation of contracts is dealt with in Arts 14–24 CISG. The buyer's remedies for breach of contract are to be found in Arts 45–52, the seller's remedies in Arts 61–5.

40 On the battle of forms see Ulrich G Schroeter in Schwenzer, *Commentary* (n 24) Art 19 paras 31–51; on the applicable rate of interest see Klaus Bacher in Schwenzer, *Commentary* (n 24) Art 78 paras 26-43.

Sale of Goods[41] and the 2005 United Nations Convention on the Use of Electronic Communications in International Contracts,[42] have at least not attracted as many members as the CISG, thereby also diminishing their unifying effect.

In addition to the CISG, UNCITRAL has embarked upon the unification of many other areas of international trade. Some of these instruments again touch upon various questions of General Contract Law,[43] especially the 1974 Convention on the Limitation Period in the International Sale of Goods, the 1983 Uniform Rules on Contract Clauses for an Agreed Sum Due upon Failure of Performance, the 1992 UNCITRAL Legal Guide on International Countertrade Transactions, and the 2005 United Nations Convention on the Use of Electronic Communications in International Contracts. However, this still leaves important areas to domestic law.

UNIDROIT Principles

On a global scale, UNIDROIT has engaged in elaborating Principles of International Commercial Contracts (PICC).[44] Whereas the 1994 version of the UNIDROIT Principles mostly covered the areas already dealt with under the CISG, and in addition validity issues, the 2004 version also addressed authority of agents, contracts for the benefit of third parties, set-off, limitation periods,

---

41 See for text and status <www.uncitral.org/uncitral/en/uncitral_texts/sale_goods/1974Convention_limitation_period.html>.

42 See for text and status <www.uncitral.org/uncitral/uncitral_texts/electronic_commerce/2005Convention.html>.

43 1974 Convention on the Limitation Period in the International Sale of Goods; 1978 United Nations Convention on the Carriage of Goods by Sea – the 'Hamburg Rules'; 1980 United Nations Convention on International Multimodal Transport of Goods; 1983 Uniform Rules on Contract Clauses for an Agreed Sum Due upon Failure of Performance; 1988 United Nations Convention on International Bills of Exchange and International Promissory Notes; 1991 United Nations Convention on the Liability of Operators of Transport Terminals in International Trade; 1992 UNCITRAL Legal Guide on International Countertrade Transactions; 1992 UNCITRAL Model Law on International Credit Transfers; 1995 United Nations Convention on Independent Guarantees and Stand-by Letters of Credit; 1996 UNCITRAL Model Law on Electronic Commerce with Guide to Enactment, with additional article 5 bis as adopted in 1998; 2001 UNCITRAL Model Law on Electronic Signatures with Guide to Enactment; 2001 United Nations Convention on the Assignment of Receivables in International Trade; 2005 United Nations Convention on the Use of Electronic Communications in International Contracts; 2007 UNCITRAL Legislative Guide on Secured Transactions; 2007 Promoting confidence in electronic commerce: legal issues on international use of electronic authentication and signature methods; 2008 United Nations Convention on Contracts for the International Carriage of Goods Wholly or Partly by Sea – the 'Rotterdam Rules'; 2010 UNCITRAL Legislative Guide on Secured Transactions: Supplement on Security Rights in Intellectual Property.

44 See for further information on the PICC n 26.

assignment of rights and contracts, and transfer of obligations. Finally, the 2010 version contains a chapter on illegality and a section on conditions as well as detailed rules on the plurality of obligors and obligees and on the unwinding of contracts. Thus, the PICC 2010 now cover all areas that are perceived as contract law in most legal systems. Still, the practical importance of the PICC is rather limited, as they are an opt-in instrument being applicable by the parties' choice of law only.[45] Surveys suggest that in international commercial contracts the PICC are chosen in only 0.6 per cent of all cases.[46] Furthermore, the PICC being soft law, many domestic courts will not even accept such a choice of law.[47]

Furthermore, there are some shortcomings concerning the content of the PICC. The terminology used by the PICC is not always in line with the one used by CISG. For example, where the CISG uses the word avoidance for breach of contract the PICC instead uses the word termination[48] whereas avoidance is used in relation to defects of intent,[49] which would otherwise also be called rescission. This certainly gives rise to misunderstanding and confusion.[50] As the circle of representatives at UNIDROIT is not as inclusive as at UNCITRAL, the PICC display a certain tendency towards Civil Law concepts. The frequent use of good faith[51] is hardly acceptable to many Common Law lawyers. Likewise, there are too many provisions known to French legal systems only but unknown to both Common Law as well as Germanic systems, such as the rules on *astreinte*, a private penalty,[52] or those on conditions.[53]

4 Regional Instruments on Contract Law

On a regional level, a number of initiatives can be discerned. Several approaches can be found in Europe which all aimed at a European Civil Code or at least a European Contract Law. First and foremost, the Principles of European Contract Law (PECL) shall be mentioned here.[54] Starting with preparatory work in the 1980s, the PECL were published in three parts (1995, 1999, 2003),

---

45   cf the Preamble of the PICC.
46   See Simon Greenberg, Christopher Kee and J Romesh Weeramantry, *International Commercial Arbitration: An Asia-Pacific Perspective* (Cambridge University Press 2011) para 3.140.
47   Ralf Michaels in Stefan Vogenauer and Jan Kleinheisterkamp (eds), *Commentary on the UNIDROIT Principles of International Commercial Contracts (PICC)* (OUP 2009) Preamble I para 7.
48   See Chapter 7, Section 3 PICC, titled 'Termination'.
49   See Chapter 3, Section 2 PICC, titled 'Grounds for Avoidance'.
50   See also Schwenzer, Hachem and Kee (n 8) para 47.09.
51   See Arts 1.7, 4.8, 5.1.2, 5.3.3, 5.3.4 PICC.
52   Art 7.2.4 PICC; see also Schwenzer, Hachem and Kee (n 8) para 43.67–43.68.
53   See Chapter 5, Section 3 PICC.
54   For further information on PECL see n 7.

Part I covering performance, non-performance and remedies, Part II covering formation, agency, validity, interpretation, content and effects of contracts, and Part III covering plurality of parties, assignment of claims, substitution of the debtor, set-off, limitation, illegality, conditions, and capitalization of interest. The PECL have a clear European focus, but also take into account the US–American Uniform Commercial Code as well as the Restatements on Contracts and Restitution.[55] Like the PICC, the PECL are so-called soft law. Although the parties at least in arbitration may choose the PECL, there are no reported cases where this has happened.

More recently, the Study Group on a European Civil Code and the Research Group on European Private Law published the Draft Common Frame of Reference (DCFR) in 2009.[56] In contrast to the PICC and the PECL, the DCFR not only addresses General Contract Law but virtually all matters typically addressed in civil codes except family law and the law of inheritance. The DCFR was, however, met with severe criticism not only with regard to the general idea of the project[57] but especially with regard to drafting and style[58] as well as specific solutions in the area of general contract and sales law.[59]

Building on the DCFR, the European Commission published a proposal for a Regulation of the European Parliament and of the Council on a Common European Sales Law (CESL) in October 2011.[60] Thus, the idea of a General Contract Law on the European level was not pursued anymore but rather narrowed down to sales law. The content of the CESL is almost identical to that of the CISG and the United Nations (UN) Limitation Convention with additional provisions on defects of consent, unfair contract terms, pre-contractual information duties, and contracts to be concluded by electronic means. Most notably, in contrast to the CISG, the CESL not only applies to b2b contracts but is in fact primarily aimed at contracts with consumers. The CESL, too, is an opt-in instrument. Throughout the European Union this proposal has been met with utmost criticism from academia as well as from practice. The future of this instrument is yet to be seen.[61]

In Europe, a few more private initiatives undertook similar projects, among them the Academy of European Private Lawyers (Pavia Group) that issued

---

55 Lando and Beale (n 7) xxvi.
56 For further information on DCFR see n 28.
57 Schwenzer, Hachem and Kee (n 8) para 3.63.
58 Horst Eidenmüller and others, 'Der Gemeinsame Referenzrahmen für das Europäische Privatrecht: Wertungsfragen und Kodifikationsprobleme' (2008) Juristenzeitung 529, 549; Ulrich Huber, 'Modellregeln für ein Europäisches Kaufrecht' (2008)16 Zeitschrift für Europäisches Privatrecht 708, 742.
59 Huber (n 58) 744; Ingeborg Schwenzer and Pascal Hachem, 'Drafting New Model Rules on Sales: CFR as an Alternative to the CISG?' (2009) 11 European Journal of Law Reform 459.
60 For further information on CESL see n 29.
61 See on the whole Schwenzer, 'The Proposed European Sales Law' (n 29).

the Preliminary Draft for a European Code (2001)[62] and the Trento Common Core Project.[63]

In Africa, first regard is to be given to the OHADA's Uniform Act on General Commercial Law (1998, amended 2011).[64] As mentioned above, the sales part of this act strongly relies on the CISG, although it contains certain modifications. Unfortunately, the 2011 amendments have implemented additional concepts stemming from French law and thus blurring the clear concepts achieved by the CISG.[65] In addition to this act, OHADA initiated works on a Uniform Act on Contract Law. A draft was prepared in cooperation with UNIDROIT and published in 2004, heavily drawing on the PICC.[66] At the time being, the future of this project is uncertain. Considerations for the harmonization of contract law based on the current international experience are also voiced in the framework of the East African Community.

Another recent private initiative aiming at the elaboration of Principles of Asian Contract Law (PACL) can be found in Asia since 2009. Among others, participants come from Cambodia, Vietnam, Singapore, PRC, Japan, and South Korea. Until today, the chapters on formation, validity, interpretation, performance and non-performance of the contract have been finalized.[67]

Likewise, in Latin America, general contract principles are being developed since 2009 within the framework of the Proyecto sobre Principios Latinoamericanos de Derecho de los Contratos hosted by a Chilean university. The countries covered up to now are Argentina, Uruguay, Chile, Colombia and Venezuela. However, the European approach seems to be considered as well.[68] In 2011 the biannual Conference of Private Law teachers in Latin America recommended working towards a uniform Civil Code for the Latin American region and to take the work of the above mentioned Pavia Group as a starting point.[69]

---

62 For further information on the so-called Pavia Draft of a European Contract Code see Giuseppe Gandolfi, 'The Academy of European Private Lawyers and the Pavia Draft of a "European Contract Code"', <http://ec.europa.eu/consumers/cons_int/safe_shop/fair_bus_pract/cont_law/stakeholders/5-20.pdf>.

63 For further information on the Trento Common Core Project see <www.common-core.org/>.

64 For further information on the AUDCG see n 25.

65 cf Schwenzer, Hachem and Kee (n 8) para 3.40.

66 OHADA Uniform Act on Contract Law, Preliminary Draft (2004) <www.unidroit.org/english/legalcooperation/OHADA%20act-e.pdf>.

67 For further information on the PACL see <www.fondation-droitcontinental.org/jcms/c_7718/projet-commun-de-droit-des-contrats-en-asie-du-sud-est>.

68 For further information on this project see <www.fundacionfueyo.udp.cl/archivos/Proyecto%20sobre%20Principios%20latinoamericanos%20de%20derecho%20de%20los%20contratos.pdf>.

69 See Luis FP Leiva Fernandez, 'Autour d'un "Code des contrats": Le Congrès des civilistes latino-américains à Tucuman' (2012) 64 Revue internationale de droit comparé 334 <http://www.unisob.na.it/universita/facolta/giurisprudenza/age/leiva.pdf>.

Along these initiatives, a trend aiming at building common regional law by using global texts also exists, for instance in the framework of the North American Free Trade Agreement (NAFTA), and now also in the framework of the Dominican Republic – Central America Free Trade Agreement (DR-CAFTA).[70]

Regional endeavours to harmonize and unify General Contract Law, however, cannot fulfill the needs of international trade.[71] Rather, different legal regimes in different regions lead to fragmentation. Instead of saving transaction costs and thus facilitating cross-border trade, international contracting may become even more complicated. Regional unification adds one more layer in addition to domestic rules and the well-established instrument of the CISG. Additionally, in many instances, not only does the terminology used in the General Contract Law instruments differ from that of the CISG, which in itself leads to confusion, but frequently, there will also be contradicting solutions to one and the same legal problem. Finally, regionalization of legal systems reduces the number of cases decided on a truly international level and hence has a negative impact on the predictability of the outcomes.

5 International Chamber of Commerce

For decades, important contributions to the harmonization of international trade law have emanated from the International Chamber of Commerce (ICC). As far back as 1936, the ICC published the International Commercial Terms (Incoterms®). Their latest version, the eighth edition, dates from 2010.[72] Although in many sales contracts they are agreed upon and thus are of significant practical importance, Incoterms® cover only a small fraction of the parties' obligations in an international sales contract. With the Uniform Customs and Practice for Documentary Credits (UCP), the ICC has created another important instrument to facilitate international trade.[73] Finally, the ICC provides innumerable model contracts and clauses for use in various types of international commercial transactions.[74]

---

70   cf Stephen Zamora, 'NAFTA and the Harmonization of Domestic Legal Systems: The Side Effects of Free Trade' (1995) 12 Arizona Journal of International and Comparative Law 401; see also Craig L Jackson, 'The Free Trade Agreement of the Americas and Legal Harmonization' ASIL Insights June 1996 <www.asil.org/insight3.cfm>.

71   See also McKendrick (n 5) 29.

72   See on the Incoterms® 2010 Jan Ramberg, *ICC Guide to Incoterms 2010* (ICC 2011).

73   See on the latest version of the UCP, UCP 600, International Chamber of Commerce, *Commentary on UCP 600* (ICC 2007).

74   See, for example, International Chamber of Commerce, *The ICC Model International Sale Contract* (ICC 2013) and International Chamber of Commerce, *ICC Force Majeure Clause 2003, ICC Hardship Clause 2003* (ICC Publishing S.A. 2003), free download of the English and French versions at <www.iccbooks.com/Product/ProductInfo.aspx?id=233>.

6 Possible Future Work on Global Contract Law

All the endeavours described above clearly demonstrate the urgent need to further harmonize if not unify General Contract Law.

UNCITRAL would be the most appropriate place for such a project which falls squarely within UNCITRAL's mandate. According to General Assembly Resolution 2205 (XXI), para. 8: "[t]he Commission shall further the progressive harmonization and unification of the law of international trade by: (a) Co-ordinating the work of organizations active in this field and encouraging co-operation among them".[75] Whereas any regional endeavour might mainly focus on the laws of the respective countries involved, UNCITRAL has the chance to embark upon a more truly global reflection. Indeed, UNCITRAL is the only forum with universal participation, that is, all the regions of the world have a chance to contribute on equal footing.[76] This is the reason why in 2012 Switzerland made a proposal for the 45th session of UNCITRAL on possible future work by UNCITRAL in the area of international contract law.[77] However, this proposal did not suggest how the possible future work should be conducted; especially what kind of instrument should be aimed at if one were to come to the conclusion that such future work is desirable and feasible. Let me give some thoughts on this question, emphasizing that I am speaking entirely for myself and in no way voicing the official Swiss opinion.

In principle, there is the choice between a convention and a model law. A convention is designed to unify law by establishing binding legal obligations.[78] Its aim is to achieve a very high level of harmonization.[79] Although there may be the possibility of having some reservations allowing State Parties a certain but very limited degree of choice, such reservations are easily discernible without the need to have recourse to the respective domestic law. Thus, a convention provides the highest level of predictability for private parties. In contrast, a model

---

75 General Assembly Resolution 2205 (XXI), 17 December 1966 <http://www.un.org/ga/search/view_doc.asp?symbol=A/RES/2205%28XXI%29&Lang=E&Area=RESOLUTION>.

76 UNCITRAL's membership comprises states from Africa, Asia, Eastern Europe, Western Europe, Latin America and the Caribbean, thereby ensuring that the main economic and legal systems of the world are represented. For an overview of the today 60 member states see United Nations Commission on International Trade Law, *A Guide to UNCITRAL: Basic Facts about the United Nations Commission on International Trade Law* (2013), 37–41 (Annex II) <www.uncitral.org/pdf/english/texts/general/12-57491-Guide-to-UNCITRAL-e.pdf>.

77 United Nations Commission on International Trade Law, 'Possible future work in the area of international contract law: Proposal by Switzerland on possible future work by UNCITRAL in the area of international contract law', 45th session, New York, 25 June – 6 July 2012, A/CN.9/758 (8 May 2012) <www.uncitral.org/uncitral/commission/sessions/45th.html>.

78 UNCITRAL, *A Guide to UNCITRAL* (n 76) 13.

79 ibid 14.

law only provides for a legislative text that is recommended to State Parties.[80] It is used where State Parties want to retain flexibility in implementing or where strict uniformity is not desirable or necessary.[81] Furthermore, a model law may be finalized and approved by UNCITRAL at its annual session whereas a convention still, in principle, necessitates a diplomatic conference.[82] Although, at the political level it may be certainly easier to convince state governments to agree to a model law allowing them more leeway, the needs of international commerce clearly militate in favour of a convention. Even if states were to implement a model law, they could deviate from the text of such a model law which would make it difficult to ascertain the content of the applicable law in a specific case. Moreover, there is no obligation for courts of a state that has implemented a model law to regard its international character and the need to promote uniformity in its interpretation, as it is nowadays provided for in any international convention.[83] Thus, a statute implementing a model law *is* purely domestic law and is legitimately interpreted against the respective domestic background. If a model law may bring about some harmonization at the beginning this will soon be lost after some time. This can especially be expected in a traditional field such as contract law where firm dogmatic conceptions and convictions prevail that have been shaped over centuries and that every lawyer has internalized from the very first day in law school.

The scope of the envisaged instrument on General Contract Law should be similar to that of the CISG. That means in the first place that the instrument should only be concerned with international contracts but not with purely domestic ones. There is no reason and it is not the mandate of UNCITRAL to interfere with domestic relationships.[84] If a state feels the need to simplify the situation for its citizens by having the same law applied to domestic as well as to international contracts it is free to do so and implement correspondent domestic legislation as some states already have chosen in the relation to the CISG.[85]

Like the CISG, the instrument on General Contract Law should be confined to b2b contracts without touching business-to-consumer (b2c) relationships. Except for internet transactions that become more and more international, b2c contracts remain mostly domestic contracts. Consumer protection asks for mandatory rules which stands in sharp contrast to the need for freedom of contract in b2b contracts. It is not possible to juggle the needs of both – consumers and businesses – in one single instrument. The futility of such an endeavour has been demonstrated lately by the draft of a CESL.[86] Furthermore, the level of consumer protection still differs considerably around the world; an international *consensus* in this field probably

---

80 ibid.
81 ibid.
82 ibid 15.
83 See only Art 7(1) CISG.
84 cf for UNCITRAL's mandate UNCITRAL, *A Guide to UNCITRAL* (n 76) 1–2.
85 cf nn 31–37.
86 See Schwenzer (n 29).

cannot be achieved during the decades to come. Finally, consumer protection is better served by procedural tools such as class action and online dispute resolution than by mandatory substantive law rules.

Having regard to the areas already covered by the CISG – especially contract formation, interpretation and remedies for breach of contract – it can be expected that the CISG rules are also well suited for other contracts. Even long-term contracts can be accommodated by the existing CISG rules on contracts for delivery of goods by installments.[87] If the need were to be felt to exclude certain contracts from the instrument, such as maybe labour contracts or insurance contracts, this could be achieved on the one hand on a general level by a rule similar to Art. 2 CISG, excluding certain contracts from the scope of application of the instrument; and on the other hand, by providing for reservations allowing individual states to exclude certain contracts. Finally, the contract law instrument like the CISG[88] would be an opt-out instrument enabling the parties themselves to decide if they do not want these rules to apply to their contract.

As regards further areas of contract law that should be addressed it is clear that the future uniform contract instrument should cover as many areas as possible. However, there are some fields where unification is more urgent than in others. The most important area where the gaps left by the CISG are most unfortunate because they endanger uniformity already reached is questions of validity. Although it is now unanimously held that the CISG itself defines what is a question of validity left to domestic law and what is not,[89] many day-to-day contract problems are issues of validity. To name but a few; questions of consent, such as mistake, undue influence or fraud; and validity of individual clauses and standard terms, such as gross disparity, burdensome obligations, exclusion and limitation of liability clauses as well as fixed sums, that is, penalty and liquidated damages clauses.[90] It is extremely burdensome to have these questions answered by domestic law which might well lead to frictions with unified law. Also very important are issues of consequences of unwinding of contracts[91] and set-off.[92] Other areas of contract law, such as third party rights, assignment and delegation, or joint and several obligors and obligees might not be at the forefront of desirability for unification.

If one considers working on further unification of contract law, the route to be followed seems to be pretty clear. The starting point must be the CISG. It has

---

87   Art 73 CISG.

88   Art 6 CISG.

89   Ingeborg Schwenzer and Pascal Hachem in Schwenzer, *Commentary* (n 24) Art 4 para 31 with references.

90   For an overview on how the issues of formation and validity of sales contracts are dealt with in different legal systems see Schwenzer, Hachem and Kee (n 8) paras 9.01–22.25.

91   For an overview on how the unwinding of contracts is dealt with in the different legal systems see ibid paras 50.01–50.36.

92   For a comparative discussion on set-off see Christiana Fountoulakis, *Set-off Defences in International Arbitration: A Comparative Analysis* (Hart Publishing 2011).

received such tremendous acceptance that anything that might interfere with it must be refrained from. Other UNCITRAL instruments, such as the 1974 Limitation Convention or the 1983 Uniform Rules on Contract Clauses for an Agreed Sum Due upon Failure of Performance, should be taken in due consideration and it should be discussed whether they should be amended. Certainly, of utmost importance are the PICC. Most valuable work has been completed by UNIDROIT and any duplication of efforts must be prevented. In essence, we face a similar situation as in 1968 when UNCITRAL started working on the CISG, drawing heavily on the previous work done by UNIDROIT that had led to the Hague Conventions on the sale of goods, the Uniform Law on the Formation of Contracts for the International Sale of Goods (ULF) and the Uniform Law on the International Sale of Goods (ULIS) respectively.[93] However, as has been mentioned before, there are certain contradictions between the CISG and the PICC that need to be eliminated;[94] in other areas the possible acceptance of the PICC rules at a global level must be carefully scrutinized and discussed.

Having regard to what already has been achieved at the international level, a global contract law appears to be feasible within a reasonable amount of time and without consuming too many resources needed elsewhere.

7 Improvements by a Global Contract Law

How would the global picture for internationally contracting parties change if we had an UNCITRAL instrument on General Contract Law?

First, this instrument – just like the CISG – could be expected to represent a good compromise between Common and Civil Law.[95] It would be acceptable to any party regardless of its own legal background. It would be a truly neutral law.

Second, it would be drawn up in the six UN languages and would be translated into the languages of the states adopting this instrument and thus be readily available in court and arbitral proceedings rendering costly translations and expert testimony superfluous. Like the CISG, it could serve as a model for further harmonization of contract law on a domestic level. And it could be used to teach traders that cannot afford in-house counsel or legal advice the basics of contract law.

Third, it would lead to much more predictability in international contracts. It can be expected that the same mechanisms that now support and enhance the uniform application and interpretation of the CISG will also play a decisive role

---

93 For more information on the drafting history of the CISG see Peter Schlechtriem, *Uniform Sales Law – The UN-Convention on Contracts for the International Sale of Goods* (Manzsche Verlags- und Universitätsbuchhandlung 1986) 17–21.

94 cf nn 48–53.

95 cf for the CISG Ulrich Magnus, 'The Vienna Sales Convention (CISG) between Civil and Common Law – Best of all Worlds?' (2010) 3 Journal of Civil Legal Studies 67–98.

for such an instrument. It must be recalled that by now we have about 3,000 published cases on the CISG,[96] we count about 4,000 publications freely accessible on the internet,[97] we have CLOUT – Case Law on UNCITRAL texts,[98] we have the UNCITRAL Digest[99] and further institutions world-wide such as the CISG Advisory Council[100] that strive to guard uniformity. Commentaries with article-by-article comments will be published in different languages. Uniform standard forms that facilitate contracting will soon emerge on the basis of such an instrument and further add to predictability.

All in all it can be expected that an UNCITRAL instrument on General Contract Law may considerably save transaction costs. It may help companies with lesser funds to be able to pursue their legal rights under an international contract and thus further promote international trade. Finally, it can support the rule of law world-wide.

---

96 See for cases on the CISG, for example, the online case database CISG-online <www.cisg-online.ch> and the Pace Law School CISG database <www.cisg.law.pace.edu>.

97 See for publications freely accessible on the internet, for example, the online collection of scholarly writings at the Pace Law School CISG database <www.cisg.law.pace.edu>.

98 See for CLOUT <www.uncitral.org/uncitral/en/case_law.html>.

99 See for the UNCITRAL Digest <www.uncitral.org/uncitral/en/case_law/digests.html>.

100 For further information on the CISG Advisory Council and for the CISG Advisory Council Opinions see <www.cisgac.com>.

Chapter 4
The Challenges of Good Faith in Contract Law Codification

Therese Wilson

1 Introduction

In this chapter I will argue that in any codification or restatement of Australian contract law there should be some focus on 'internationalisation' of contract law, including the incorporation of a good faith obligation as is found in most civil law codes and a number of international instruments.

The internationalisation of Australian contract law is an important consideration in a context where Australians are increasingly trading internationally, Australian law firms are merging with international firms, and there is a desire to attract international litigation and arbitration to Australia.

Common lawyers have resisted the impost of good faith upon their contract law, citing a lack of clarity surrounding the good faith obligation. It will be argued that, in reality, the obligation to act in good faith is not so far removed from, and is no more or less difficult to clearly articulate than, an obligation to act with good conscience under the unconscionability principle. To better understand the common law resistance to good faith, it will be viewed through the lens of systems theory. It will be argued that, while good faith cannot be neatly transplanted into the contract law of a common law country, it can develop and evolve within the common law system and in turn influence development and evolution of the principle in civil law systems, potentially leading over time to international understandings of the concept. This is, in a sense, not unlike the experiment that has been the United Nations Convention on Contracts for the International Sale of Goods (CISG), which has seen lawyers from different systems reach compromises and strive towards common understandings of the provisions under the convention.[1]

---

1   Although it is acknowledged that this compromise did not extend to the inclusion of a good faith obligation under the CISG. The 'common understandings' referred to have been assisted by the publication of commentaries on the CISG, such as John Honnold and Harry Flechtner, *Uniform Law for International Sales Under the 1980 United Nations Convention* (Alphen aan den Rijn, Wolters Kluwer, 4th Edition, 2009); and Peter Schlechtriem and Ingeborg Schwenzer, *Commentary on the UN Convention on the International Sale of Goods (CISG)* (New York, Oxford University Press, 3rd Edition, 2010). Publication of a commentary on international understandings and implementation of the good faith doctrine

2 Internationalisation as an Important Consideration in a Codification Project

When a common law country such as Australia considers embarking upon a codification or restatement of its contract law,[2] it is pertinent to ask whether it should seek to *reform* its contract law at the same time. Such reform might be informed by a desire to 'internationalise' the law. This is in a context where Australians increasingly trade internationally and where Australian law firms are increasingly merging with international law firms.[3] There is seen to be a risk of 'being left behind' by the world, if Australia's contract law does not conform to basic international expectations, including for example an obligation of good faith in contract negotiation, performance and termination. In arguing for recognition of the good faith obligation in Australian contract law, Finn has asserted that:

> If contract as an institution is to have integrity, if Australian contract law is to maintain its standing in the global arena, it must, in my view, have effective legal safeguards against undue exploitation and advantage-taking in contract formation.[4]

Whether or not any codification or restatement should include reform so as to recognise a good faith obligation, there are those who are opposed to the

---

would be a most worthwhile undertaking, particularly given that the UK has now had two decades to come to terms with good faith following the European Economic Community Council Directive 93/13/EEC regarding unfair terms in consumer contracts. Australian courts also have to consider good faith in relation to consumer law, for example as one of the factors relevant to determining unconscionability under section 21 Australian Consumer Law. A commentary which could incorporate UK interpretations of good faith alongside civil law interpretations would be a valuable international resource.

    2   It has been suggested in relation to the review of Australian contract law that a restatement of principles rather than a codification of contract law would be more appropriate. See for example Luke Nottage, 'The Government's Proposed 'Review of Australian Contract Law': A Preliminary Positive Response': <http://www.ag.gov.au/Consultations/Documents/SubmissionstotheReviewofAustralianContractLaw/Submission%20008%20-%20Contract%20Law%20Review%20-%20Dr%20Luke%20Nottage.pdf> accessed 8 April 2013; and Bryan Horrigan, Emmanuel Laryea, Lisa Spagnolo, 'Reviewing Australia's Contract Law: A Time for Change?', <http://www.ag.gov.au/Consultations/Documents/SubmissionstotheReviewofAustralianContractLaw/Submission%20035%20-%20Contract%20Law%20Review%20-%20Horrigan%20Laryea%20Spagnolo.pdf> accessed 8 April 2013.

    3   Ibid.

    4   Paul Finn, 'Internationalisation or Isolation: The Australian Cul De Sac? The Case of Contract Law' in Elise Bant and Matthew Harding (eds), *Exploring Private Law* (Cambridge University Press 2010) 41, 64.

idea of codification per se, arguing that the common law for all of its 'untidy complexity'[5] is superior:

> ... it is better to have a feast of contrasting sources, festering with ideas, than a simple hygienic package, wrapped in polythene, insulated ... from differences in analysis and on points of detail.[6]

Carter and Peden have similarly argued that:

> ... Australian common law is not a code. It does not always provide a neat list of features, inclusions and exclusions. This does not mean it is inferior. It merely requires lawyers and judges to explain what is inherent in our law.[7]

They also argue that good faith is already implicit in existing contract law principles and does not need to be separately articulated, either by implication of terms or through codification.[8]

The difficulty for Australian contract law, however, is that the Australian courts have failed to clarify the existence (or non-existence) or scope of any good faith obligation, or its relationship to the existing doctrine of unconscionability. Determining whether or not a good faith obligation exists within Australian contract law, and the scope of any such obligation, may be of significant importance to Australia's trading partners. The Contract Law of the People's Republic of China, for example, places considerable emphasis on the principle of good faith.[9]

It is noteworthy that the CISG does form part of Australia's law relating to international sales contracts.[10] Article 7 (1) CISG does not go so far as to impose good faith obligations on contracting parties,[11] however it does requires good faith to be used as a principle in interpreting obligations under the CISG.[12]

---

5 Robert Goff, 'The Search for Principle' in William Swadling and Gareth Jones (eds), *The Search For Principle* (Oxford University Press 1999) 313.

6 Ibid.

7 John Carter and Elisabeth Peden, 'Good Faith in Australian Contract Law' (2003) 19 Journal of Contract Law 155, 171.

8 Ibid

9 Wang Liming and Xu Chuanxi, 'Fundamental Principles of China's Contract Law' (1999) 13 Columbia Journal of Asian Law 1, 15–19.

10 Through legislation such as the Sale of Goods (Vienna Convention) Act 1986 Qld.

11 See Ingeborg Schwenzer, 'The Proposed Common European Sales Law and the Convention on the International Sale of Goods' (2012) 44 (4) Uniform Commercial Code Law Journal. 457, 463; John Honnold and Harry Flechtner, *Uniform Law for International Sales under the 1980 United Nations Convention*, 4th Edition (Kluwer Law International 2009), 133–136; and Peter Schlechtriem and Petra Butler, *UN Law on International Sales: The UN Convention on the International Sale of Goods* (Springer 2009), 50.

12 See discussion in Allan Farnsworth, 'Duties of Good Faith and Fair Dealing Under the UNIDROIT Principles, Relevant International Conventions, and National

This was recognised in 1992 by Priestley JA sitting on the New South Wales Court of Appeal in the matter of *Renard Constructions (ME) Pty Ltd v Minister for Public Works*.[13] Priestley JA referred to article 7 (1) of the CISG as demonstrating international recognition of the principle of good faith, and found that 'reasonableness in performance', which equated to European notions of good faith, should be implied as a contract term under Australian contract law. This position was endorsed in two subsequent New South Wales Court of Appeal decisions,[14] for example with findings that termination rights must be exercised in good faith. This position has not, however, been endorsed by the Australian High Court.[15] Further, the Victorian Supreme Court has rejected the implication of a duty of good faith. Warren CJ stated in *Esso Australia Resources Pty Ltd v Southern Pacific Petroleum NL*[16] that:

> If a duty of good faith exists, it really means that there is a standard of contractual conduct that should be met. The difficulty is that the standard is nebulous. Therefore, the current reticence attending the application and recognition of a duty of good faith probably lies as much with the vagueness and imprecision inherent in defining commercial morality. The modern law of contract has developed on the premise of achieving certainty in commerce. If good faith is not readily capable of definition then that certainty is undermined. ... Ultimately, the interests of certainty in contractual activity should be interfered with only when the relationship between the parties is unbalanced and one party is at a substantial disadvantage, or is particularly vulnerable in the prevailing context ... If one party to a contract is more shrewd, more cunning and out-manoeuvres the other contracting party who did not suffer a disadvantage and who was not vulnerable, it is difficult to see why the latter should have greater protection than that provided by the law of contract.

This statement prefers the application of the unconscionability doctrine (through requiring substantial disadvantage on the part of one party before court intervention is warranted) rather than the principle of good faith in regulating the conduct of contracting parties. It is also consistent with the narrow view of unconscionability adopted by the Australian High Court in *Australian Competition and Consumer*

Laws', (1995) 3 Tulane Journal of International and Comparative Law 47, 55; and in Paul Powers, 'Defining the Undefinable: Good Faith and the United Nations Convention on Contracts for the International Sale of Goods', (1998–1999) 18 Journal of Law and Commerce 333, 342–343.

13   (1992) 26 NSWLR 234

14   *Alcatel Australia Ltd v Scarcella* (1998) 44 NSWLR 349 at 368-9; *Burger King Corp v Hungry Jack's Pty Ltd* (2001) 69 NSWLR 558.

15   See discussion in Andrew Stewart, 'What's Wrong with the Australian Law of Contract?' (2012) 29 Journal of Contract Law 74, 84.

16   [2005] VSCA 228.

Commission v C G Berbatis Holdings Pty Ltd,[17] which will be further discussed below. One wonders whether Australia's Chinese, US and European trading partners would be accepting of this approach, and whether or not that matters. Contracts between, for example, Australian and Chinese traders may, of course, be governed by the CISG or another choice of law, but if it is considered economically desirable for Australian law to be the preferred choice of law, with a view to attracting international litigation and arbitration to Australia, then it probably it does matter.[18]

3 Understandings of Unconscionability

Australian contract law primarily regulates what might be regarded as poor or unreasonable conduct by a contracting party, through the doctrine of unconscionability.

Carter and Peden argue that there is no need to imply a good faith obligation into contracts under Australian law as such an obligation is already to be found in existing contract principles, and that in any event, doctrines such as the unconscionability doctrine deal adequately with poor behaviour:

> Unconscionability, in particular, has been used in the past where there are legitimate concerns about a contracting party's behaviour that would not necessarily fall foul of other contract rules. Courts do not need to resort to manipulating or misapplying the tests for implying terms in order to incorporate 'good faith'.[19]

Unconscionability is said to be used in 'three senses' under Australian contract law:

> The first-order sense of the underlying principle according to which the law of equity intervenes ... the second-order sense of the touchstone for specific equitable doctrines and remedies such as imposing a constructive trust ... creating an estoppel ... the third-order sense of the specific equitable cause of action associated with doctrines like ... taking advantage of someone's special disadvantage.[20]

The first and second order senses might bear the closest resemblance to the civil law concept of good faith in so far as they are concerned with preventing conduct

---

17 (2003) 197 ALR 153.
18 See also discussion on this in Nottage, 'The Government's Proposed 'Review of Australian Contract Law': A Preliminary Positive Response' (n2).
19 Carter and Peden, 'Good Faith in Australian Contract Law' (n7), 171–172.
20 Bryan Horrigan, 'Unconscionability Breaks New Ground- Avoiding and Litigating Unfair Client Conduct after the ACCC Test Cases and Financial Services Reforms' (2002) 7 Deakin Law Review 73, 75.

which goes against good conscience. This tends not to be overly-prescriptive, but conforms to equity's original goal of achieving individual justice, preferring substance and intention over form.[21] An unconscionable assertion of strict legal rights can, for example, lead to the imposition of a remedial constructive trust,[22] or can lead to a party being estopped from asserting strict legal rights where the other party has acted to their detriment in reliance on a fundamental assumption that the first party has knowingly created.[23]

The third order sense – unconscionable dealing – is more prescriptive, and is a 'vitiating factor' giving rise to a right to rescind a contract. This focuses on conduct at the pre-contractual negotiation stage. As stated by Deane J in *Louth v Diprose*:[24]

> Unconscionable dealing extends generally to circumstances in which (i) a party to a transaction was under a special disability in dealing with the other party to the transaction with the consequence that there was an absence of any reasonable degree of equality between them and (ii) that special disability was sufficiently evident to the other party to make it prima facie unfair or 'unconscionable' that that other party procure, accept or retain the benefit of, the disadvantaged party's assent to the impugned transaction in the circumstances in which he or she procured or accepted it.

The High Court of Australia made it clear in *Australian Competition and Consumer Commission v C G Berbatis Holdings Pty Ltd*[25] that no special disability or disadvantage such as to give rise to a claim in unconscionability would be found merely because of an inequality of bargaining power. Gleeson CJ, in the majority, stated that:

> A person is not in a position of relevant disadvantage, constitutional, situational, or otherwise, simply because of inequality of bargaining power. Many, perhaps even most, contracts are made between parties of unequal bargaining power, and good conscience does not require parties to contractual negotiations to forfeit their advantages, or neglect their own interests ... Unconscientious exploitation of another's inability, or diminished ability, to conserve his or her own interests is not to be confused with taking advantage of a superior bargaining position.[26]

---

21 Peter Young, Clyde Croft and Megan Smith, *On Equity* (Lawbook Company 2009), 11–15.
22 See, for example, *Muschinski v Dodds* (1985) 160 CLR 583.
23 See, for example, *Waltons Stores (Interstate) Ltd v Maher* (1988) 164 CLR 387.
24 (1992) 175 CLR 621 at para 11.
25 (2003) 197 ALR 153.
26 Ibid, paras 11 and 14.

As a result, a lessee's need to renew a lease in order to sell the business which occupied the lease, was not enough to render the lessor's 'hard bargain' in requiring the lessee to discontinue certain legal action against the lessor before extending the lease, unconscionable. Bigwood has argued that the High Court in *Berbatis* incorrectly focused on a lack of 'impaired judgment' to dismiss any serious disadvantage, whereas it should have focused on 'impaired volition', that is, a lack of any real or meaningful choice.[27] This would seem to accord more with the US concept of unconscionability as included in the Uniform Commercial Code (UCC).[28] Judge Skelly Wright linked unconscionability under the UCC to a lack of meaningful choice in *Williams v Walker-Thomas Furniture Co*, as follows:

> Unconscionability has generally been recognized to include an absence of meaningful choice on the part of one of the parties [procedural unconscionability] together with contract terms which are unreasonably favourable to the other party [substantive unconscionability].[29]

The annotations to section 208 of the US Restatement (Seconds) of Contracts include the following recognition of 'meaningful choice' as a consideration, although it is confirmed that inequality in bargaining positions will not in and of itself give rise to a finding of unconscionability:

> ***Weakness in the bargaining process.*** A bargain is not unconscionable merely because the parties to it are unequal in bargaining position, nor even because the inequality results in an allocation of risks to the weaker party. But gross inequality of bargaining power, together with terms unreasonably favorable to the stronger party, may confirm indications that the transaction involved elements of deception or compulsion, or may show that the weaker party *had no meaningful choice, no real alternative*, or did not in fact assent or appear to assent to the unfair terms. [*Italics inserted*]

A different approach to unconscionability, or an application of good faith principles, may have resulted in a different outcome in *Berbatis* as will be explored below.

---

27 Rick Bigwood, 'Case Note: Australian Competition and Consumer Commission v C G Berbatis Holdings Pty Ltd. Curbing Unconscionability: Berbatis in the High Court of Australia' (2004) 28 Melbourne University Law Review 203, 230.

28 Section 2-302 Uniform Commercial Code as discussed in Craig Horowitz, 'Reviving the Law of Substantive Unconscionability: Applying the Implied Covenant of Good Faith and Fair Dealing to Excessively Priced Consumer Credit Contracts', (1985–1986) 33 UCLS Law Review, 940, 940.

29 350 F.2d 445 (D.C. Cir.1965) quoted and discussed in Horowitz, 'Reviving the Law of Substantive Unconscionability: Applying the Implied Covenant of Good Faith and Fair Dealing to Excessively Priced Consumer Credit Contracts' (n28), 941.

4 Understandings of Good Faith

In this part, current understandings of 'good faith' will be explored. A key articulated criticism of the good faith doctrine, fuelling concern amongst common lawyers, is that it is too vague and 'undefinable.' Arguably, however, it is no less 'definable' than the doctrine of unconscionability used in what Horrigan has referred to above as the first and second-order senses – essentially a prohibition on asserting strict legal rights where to do so would go *against 'good conscience'*.

The argument that the good faith doctrine is too vague and 'undefinable' led to what has been described as a 'strange arrangement,' an 'awkward compromise' and 'a rather peculiar provision' in the CISG.[30] As Schwenzer explains, the interest of maintaining certainty as to obligations under the CISG, resulted in the civil obligation of good faith being omitted, and good faith merely being referred to in Article 7 (1) CISG as an interpretive tool:

> It is one of the most salient features of English commercial law that it strongly favours certainty over fairness whereas many civil law legal systems tend to rely on notions of good faith and fair dealing. It was against this background that in the CISG 'the observance of good faith in international trade' was only inserted in Art. 7 (1) CISG as one criterion among others to be taken into consideration in interpreting the Convention.[31]

Examples of where the obligation of good faith dealing in contract are to be found include the German Civil Code, the Contract Law of the People's Republic of China, the UCC, the UNIDROIT Principles, the Principles of European Contract Law (PECL), and the recently adopted Common European Sales Law (CESL). The good faith concept was imposed upon members of the European Economic Community (including the UK) under the European Economic Community Council Directive 93/13/EEC of 5 April 1993 on unfair terms in consumer contracts; and is being considered for inclusion in unfair contracts law reform by the British Columbia Law Institute. A key difference between the US and British Columbian approach on the one hand and the European and Chinese approaches on the other, is that the US and proposed BC good faith duty only applies to contract performance, whereas the European and Chinese approaches extend this duty to pre-contractual negotiations. This could in part be due to the availability of the unconscionability doctrine with respect to pre-contractual negotiations in common law countries.

---

30 Allan Farnsworth, 'Duties of Good Faith and Fair Dealing Under the Unidroit principles, Relevant International Conventions, and National Laws', (1995) 3 Tulane Journal of International and Comparative Law 47, 55.

31 Schwenzer, 'The Proposed Common European Sales Law and the Convention on the International Sale of Goods' (n11), 463.

The Contract Law of the People's Republic of China

Article 6 of The Contract Law of the People's Republic of China provides as follows:

> Article 6 Good Faith
> The parties shall abide by the principle of good faith in exercising their rights and performing their obligations.

Liming and Chuanxi explain this duty as follows:

> The principle of good faith (... literally honesty and trustworthiness) requires parties to a civil act to conduct themselves honourably, to perform their duties in a responsible manner, to avoid abusing their rights, to follow the law and common business practice.[32]

This is said to be a central aspect of Chinese commercial law, consistent with the significant influence of Confucianism upon Chinese law.[33] The good faith duty applies to contract formation, performance, modification, termination and post-contractual conduct.[34]

The Contract Law itself contains examples of good faith requirements at each stage of the contracting process, for example, stating that pre-contractual negotiations should not take place merely to prevent a contract with a third party, and false statements or misrepresentations should not be made in the course of those negotiations, in accordance with Article 42:

> Article 42 Pre-contract Liabilities
> Where in the course of concluding a contract, a party engaged in any of the following conducts, thereby causing loss to the other party, it shall be liable for damages:
> (i) negotiating in bad faith under the pretext of concluding a contract;
> (ii) intentionally concealing a material fact relating to the conclusion of the contract or supplying false information;
> (iii) any other conduct which violates the principle of good faith.

In contract performance itself, there is understood to be an obligation to give effect to the parties' intentions and not to insist on strict compliance with the terms of a contract which may be 'unclear, insufficient or lacking', for example by providing goods of a reasonable quality within a reasonable time, notwithstanding that there is no clear contractual obligation to do so.[35]

---

32 Liming and Chuanxi, 'Fundamental Principles of China's Contract Law' (n9), 15.
33 Ibid.
34 Ibid, 16.
35 Ibid, see discussion at 19.

In relation to termination, the Contract law requires that this should only be permitted where the purpose of the contract has been frustrated, not on the basis of some 'technical' breach.[36] Post-termination, Article 92 provides as follows:

> Article 92 Post-discharge Obligations
> Upon discharge of the rights and obligations under a contract, the parties shall abide by the principle of good faith and perform obligations such as notification, assistance and confidentiality, etc. in accordance with the relevant usage.

None of these obligations seem to be particularly difficult to understand or to apply.

German Civil Code

Section 242 German Civil Code (known as the 'Treu und Glauben' provision) states that 'an obligor has a duty to perform according to the requirements of good faith, taking customary practice into consideration'. This obligation extends to 'the commencement of contract negotiations' by virtue of section 311 (2) (1) German Civil Code. While good faith is not defined in the Code itself, it is said that reference to it in the Code has:

> ... spawned a mass of case law, resulting in an annotation, the sheer volume of which has come to dwarf the provision itself.[37]

This would suggest a certainty of interpretation at least comparable to the allegedly 'certain' but at the same time gloriously 'messy' common law, 'festering with ideas'.[38] It does, however, represent a different approach to legal interpretation and analysis than is followed in common law systems, which will be discussed below in the context of systems theory.

The UCC and the Restatement (Second) of Contracts

Under the UCC and the Restatement (Second) of Contracts, US law imposes an obligation of good faith, although not one extending to pre-contractual negotiations. Rather the obligation is limited to contract performance and enforcement:

> § 205. DUTY OF GOOD FAITH AND FAIR DEALING
>
> Every contract imposes upon each party a duty of good faith and fair dealing in its performance and its enforcement.

---

36 Ibid, see discussion at 19.
37 Farnsworth, 'Duties of Good Faith and Fair Dealing Under the Unidroit principles, Relevant International Conventions, and National Laws' (n30), 50.
38 Robert Goff, 'The Search for Principle' (n5).

Comment:

> a. Meanings of 'good faith.' Good faith is defined in Uniform Commercial Code § 1-201(19) as 'honesty in fact in the conduct or transaction concerned.' 'In the case of a merchant' Uniform Commercial Code § 2-103(1)(b) provides that good faith means 'honesty in fact and the observance of reasonable commercial standards of fair dealing in the trade.' The phrase 'good faith' is used in a variety of contexts, and its meaning varies somewhat with the context. Good faith performance or enforcement of a contract emphasizes faithfulness to an agreed common purpose and consistency with the justified expectations of the other party; it excludes a variety of types of conduct characterized as involving 'bad faith' because they violate community standards of decency, fairness or reasonableness. The appropriate remedy for a breach of the duty of good faith also varies with the circumstances.
>
> c. Good faith in negotiation. This Section, like Uniform Commercial Code § 1-203, does not deal with good faith in the formation of a contract.

The reference to 'faithfulness to an agreed common purpose and consistency with the justified expectations of the other party' are consistent with general understandings of good faith in other jurisdictions and also with the equitable preference for substance over form in equity, with which common lawyers would be familiar.

The Unidroit Principles

Article 1.7 of the Unidroit Principles 2010 provides that:

> (1) Each party must act in accordance with good faith and fair dealing in international trade.
>
> (2) The parties may not exclude or limit this duty.

The notes to this confirm that the parties must act in good faith throughout the life of the contract, including in the negotiation process. Interestingly, an abuse of rights is given as a typical example of breach of good faith. This equates to an unconscionable adherence to strict legal rights, as understood by common lawyers.

Article 2.1.15 Unidroit Principles 2010 deal with good faith obligations during negotiations and state that:

> (1) A party is free to negotiate and is not liable for failure to reach an agreement.
>
> (2) However, a party who negotiates or breaks off negotiations in bad faith is liable for the losses caused to the other party.

(3) It is bad faith, in particular, for a party to enter into or continue negotiations when intending not to reach an agreement with the other party.

Examples given in the notes regarding bad faith negotiating include entering into negotiations without any intention of concluding an agreement for example to stop a third party competitor securing the contract; or misrepresenting facts or not disclosing facts which should have been disclosed given the nature of the parties and/or their contract.

European Economic Community Council Directive 93/13/EEC

This 1993 directive was concerned with achieving uniformity in consumer protection regulation amongst European Economic Community member states, in order to facilitate competition between, and overcome market distortions in, consumer markets that would otherwise be operating under different laws. Article 3 (1) provides:

> A contractual term which has not been individually negotiated shall be regarded as unfair if, contrary to the requirement of good faith, it causes a significant imbalance in the parties' rights and obligations arising under the contract, to the detriment of the consumer.

The directive then contains a list of indicative terms that would be regarded as unfair, that is, contrary to the good faith requirement, at contract formation stage. These include unreasonably limiting liability, making an agreement binding on a consumer but not a supplier, permitting sums paid by a consumer to be retained by a supplier even where the supplier decides not to perform the contract, and limiting a consumer's rights of action, for example through an arbitration clause.

British Columbia Law Institute Report on Proposals for Unfair Contracts Relief, Report No. 60

This report, published in September 2011, recommends the inclusion of an obligation of good faith in the performance of contracts in a draft *Contract Fairness Act*. This obligation does not extend to pre-contractual negotiations. The draft provision reads:

> **Duty of good faith 10.** Every contract imposes upon each party a duty of good faith in its performance.

Good faith is actually defined in the definitions section, section 1:

> **'Good faith'** means the duty to (a) exercise discretionary powers conferred by a contract reasonably and for their intended purpose, (b) cooperate in securing

performance of the main objects of the contract, and (c) refrain from strategic behaviour designed to evade contractual obligations.

Including such a definition in legislation is a good example of a common lawyer's approach to a civil law concept such as good faith, as will be discussed below. This was acknowledged by the BCLI as follows:

> This brings the law of British Columbia into line with that of the United States, Quebec, and continental Europe. What distinguishes the *Contract Fairness Act* from the law in those other jurisdictions is that this act contains a legislative definition of *good faith*.

Principles of European Contract Law

Article 1:201 PECL contains the general requirement of good faith dealing as follows:

> Article 1:201: Good Faith and Fair Dealing
>
> (1) Each party must act in accordance with good faith and fair dealing.
>
> (2) The parties may not exclude or limit this duty.

Specifically in relation to pre-contractual negotiations, Article 2:301 PECL is identical to Article 2.1.15 Unidroit Principles 2010, set out above.

Common European Sales Law

The CESL is designed to be an 'opt-in' instrument for contracting parties to choose as the governing law of their contract. The CESL as adopted by the European Parliament on 26 February 2014 imposes an obligation of good faith and fair dealing upon contracting parties articulated as follows:

> Article 2
>
> Good faith and fair dealing
>
> (1) Each party has a duty to act in accordance with good faith and fair dealing.
>
> (2) Breach of this duty may preclude the party in breach from exercising or relying on a right, remedy or defence which that party would otherwise have, or may make the party liable for any loss thereby caused to the other party.
>
> (3) The parties may not exclude the application of this Article or derogate from or vary its effects.

The CESL defines 'good faith and fair dealing' as:

> ... a standard of conduct characterised by honesty, openness and, in so far as may be appropriate, reasonable consideration for the interests of the other party to the transaction or relationship in question; ...

The limitations of the good faith doctrine as a source of liability under the CESL are made clear in Recital 31, as follows:

> The general principles of good faith and fair dealing should set a standard of conduct which ensures an honest, transparent and fair relationship. While it precludes a party from exercising or relying on a right, remedy or defence which that party would otherwise have, the principle as such should not give rise to any general right to damages.

It has been argued that the inclusion of the good faith obligation in the CESL goes beyond what will be acceptable to common lawyers or traders from common law countries, as it will reduce clarity and predictability with regard to the duties imposed upon the parties.[39] That is undoubtedly a complaint often made by common lawyers, as noted by Stewart with regard to the inclusion of a good faith obligation as part of any proposed codification of Australian contract law:

> It is true that many Australian lawyers are suspicious of the concept of good faith and fair dealing, or at least are not persuaded that it adds very much to the common law armoury for policing contractual behaviour. The inclusion of such a concept in any new code is likely to be a source of disquiet and opposition – regardless of how well accepted it may be in other jurisdictions.[40]

Based upon clear principles that can be gleaned from an overview of good faith provisions in civil codes and international instruments, particularly when compared with the common law's failure to clearly resolve issues such as the existence and scope of any good faith obligation in Australian contract law,[41] it appears that the suspicion and disquiet to which Stewart refers cannot be justified and can in fact be overcome.

Certainly, a recent judgment of the England and Wales High Court (Queen's Bench Division) gives some hope to the prospect of acceptance of the good faith principle in common law jurisdictions. In *Yam Seng Pte Limited (A company registered in Singapore) v International Trade Corporation*

---

39 See discussion in Schwenzer, 'The Proposed Common European Sales Law and the Convention on the International Sale of Goods' (n11), 463, 479.

40 Andrew Stewart, 'What's Wrong with the Australian Law of Contract?' (2012) 29 Journal of Contract Law 74, 89.

41 Ibid, 84–85.

Limited[42] Justice Leggatt found that a duty of good faith could be implied into a commercial contract based on the presumed intentions of the parties, taking into account the relevant background against which the contract was made, including shared values and norms of behaviour. Those norms, he said, included an expectation of honesty and fidelity to the parties' bargain. It was held by Justice Leggatt that an implied duty, based on a core expectation of honesty, that the Defendant would not knowingly provide false information on which the Plaintiff was likely to rely, had been breached.

A remaining possible difficulty with the incorporation of a good faith doctrine into a common law system is, however, that legal systems will naturally repel, or at least modify, concepts imposed upon them with which they are not comfortable, as will be discussed below.

5 Commonalities and Differences and the Problems with 'Systems'

In this part I will consider the extent to which the doctrine of unconscionability and good faith principles might work together, and the extent to which the civil law concept of good faith might in fact be used to enhance and develop the law regulating the conduct of contracting parties as part of any review of Australian contract law. In this regard it is noted that many Australian statutes do now include reference to good faith, in particular in section 21 of the Australian Consumer Law which prohibits unconscionable conduct in connection with goods or services and lists as one of the factors to which a court may have regard in determining unconscionability, the 'extent to which the supplier and customer acted in good faith'. The prohibition is on unconscionable conduct 'in connection with' the supply or acquisition of goods or services, and would thus apply to all stages of the contracting process including pre-contractual negotiations, performance and termination.

Conduct During Pre-contractual Negotiations

The 'third order sense' in which unconscionability is used relates to pre-contractual negotiations and allows one party to rescind a contract where the other party has taken unconscionable advantage of the first party's serious disability or disadvantage in entering into the transaction. Damages remedies and civil penalties are also now available for such conduct under the Australian Consumer Law.

In *Berbatis* as discussed above, the Australian High Court did not give consideration to one party's lack of meaningful choice when entering into the transaction in question. Had the court defined unconscionability to include taking advantage of another party's lack of meaningful choice, as appears to be possible in the US under the Restatement and the UCC, the outcome of the case may have been

---

42 [2013] EWHC 111 (QB).

different. Further, had the obligation of good faith in pre-contractual negotiations been applied, concepts consistent with substance over form, not abusing rights, consistency with the justified expectations of the parties, and behaving reasonably, may also have led to a different outcome.

A general restatement of parties' obligations in the course of pre-contractual negotiations could incorporate a nuanced unconscionability doctrine and good faith principles, and give clarity to the circumstances in which a contract is liable to be set aside or damages be found payable. This could extend beyond the prohibition on taking advantage of a serious disadvantage under 'unconscionable dealing', to circumstances of negotiating with no intention of contracting (for an ulterior purpose), and misrepresentation of facts (already recognised as a ground for rescission under common law and applied under Chinese law, the Unidroit Principles and PECL as a breach of good faith obligations) or failure to disclose facts where the nature of the parties or their contract warrants such disclosure. This would provide clear and comprehensive guidance as to the circumstances in which obligations during pre-contractual negotiations have been breached, and would render Australian law more consistent with international understandings.

Conduct in Contract Performance

Applying the 'second order sense' of unconscionability– an unconscientious assertion of strict legal rights – the conduct of contracting parties during performance can be regulated through an estoppel. This prevents a party from asserting a strict legal right where they have been responsible for the other party acting to their detriment in reliance on a fundamental assumption contrary to that right. A Restatement could clearly frame the estoppel remedy as one available in these circumstances, and could then incorporate civil law understandings of good faith performance obligations giving rise to a damages remedy. This would require performing in a manner which respects the parties' intentions and justified expectations under the contract, as well as common usages in that trade or industry.

Conduct in Contract Termination

Again, an unconscientious assertion of the right to terminate a contract on a technical ground, and against the parties' fundamental assumptions, would arguably give rise to an estoppel. It could equally give rise to damages for a breach of the good faith obligation, where a party purports to terminate other than for a breach which frustrates the purpose of the contract (to follow the Chinese approach).

The suggestions above with regard to an incorporation of good faith principles into Australian contract law are designed to provide brief examples of possible approaches but not to suggest that this could be done seamlessly or easily. There is a broader issue to be considered in this part, and that is the difficulty with seeking to 'transplant' legal concepts and approaches from one legal system into another, in this case from a civil law system into a common law system. It will be suggested that this is not an insurmountable challenge, and may lead to creative responses which enhance the organic development of a legal doctrine such as good faith.

Issues in Incorporating Good Faith Concepts into a Common Law System of Contract Law

Systems theory provides a useful lens through which to see the issues that might arise as part of the process of incorporating good faith principles into Australian contract law. Teubner notes that we have a complex and 'functionally differentiated society' where different organisations and institutions are carrying out different functions and using their own language and norms to do so.[43] In this respect, organisations and systems, including legal systems, are likened to biological organisms with autopoietic properties, in that they reproduce themselves within a 'self-referential', 'closed' space. They exist and reproduce their elements autonomously, and are not open to permeation by external influences.[44]

Following the 1993 EEC Council directive referred to above, Teubner wrote an interesting article specifically investigating the purported 'transplant' of good faith into UK law from a systems theory perspective.[45] He referred to this not as a neat 'transplant', but rather a legal 'irritant' which would lead to unexpected developments in the law.

'Legal irritants' cannot be domesticated; they are not transformed from something alien into something familiar, not adapted to a new cultural context, rather they will unleash an evolutionary dynamic in which the external rule's meaning will be reconstructed and the internal context will undergo fundamental change.[46]

In essence, when a foreign legal principle is imported into a system which operates according to its own norms and understandings, the system will be irritated and will respond by re-shaping and re-moulding that principle, leading to divergences from the original principle. This is largely due to the different approaches to legal expression and interpretation as between civil and common law systems. Teubner notes that good faith tends not to be well-defined within civil law codes and that:

> The specific way in which continental lawyers deal with such a 'general clause' is abstract, open-ended, principle-oriented, but at the same time strongly systematised and dogmatised. This is clearly at odds with the more rule-oriented,

---

43 Gunther Teubner, 'Substantive and Reflexive Elements in Modern Law' (1983) 17(2) Law and Society Review 239, 244.

44 Gunther Teubner, *Dilemmas of Law in the Welfare State* (Walter de Grutyer 1986) discussed in Bronwen Morgan and Karen Yeung, *An Introduction to Law and Regulation* (Cambridge University Press 2007), 69–71.

45 Gunther Teubner, 'Legal Irritants: Good Faith in British Law or How Unifying Law Ends Up in New Divergences,' (1998) 61(1) The Modern Law Review 11.

46 Ibid 12.

technical, concrete, but loosely systematised British style of legal reasoning, especially when it comes to interpretation of statutes.[47]

Good examples of this are the lack of definition of good faith in the German Civil Code, but the voluminous annotation to it which dogmatises the concept; and the inclusion of a definition of good faith in the British Columbia Law Institute's draft legislation, which if enacted would no doubt be 'loosely systematised' and analysed through the 'messiness' of common law judgments. This may well result in divergent meanings being given to the concept of 'good faith' in different systems.

The question is whether such divergences are in fact a bad thing. As has occurred in what I have referred to as the 'CISG experiment', it may be possible for different systems to cross-pollinate or indeed cross-irritate one another to the point that shared understandings are reached over a period of time.

6 Conclusion

In advocating for 'internationalisation' of Australian contract law, for example through the inclusion of the good faith principle, this chapter does not seek to unnecessarily apologise for any differences between Australian law and internationally accepted principles. Carter and Peden have asserted that:

> It seems clear that there are some who see Australian contract law as the 'poor relation' in comparison with other jurisdictions when it comes to good faith. A term of good faith is then implied almost by way of apology to the parties.[48]

By the same token, civil lawyers should not feel obliged to unnecessarily apologise for the good faith 'impost' on the alleged certainty of the common law, and argue against its inclusion in international instruments.[49]

The fact is that an obligation to act in good faith is not so far removed from, and is no more or less difficult to clearly articulate than, an obligation to act with good conscience. Further, the historical role of equity in achieving justice and fairness and substance over form in the face of unconscientious assertions of strict common law rights would lead most common lawyers to have no difficulty in understanding and applying good faith principles as articulated in civil law codes and international instruments. On that premise, and because of the reality of international trade and the desirability of attracting international litigation and arbitration to Australia, any codification or restatement of Australian contract law should involve an incorporation of good faith principles.

---

47 Ibid 19.
48 Carter and Peden, 'Good Faith in Australian Contract Law' (n7), 171.
49 See for example Schwenzer, 'The Proposed Common European Sales Law and the Convention on the International Sale of Goods' (n11).

In any common law system there will necessarily be a re-shaping and re-moulding of the good faith principle using the common law method, but through 'cross-irritation' between common law and civil law systems, there may be some organic development of the principle across systems to a point where in time, we might all be speaking the same language.

PART III
Regional Perspectives

Chapter 5
Codification Mania and the Changing Nation State: A European Perspective[1]

Hans-W. Micklitz

1 The Argument

Over the last 60–70 years we can observe a trend towards the codification of private law.[2] Nation-building by former colonies in the aftermath of the Second World War and nation-building after the breakdown of communism in Middle and Eastern Europe,[3] or in South Eastern Europe,[4] or the Mediterranean democratic transformation goes hand in hand with civil code-building.[5]

---

1 This paper, which has been written in the context of the ERC project on European Regulatory Private Law (n.269722), condenses and develops ideas I have already presented elsewhere. (1) on European private law: 'The Visible Hand of European Private Law', in Piet Eeckhout and Takis Tridimas (eds), *Yearbook of European Law 2009*, Volume 28 (Oxford University Press, 2010) 3–60; (2) on European private legal order building and European constitution building: 'Failure or Ideological Preconceptions? Thoughts on Two Grand Projects: the European Constitution and the European Civil Code', in Kaarlo Tuori and Suvi Sankari (eds), *The Many Constitutions of Europe* (Ashgate 2010), 109–142; (3) on social justice and European legal culture (ed.), *The Many Concepts of Social Justice in European Private Law* (Elgar 2011), and 'The (Un)-Systematics of (private) Law as an Element of European Legal Culture', in Geneviève Helleringer and Kai Purnhagen (eds), *Towards a European Legal Culture* (Beck/Hart/Nomos 2013); (4) on the European Union as a Market State: with Dennis Patterson, 'From the Nation State to the Market: The Evolution of EU Private Law', in Bart van Vooren, Steven Blockmans, Jan Wouters (eds) *The EU's Role in Global Governance: The Legal Dimension* (Oxford University Press, 2013), 59–78.; (5) on the drivers behind the transformation: with Yane Svetiev, 'Transformation(s) of private law', in H-W Micklitz and Yane Svetiev, European Regulatory Private Law: The Paradigms Tested, EUI-ERC Working Papers 2014/04 69.

2 Reiner Schulze and Fryderyk Zoll (eds), *The Law of Obligations in Europe, A New Wave of Codifications* (Sellier, 2013).

3 Norbert Reich, 'Transformation of Contract Law and Civil Justice in the New EU Member States: The Example of the Baltic States, Hungary and Poland', in Fabrizio Cafaggi (ed.), *The Institutional Framework of European Private Law* (Oxford University Press, 2006), 271.

4 Marija Karanikic, Hans-Wolfgang Micklitz, Norbert Reich, *Modernising Consumer Law, The Experience of the Western Balkan* (Nomos, 2012).

5 Both the European Union via the European Commission and national development aid agencies are involved in the reform of national private law, broadly interpreted as later explained.

Nearly in parallel to these developments we have to recognize the fading importance of the Nation State, at least since the 1970s. There is no agreement on the concrete form and the implications of what is emerging. The new State might be called the Market State (Bobbitt,[6] Afilalo/Patterson,[7] Sassen[8]) or Gewährleistungsstaat (the State which guarantees the working conditions under which companies are operating in an ever more globalized world (Franzius,[9] Folke-Schuppert[10]). However, there is consensus on the fact that the State is *transforming*. There is and there will be disagreement about the degree to which the State is changing and whether it really makes sense to draw parallels between the nation states of the European Union (EU), where the transformation is more visible, and the transformations in the US and in China, where Nation State ideologies seem to be at the forefront of the political agenda. I understand and I take the EU as a blueprint for the new format of the post-Nation State, the *Market State*.

My focal point is private law understood as a composition of *traditional* codified Nation State private law, or common law, and what I call *regulatory* private law, in the European context, European regulatory private law. The bifurcation between the two types of private law, the traditional private law and the regulatory private law, reflects the changing character of the State. Traditional private law is inherently linked to Nation State-building. It is a product of the first half of the nineteenth century. Regulatory private law goes together with the rise of the industrial age in the second half of the nineteenth century, first in the form of the regulatory State, later through the welfare State. The EU gives regulatory private law a different twist, since it employs private law making for one dominant purpose – the completion of the internal market. It is this instrumentalization of private law, for one dominant purpose, which is the innovative element in the rise of the new European private law.

What is going on in the EU is not only relevant for the 28 Member States. It has a large impact on the rest of the world. The so-called *Brussels effect*[11] means that Europe, due to its large population (550 million people) and its strong buying power (as a result of its high average income per capita) is able to impose

---

6 Philip Bobbitt, *The Shield of Achilles: War, Peace and the Course of History* (Knopf, 2002).

7 Dennis Patterson and Ari Afilalo, *The New Global Trading Order* (Cambridge University Press, 2008).

8 Saskia Sassen, *Denationalization: Territory, Authority and Rights in a Global Digital Age* (Princeton University Press, 2005).

9 Claudio Franzius, 'Der Gewährleistungsstaat', (2008) 99 Verwaltungsarchiv 351–379.

10 Gunnar Schuppert, *Der Rechtsstaat unter den Bedingungen informaler Staatlichkeit. Beobachtungen und Überlegungen zum Verhältnis formeller und informeller Institutionen. Schriften zur Governance-Forschung*, Bd. 23. (Nomos, 2011).

11 Anu Bradford, 'The Brussels Effect', (2012) 107 Northwestern University Law Review 1–68.

regulatory standards on the rest of the world. These *regulatory standards* can take different forms. They may be regulatory mandatory private law, such as consumer sales guarantees in Directive 99/44/EC, which have to be respected by American producers of consumer goods like Apple.[12] They may be the product of co-regulation, where the EU defines a binding frame which has to be completed by industrial and trade organizations, such as in the field of standardization of goods, of food safety and the like.[13] They may result from self-regulation without any direct or indirect statutory EU regulatory impact. Here, hard empirical evidence about the particular role of European companies and European service providers is lacking. Intuitively, one would assume that self-regulation is the product not only of rule-production beyond the State but even beyond Europe.[14]

Building on these observations, I intend to investigate the obvious tension between the two trends, the changing nature of the Nation State and what I tend to call *codification mania*. Again, I will use the EU as a model to underpin my argument. The failure of the two grand projects of the first decade of the twenty-first century, the so-called European Constitution and the European Civil Code, demonstrate in a nutshell all the difficulties in developing a post-Nation State private legal order that complies with the demands of the Market State. In Europe, we can observe the bifurcation between two types of private law: the silent move and increase of regulatory private law, which lies at the heart of the Brussels effect, and the noisy debate around the *Academic* Draft Common Frame of Reference (DCFR),[15] the *Political* DCFR,[16] now 'perhaps/probably' being transformed into

---

12 Mateja Djurovic, 'The Apple Case : The Commencement of Pan-European Battle Against Unfair Commercial Practices', (2013) European Review of Contract Law 253; Mateja Djurovic and Hans-Wolfgang Micklitz, 'The Apple Case – How a US Company is Challenging European Consumer Law Standards', forthcoming; Hans-Wolfgang Micklitz, 'Is Chinese law enforcement a model for Europe? – No!', see <http://www.consumatoridirittimercato.it/author/micklitz>, last accessed on 30 October 2013.

13 Anu Bradford, fn. 11, analyses competition law, data protection, environmental protection and food safety as examples.

14 See the empirically motivated research by Fabrizio Cafaggi, 'Private Regulation and European Private Law' in Arthur Hartkamp, Martijn Hesselink, Ewoud Hondius, Chantal Mak, Edgar Du Perron (eds), *Towards a European Civil Code* (Kluwer Law International, 2011), 91–126.

15 Christian von Bar, Eric Clive, Hans Schulte-Nölte, Hugh Beale, Johnny Herre, Jerôme Huet, Matthias Storme, Sthephen Swann, Paul Varul, Anna Veneziano, Fryderyk Zoll (eds), *Principles, Definitions and Model Rules of European Private Law* (Sellier München, 2009), prepared by the Study Group on a European Civil Code and the Research Group on EC Private Law (Acquis Group).

16 'A European contract law for consumers and businesses: Publication of the results of the feasibility study carried out by the Expert Group on European contract law', see <http://ec.europa.eu/justice/contract/files/feasibility_study_final.pdf>, last accessed 27 June 2014; see the contributions in: Reiner Schulze and Jules Stuyck (eds) *Towards a European Contract Law* (Sellier, 2011).

the Common European Sales Law (CESL),[17] mainly designed for intra-European internet sales between businesses and between businesses and consumers.

I will use as a categorical frame the three functions of codification identified by J Maillet in The Historical Significance of French Codification:[18]

1. to *expose* the law in order to present the existing or desired law in a comprehensive, rational and systematic way;
2. to *unify* the law in order to eliminate territorial diversity and abolish diverging law; and
3. to *modify* the nature of the law, using the law to build a Nation State.

This will allow me to embark on questions with regard to a) is it possible, feasible and does it make sense to develop a rational body of law today? Where is the extensive discussion of private law beyond the State,[19] be it new modes of contract law (Cafaggi/Muir Watt),[20] contract governance (Grundmann/Möslein/Riesenhuber),[21] transnational private law,[22] with regard to b) are we returning to the middle ages (Jansen),[23] where the true question was one of the authority of the law and not 'who codifies'? And with regard to c) what should private law look like in a globalized world in which the Nation State may adopt private-law rules which are of limited importance for transnational transactions? What kind of role could the EU as Market State play and what kind of role is it perhaps already playing? Is the EU the Market State, the laboratory from which lessons can be learned beyond Europe?

The hypothesis which I would like to present is that if we transfer Maillet's three paradigms to the European level and take them seriously, codification in

---

17 COM (2011) 635 final of 11.10.2011.

18 Jean Maillet, 'The Historical Significance of French Codification' (1969–1970) 44 Tulane Law Review 681.

19 Ralf Michaels and Nils Jansen, 'Private Law Beyond the State? Europeanization, Globalization, Privatization' (2006) 54 American Journal of Comparative Law 843; Nils Jansen and Ralf Michaels, *Beyond the State: Rethinking Private Law* (Mohr/Siebeck, 2008).

20 Fabrizio Cafaggi and Horatia Muir Watt (eds), *Making European Private Law* (Elgar, 2008); Fabrizio Cafaggi and Horatia Muir Watt (eds), *The Regulatory Functions of European Private Law* (Elgar, 2010).

21 Stefan Grundmann, Florian Möslein, Karl Riesenhuber (eds), *Contract Governance – Dimensions in Law and Interdisciplinary Research*, forthcoming (Oxford University Press, 2014).

22 Special Issue on theories of transitional law (édition spéciale relative aux théories du droit transnational RIDE (Revue Internationale de Droit Economique 3–4 2013) with contributions of the protagonists of the international debate.

23 Nils Jansen, 'Legal Pluralism in Europe: National Law, European Legislation and Non-legislative Codifications', in Leone Niglia (ed.), *Pluralism and European Private Law* (Hart Publishing, 2013) 109; from the same author, *The Making of Legal Authority Non Legislative Codifications in Historical and Comparative Perspective* (Oxford University Press, 2010).

the post-Nation State era must look different from nineteenth-century thinking and ideology, which is enshrined in codification projects. What is needed is a new architecture for private law-building – a flexible system that cuts across the new and the old private law and that encompasses national as well as supranational elements.

2 The European Market State and European (Regulatory) Private Law

The EU Market State

The European Constitution and the European Civil Code were conceived at a time in history when the Nation State entered a new historical era, that of the Market State. The design of the Market State and its impact on the EU in its constitutional and its private law design is part of a bigger and more long-term project in which I am engaged with my colleague Dennis Patterson.

The 1986 Single European Act constituted the break-even point in the development of European integration. The 1985 White Paper on the Completion of the Internal Market[24] provided the necessary legitimacy for the European legislator to use and to instrumentalize law as a means to open up and to shape markets. This is what can be identified as the birth of the EU Market State.

> With a view to regulatory integration, the main features of the EU Market State are the following: the shift from private into public – the State outsources its regulatory functions; the shift from law and regulation to regulation and outsourcing privatisation, such as may be observed in the areas of utilities, transportation and healthcare. The bottom line: sovereignty loses its Nation State force as the State shifts away from providing top-down regulatory and welfare entitlements to fostering and preserving market conditions for the maximisation of economic opportunity.[25]

Private law is submitted to the overall objective of the internal market. This private law is not the private law enshrined in the big codifications of the nineteenth century that characterized the State Nation and later the Nation State. Instead, it is what I call *regulatory private law*. The transformation of the Nation State private legal orders into a Market State European private legal order produces a diversification of private law regimes. On the one hand, there are the Nation State private legal orders that lose importance in practice and that serve, simultaneously, as a source of inspiration for the new regulatory design. On the other hand, there is the Market State European private legal order *in statu nascendi*, which unites the *formal* and the *informal authority* of

---

24 COM (1985) 310 final.
25 I am summing up the essence of our argument.

private law-making;[26] the making of private law through the EU legislator via regulations and directives, in combination and in cooperation with non-State actors, a European private law which hardly fits into well-established national categories of what private law should look like and how it should be understood.

Private Law as Economic Law

Private law is understood as economic law,[27] covering not only contract and tort, or systematically speaking the Continental codifications, but also public and private regulation of the economy.

This broad concept of private law is crucial for the development of a deeper understanding of the ongoing transformation process of Nation States to Market States, as well as of the particular role and function of the EU. The traditional national private legal orders, with their focus on contract and tort, represent the *State Nation* and later the *Nation State* variant of private law. They emerged from and are deeply rooted in the State Nation and Nation-State building process of the eighteenth and nineteenth centuries in Continental Europe. The starting point is private autonomy, freedom of contract, *la liberté de la volonté*. The actors are private individuals, private economic actors, originally primarily operating within the territorial boundaries of the State. The States claim the authority to adopt private legal rules in their territories. Local law and *droit commun* should no longer be applicable side by side. Private law became nationalized. The grand codifications of the early nineteenth and late nineteenth century were meant to overcome the informal authority of private law as it stood in the seventeenth and eighteenth centuries. The result was an enormous gain in economic efficiency and legal coherence.[28] In the early nineteenth century, private international law constituted the conceptual answer to the building of national private legal orders as a means and a technique to decide on the applicable law in cross-border transactions.

The Step Ahead – European Regulatory Private Law

Not being a State, the EU was never concerned with the political and ideological underpinnings of private law as a means and tool for State-building purposes,

---

26 See the references to Nils Jansen, 'Pluralism in a new Key – Between Plurality and Normativity', in Leone Niglia (ed.), fn. 23, 248.

27 Heinz-Dieter Assmann, Gert Brüggemeier, Dieter Hart, Christian Joerges, *Wirtschaftsrecht als Kritik des Privatrechts. Beiträge zur Privat- und Wirtschaftsrechtstheorie* (Athenäum 1980).

28 See the distinctively different positions of Nils Jansen, fn. 26, stressing the risk of legal pluralism which has been historically overcome through the grand codifications and Jan Smits, who conceives of pluralism as an opportunity in todays' world and who, therefore, promotes the disconnection of jurisdiction and applicable law, 'A Radical View of Legal Pluralism' in Leone Niglia (ed.), fn. 23, 161.

such as private autonomy or freedom of contract, laying down ground rules for the development of a capitalist economy. The overall project of the European integration process[29] was, first, the common market, and, later, the internal market and, only gradually, the building of a legal order that reached beyond mere economic transactions – the shaping of a *social order*, a citizen order or even a constitution. Private law – except for family law – may by and large be associated with economic transactions with a social outlook, as enshrined in consumer law and anti-discrimination law.

In European private law, the internal market rhetoric sets the tone. Here, the EU appears as a *regulator*, whether through the European Court of Justice (ECJ), which is challenging national economic rules that hinder free trade in products, services, capital or persons, or through the EU legislator, which is adopting horizontal or vertical market-related rules on private transactions, often by way of new modes of governance.[30] The regulatory private law, in its negative variant through the impact of the four freedoms on the private law and in its positive variant through the bulk of EU rules that have been adopted in the aftermath of the Single European Act outside consumer and anti-discrimination law, deserves our utmost attention. This is the *European regulatory private law*, in which the *modern variant of the EU as a Market State* becomes clear. This private law is different from national private legal orders based on private autonomy and free will. This private law takes its form, procedure and content from being instrumentalized to build and shape markets,[31] yielding its own pattern of justice (access justice – *Zugangsgerechtigkeit*). It covers the setting of the regulatory frame through the EU institutions, the EU-driven building of new market surveillance authorities, the fine-tuning of the rules through intermediary forms of cooperation between EU and Member State institutions – whether they are called comitology, Lamfalussy process, open method of coordination, better regulation, or smart regulation – the development of new substantive legal mechanisms that reach beyond traditional private law rules and, last but not least, the enforcement of the self-standing rules through sectorial regulatory agencies which make and enforce private law through new forms of alternative

---

29 For the still dominant understanding, Pierre Pescatore, *The Law of Integration, the Emergence of a New Phenomenon in International Relations, Based on the Experience of the European Communities* (Sijthoff, 1974). For a different reading, putting emphasis on the 'historicity of politics' and the key role of the European Council in building a European polity, see Luuk van Middelaar, *The Passage to Europe, How a Continent became a Union* (Yale University Press, 2013).

30 Fabrizio Cafaggi and Horatia Muir Watt (eds) (2008) and Fabrizio Cafaggi and Horatia Muir Watt (eds) (2010), fn. 20.

31 In the German understanding of private law as economic law (*Privatrecht als Wirtschaftsrecht*), see, with regard to Europe, Christoph Schmid, *Die Instrumentalisierung des Europäischen Privatrechts durch die Europäische Union* (Nomos, 2010).

dispute settlement mechanisms, and occasionally through collective actions or through the courts in case of serious conflicts.[32]

European Regulatory Private Law and National Regulatory Private Law – What Is New?

There is an obvious argument against the distinction between *Nation* States being equated with contract and tort law, with freedom of contract and private autonomy, and *European* private law being regulatory in nature and meant to design markets. Regulation in private law is a matter that has already been discussed for more than 100 years. Otto von Gierke was one of those who defended the need for a distinction between private law and private law regulation, although, at that time, with a clear, highly political message. His analysis of the development in late nineteenth-century German law is as relevant today as it was more than 100 years ago and its substance is not limited to the German private legal order:[33]

> One perceives two systems, which are dominated by a totally different philosophy: a system of a common civil law, which enshrines the pure private law, and a bulk of special rules, which is governed by a cloudy mixture of public and private law. Here a vivid, popular, socially colored law, full of inner dynamic; there an abstract model, romanistic, individualistic, ossified in dead legal doctrine.

However, in comparison with the beginning of the twenty-first century, there are major differences in terms of substance and in terms of institutions which justify maintaining the equations – Nation States = the traditional concept of private law (contract and tort law (common law and/or codifications)) and the European Market State = the modern concept of private law (European regulatory private law). The late nineteenth century and the early twenty-first century may each be associated with a particular stage of development, in terms of Nation State versus Market State and in terms of traditional versus modern private law. At that time, the regulatory law was mainly labour and social law, which was kept outside the

---

32 I have given a much clearer picture of both the substance and the enforcement in the report I wrote for the German Juristentag 2012, 'Brauchen Konsumenten und Unternehmen eine neue Architektur des Verbraucherrechts?' (Beck, 2012). In English, 'Do Consumers and Business need a New Architecture of Consumer Law', (2013) 32(1) Yearbook of European Law 2013/2014, 266–367.

33 Otto von Gierke, *Die soziale Aufgabe des Privatrechtulius* (Springer, 1889) (author's translation): 'Man erhält nun zwei von ganz verschiedenem Geist beherrschte Systeme: ein System des gemeinsamen Civilrechts, in welchem das ‚reine' Privatrecht beschlossen liegt, und eine Fülle von Sonderrechten, in denen ein vom öffentlich Recht her getrübtes und mit öffentlichem Recht vermischtes Privatrecht waltet. H i e r lebendiges, volksthümliches, sozial gefärbtes Recht voll innerer Bewerbung – d o r t eine abstrakte Schablone, romanistisch, individualistisch, verknöchert in todter Dogmatik.'

Bürgerliches Gesetzbuch (BGB). The German BGB provided only for a basic set of rules on contracts for services, the so-called *Dienstverträge*, in spite of all the social concerns of labour lawyers who were fighting for better protection of the legal position of dependent workers.[34] It is this to which von Gierke was referring.

Today's regulatory private law cuts across all sectors of the economy and of policies. In a horizontal perspective it covers consumer law and anti-discrimination law which intrude into private law. In a vertical dimension it intrudes in the heart of contracts for financial services, telecommunications, energy (electricity, gas), (the increasingly privatized) health care services, more and more educational services and, last but not least, transport. Services account for 70 per cent of the gross income in the EU. The driving force behind all these rules, that primarily aim to open up markets, to establish competition, to liberalize former public services, and to promote privatization in former areas of public services, is undoubtedly the EU, or more precisely the European Commission. Private law issues are subordinate to other more 'important aspects' of the appropriate market design. What we can find is a large set of private law rules mainly bound to and designed for a particular sector.

This private law is regulatory law. However, 'regulatory' should not be equated with rules that quasi-automatically restrict private autonomy and freedom of contract. Its instrumental character makes it immune from easy classification. Regulatory private law contains both elements: it establishes market freedoms, thereby increasing private autonomy, and at the same time it provides for rules that set boundaries to this newly-created competitive market autonomy.[35] The 'give' and 'take' cannot be associated with the problematic distinction of private autonomy or freedom of contract exercised by private parties and the statutory intervention which takes their freedoms away. Give and take are compressed into one constitutive act. The White Paper on the Completion of the Internal Market[36] provided the European Commission with the necessary mandate and legitimation to initiate legislative measures which were mainly aimed at establishing markets. However, they, inter alia, contained a whole series of private law rules, understood as economic law.

About 100 years ago, the regulator was the Nation State, which used regulation to shape national markets for national economies. Implicit in this assumption is

---

34   See the writings from Hugo Sinzheimer, *Lohn und Aufrechnung. Ein Beitrag zur Lehre vom gewerblichen Arbeitsvertrag auf reichsrechtlicher Grundlage*, Diss. Univ. Heidelberg (Berlin, 1902); *Der korporative Arbeitsnormenvertrag* (Leipzig, 1907); *Brauchen wir ein Arbeitstarifgesetz? Rechtsfragen des Tarifvertrags* (Jena, 1913); *Ein Arbeitstarifgesetz. Die Idee der sozialen Selbstbestimmung im Recht* (München, 1916).

35   Guido Comparato and Hans-Wolfgang Micklitz, 'Regulated Autonomy between Market Freedoms and Fundamental Rights in the Case Law of the CJEU', in Ulf Bernitz, Xavier Groussot, Felix Schulyok (eds), *General Principles of EU Law and European Private Law* (Ashgate 2013) 121–154.

36   COM (1985) 310 final.

the understanding that 'legislation' or, more broadly, 'regulation *meant to* shape markets' is not an invention of the Market State. Regulatory private law already existed in the late nineteenth century. This was particularly true for the then emerging new industries, such as the chemical industry and, in today's terminology, the telecommunications industry. However, at that time, such firms were national, and they were deeply anchored in the Nation State, both economically and culturally.[37] They were operating in national markets, which was the case both for the old industries and for the new industries. The establishment of the European Economic Community in 1957 changed the economic, the political and the social environment. All in all, the European Commission has managed to get the necessary support to implement its policies to complete the internal market at all institutional levels, even in sensitive areas such as health care. It then remains for the Member States to implement and to enforce what has been decided at the EU level. Here, the relevant pieces of secondary EU law focus on the shaping of a genuine European market. They address economic actors, business and consumers, who are ready to invest in a market that offers more opportunities and better choices on both sides. The legislative means and regulatory tools, not to speak of the particular content of the rules, bear an inherently cross-border dimension. This might explain why the EU has to 'invent' new devices that fit within overall policy objective. In short, the EU regulator differs from the national regulator of 100 years ago.

There is no clear-cut moment that allows us to pinpoint when exactly the transformation from the national market to the building of a European market started. In Europe, the Single European Act may be identified as the engine for the visibly instrumental use of private law for market-building purposes. However, it needed the fall of the Berlin Wall and the collapse of communism to accelerate the building of a Market State. Transformation is a process. The new European private legal order still bears elements of the old one, and is indeed built on the old one, though only to a limited degree. A deeper look into the service sector which lies at the heart of European regulatory private law clearly reveals the differences.[38] Telecommunications, energy, transport and financial services are of paradigmatic importance. In these sectors we can identify the regulation from cradle to grave, from the opening of the markets to the management of conflicts, through an interaction between public authorities and private parties, via new modes of governance and new modes of enforcement. Regulatory private law is mostly sector-related or actor-related (consumers, customers and so on) whereas the traditional private law provides for horizontal ground rules which apply to each and every contract and tort.

---

37 Cornelius Torp, 'Von Junkern und Schlotbaronen. Zur Interpretation des deutschen Protektionismus vor 1914', (2010) 60 Saeculum 143.

38 At the EUI, there are various ongoing PhD projects working on the hypothesis: Marta Cantero, Lucila de Almeida, as documented in Hans-Wolfgang Micklitz and Yane Svetiev, 'A Self-sufficient European Private Law – A Viable Concept?', EUI Working Paper 2012/31 (ERC-ERPL 01/2012).

We are living in a transitional period in which the two orders are often still standing side by side. However, the scope of the new regulatory private law is constantly growing. It is always reaching into new areas of former public services. As a result, the inherent regulatory structures of the different service markets and the growing impact on private law become ever clearer. It is this bifurcation between the traditional private law and the regulatory private law which poses problems for codification. The last wave of private law codifications in Europe demonstrate little inclination to tackle the bifurcation upfront. If any, the relationship between codified private law and consumer law dominates the agenda. None of the issues addressed here are on the agenda of the last codification wave.[39] The Nation States in Europe, whether or not (yet) Member States of the EU, tend to preserve the deeper values, traditions and cultures of their traditional private law systems against the transformation pressure enshrined in regulatory private law.[40] The overall direction of the modernization process points towards more competition between private legal orders to make it more attractive to search for the best legal order to solve cross-border conflicts.[41]

Going Backwards – The Failed European Civil Code Project

The discussion triggered by the 2001 Communication, the work of the Study Group and of the *Acquis* Group, the merging of the two initiatives, the development of first the *Academic* DCFR in 2008/2009 and, later, the *Political* Common Frame of Reference in 2011 under the auspices of Commissioner *Reding* – also called Feasibility Study – all took place in a constitutional *competence vacuum*. The key question, whether the EU could be regarded as a form of a State that has or should have the power to adopt a European Civil Code, was set aside. The debate was framed by the European Commission. The European Commission set the tone, defined the agenda and supervised the activities.

The already existing European private law rules, the so-called private law *acquis communautaire*, formed the major source of inspiration for the codification project. In essence, the 2001 document of the European Commission listed European private international law and consumer contract law directives. The first category is conceptually speaking no more than a European variant of long-lasting attempts at the international level to agree on common standards on how the applicable law should be determined. Consumer law had raised more awareness, as the gateway for the EU to complete the internal market, long before the discussion on a European Civil Code started.

Translated into the narrative of the Nation State versus the Market State, the 2001 Communication is very much designed along the line of a Nation State

---

39 Reiner Schulze and Fryderyk Zoll (eds), fn. 2. I will come back to the relationship between codified private law and consumer law later on.
40 Sven Steinmö, *The Evolution of the Modern States* (Cambridge University Press, 2010).
41 Jan Smits, 'A Radical View of Pluralism', in Leone Niglia (ed.), fn. 23, 161.

private legal order. Two major areas are missing in the project – which obviously belong to the *acquis* but which are not mentioned. If they had been addressed, they would have demonstrated the fragility of a codification project which is deeply rooted in Nation State thinking.

The *first* is the impact of primary EU law, in particular the market freedoms, on national private law,[42] and the impact of fundamental rights on national private law, since 2000 via the Charter of Fundamental Rights which became an integral part of the European legal order with the adoption of the Treaty of Lisbon in 2009.[43] Opening the debate about the *acquis*, also as a result of ECJ case law in these areas, would have given the codification project a different direction. It would have paved the way for building a link between the then still envisaged European Constitution and the European Civil Code project, allowing for deeper reflections on the feasibility of a Civil Code in a transnational polity. The *second* is the large set of rules the EU has adopted in the field of services in order to build a European market (financial services) or to transform public services into competitive markets (energy, telecommunication, postal services, transport, health care, education). Although the narrow approach has been criticized right from its beginnings, neither the European Commission nor the *Acquis* Group which was established to execute the mandate demonstrated preparedness to change or to enlarge the working programme.

The reason why the narrow approach adopted in 2001 survived ten years of internal and external discussion might be found in the role and function of the academics who were involved in the project. We have to recall that the *Acquis* Group was composed of traditional Nation State private lawyers. There was obviously no preparedness on the side of the European Commission to take professors of EU law, or of energy, internet, telecommunications, or financial services law on board. The merging of the free-standing Study Group and the *Acquis* Group brought a new dynamic into the drafting process but did not lead to an opening up of

---

42   Ernst Steindorff, *EG Vertrag und Privatrecht* (Nomos, 1996); Christoph Schmid, *Die Instrumentalisierung des Privatrechts durch die Europäische Union* (Nomos, 2010).

43   See in a chronological order: Dawn Oliver and Jörg Fedtke (eds), *Human Rights and the Private Sphere: A Comparative Study* (Routledge, 2007); Chantal Mak, *Fundamental Rights in European Contract Law: A Comparison of the Impact of Fundamental Rights on Contractual Relationships in Germany, the Netherlands, Italy and England* (Wolters Kluwer, 2008); Stefan Grundmann (ed.), *Constitutional Values and European Contract Law* (Kluwer Law International, 2008); Gert. Bruggermeier, Aurelia Columbi Ciacchi, Giovanni Comandé (eds), *Fundamental Rights and Private Law in the European Union*, vol I, *A Comparative Overview* (Cambridge University Press, 2010); Olha Cherednychenko, *Fundamental Rights, Contract Law and the Protection of the Weaker Party* (Sellier, 2007); David Hoffman (ed.), *The Impact of the UK Human Rights Act on Private Law* (Cambridge University Press, 2011); Christoph Busch and Hans Schulte-Nölke (eds), *Fundamental Rights and Private Law* (Sellier, 2011); Hans-Wolfgang Micklitz (ed.), *Constitutionalisation of Private Law, Collected Courses of the European Academy of Private Law*, forthcoming (Oxford University Press, 2014).

the scope of the codification project. The Study Group is the successor of the *Lando* Commission, which elaborated the Principles of European Contract Law (PECL). The working method remained the same. Both distilled out of a functional comparative analysis[44] of different private legal orders a set of principles that could and should find common support not only in the academic environment but also in courts. The Study Group gave the codification project a new direction, one which the European Commission took into consideration in the 2001 Communication without actively promoting it. The Study Group stretched the mandate to its boundaries and presented the *Academic* DCFR as a fully-fledged European Civil Code. Its modern elements, which demonstrate links to regulatory private law, are enshrined in the integration of consumer and anti-discrimination law. Services were included in the project, but the services for which the EU had most actively changed the legal rules were excluded. The Academic DCFR deserves respect as it is guided by strong European idealism, by the ideology that a European Civil Code could serve to promote European integration, to build a European identity, if not a European society. However, it is exactly this largely idealistic outlook which explains its failure. It relies on the old nineteenth century codification idea to build the European future, turning a blind eye to the differences behind the nineteenth and twentieth-century Nation State and the EU as a Market State.

Summa summarum – the merger of the two groups had strengthened the Nation State understanding of a future European private law. The internal *esprit de corps* in the two groups must have been strong, at least strong enough to lead to a consistent and self-standing model for a European Civil Code. The external pressure from those in the private law community who were not involved in the drafting process might indirectly have contributed to the realization of the particular understanding of the mandate. The Study Group and the *Acquis* Group had to demonstrate the feasibility of a European Civil Code, shaped along the lines of Nation State private legal orders and respecting the *droit commun*, to the outside academic world.[45] Inside and outside pressure favoured a nineteenth-century perspective on private law, where a European Civil Code is discussed as a means to replace national and Nation State private legal orders, at least in the long run. The big question, the key question of whether a code is the appropriate means to hold the Member States of the EU together or even to deepen their relationship in a post-Nation State era is ignored. The result is then that the whole story of the European codification project,

---

44 See on the functional method, Konrad Zweigert and Hein Kötz, *Introduction to Comparative Private Law* (Mohr/Siebeck, 3rd edition, 1996). Much could be said on the limits of the method which must be understood as a typical post war attempt to promote the European integration after the Second World War, but which is unable to cope with the transformation of the Nation States.

45 See Horst Eidenmüller, Florian Faust, Hans Christoph Grigoleit, Nils Jansen, Gerhard Wagner, Reinhard Zimmermann, 'The Common Frame of Reference for European Private Law: Policy Choices and Codification Problems', (2008) 28 Oxford Journal of Legal Studies 659.

the last ten years of academic discussion, and the vast amount of publications which considerably increased the mutual understanding of our national private legal orders must also be understood, tragically enough, as a story of missed opportunities. *European messeanism*[46] does not suffice anymore to legitimize the European integration. The window of opportunity to establish the United States of Europe, which might have been open just after the fall of the Berlin Wall in the early 1990s, has been closed – if it ever existed. The future of European private law lies in the search of legal rules, mechanisms, orders and systems beyond the Nation State.

3 The Three Criteria of Maillet and the Future of Private Law

In the light of the foregoing analysis, Maillet's criteria do not seem to fit the changing economic, political, societal and legal environment. However, they are extremely valuable to highlight the potential difficulties codification has to face in the post-Nation State era.

Exposure – Systematization and Rationalization

First, I should start with a disclaimer, as I do not want to be misunderstood: systematization and rationalization are inherent to and constitutive of law. This is true for the common law and for the codified private legal orders in Europe and around the world. But is it, and will it, still be true in the emerging private law beyond the Nation State?[47] If we look at the deeper foundations behind the idea of the State, at private law as a system of a single rationality, or at the reasons for why the Market State could evolve, we have doubts.

One of the key messages of Luhmann, which Teubner[48] constantly reiterates in all his writings, is that the process of differentiation of the society cannot be turned back. There is not one single rationality, but there are subsystems which are governed by particular rationalities (referring to *lex mercatoria*, to *lex sportiva* and *lex digitalis*). This is not the only debate in legal philosophy which questions systematization and rationalization. Dickson[49] is working on a theory of EU Legal

---

46 Joseph Weiler, 'Deciphering the Political and Legal DNA of European Integration: An Exploratory Essay', in Julie Dickson and Pavlos Eleftheriadis (eds), *Philosophical Foundations of European Union Law* (Oxford University Press, 2012), 137.

47 Thomas Wilhelmsson, 'Private Law in the EU: Harmonised or Fragmented Europeanisation', (2002) 10 European Review of Journal Law 77–94.

48 Gunter Teubner, 'Global Bukowina, Legal Pluralism in a World Society', in Gunter Teubner (ed.), *Global Law Without a State* (Dartmouth, 1996).

49 Julie Dickson, 'Towards a Theory of European Union Legal Systems', in Julie Dickson and Pavlos Eleftheriadis (eds), *Philosophical Foundations of European Union Law* (Oxford University Press, 2012), 25.

Systems, which enlarges the concept of national legal systems and adapts it to the European construct. Culver and Guidice are forcefully rejecting the idea of a system and understand and interpret the EU as a legal order based on inter-institutional interaction (for example, between national and European courts, between national and European agencies and so on).[50]

In the light of these considerations, the idea of understanding European private law building as an exercise of systematization and rationalization vanishes away. If we follow Teubner, European Regulatory Private Law, even beyond the different sets of rules on regulated markets for services, should be understood as consisting of subsystems which develop their own rationality and which largely stand side by side.[51] If we follow Dickson we need to re-construct the established understanding of law as a system, as the Nation State understanding cannot be transferred to the EU, which is neither a State nor an international organization. However, it remains rather unclear what such a theory of systems would look like and what exactly it would include. Is it intended to understand European Regulatory Private Law as being one system of EU law, which connects to other systems to strive for homogeneity? If we follow Cutler/Giudice, we would have to limit systematization and rationalization to inter-institutional interaction between legal orders. Again, the question remains how an order could be defined and whether European Regulatory Private Law could and must be understood as a legal order in itself, based on inter-institutional interaction within and between the different regulated markets for services. In my concept of understanding European private law as *competitive contract law*[52] I have defended the idea that there are common denominators in regulatory private law which can be identified across the different sectors, combining vertical regulated markets with horizontal rules on consumer protection and anti-discrimination, and which can be condensed in a set of genuine *principles*.

After years of extensive research on regulatory private law I have become more sceptical about the feasibility of systematizing and rationalizing regulatory private law and I wonder whether it is not more correct to understand each regulated market as a separate subsystem (energy, telecom, financial services and so on) governed by its own rationality and requiring its own distinct systematization. If this turns out to be true, systematization and rationalization of private law at the European level would be of rather limited importance. But even if it is possible to find an

---

50 Keith Culver and Michael Guidice, 'Not a System but an Order: An Inter-Institutional View of European Union Law', in Julie Dickson and Pavlos Eleftheriadis (eds), fn. 49, 54. From the same authors, *Legality's Borders, An Essay in General Jurisprudence* (Oxford University Press, 2010).

51 See Gunter Teubner, 'Self-subversive Justice: Contingency or Transcendence Formula of Law?', (2009) 72 Modern Law Review 1–23.

52 For an early attempt Hans-Wolfgang Micklitz, 'Competitive Contract Law', (2005) 23 Penn State International Law Review 549–558, not yet taking into account the ongoing fragmentation of regulatory private law.

inner logic in European regulatory private law, to find elements of a common legal order or to understand European regulatory private law as a comprehensive subsystem which unites the different fields of regulated services, the question remains how such a systematized and rationalized European regulatory private law would fit with the traditional national private law, and, even more, if and how the two branches of private law could be connected together theoretically and conceptually: not at all (Teubner), as far as inter-institutional interaction would work (Cutler/Guidice), or even further as a system of systems (Dickson).

Certainly, systematization and rationalization of national private legal orders still remain at the forefront of the development of Nation State building and/ or adapting established codified private legal orders to the changing legal and political environment. Schulze/Zoll[53] provide for a solid account of recent trends in Europe, broadly understood. Similarly, we know that the idea of establishing a European Civil Code, largely drafted and crafted along the same lines of a national civil code based on systematization and rationalization, has failed. All that has been possible is to complete an *academic* project, whether in the form of PECL via the Lando Group, or the Academic DCFR by the Study and *Acquis* Group.

In the following I will use two examples to have a deeper look into the difficulties of systematization and rationalization in the post-Nation State. The first is consumer law, excluded in PECL,[54] but integrated in CESL and in the Dutch and German Civil Code. The second is the field of traditional services, excluded in PECL, but integrated in CESL. The new services within regulated markets do not play a role in the modernization of national civil codes as reported by Schulze/Zoll. Both examples are meant to demonstrate that systematization and rationalization cannot be a *Selbstzweck*, an end in itself. In the light of the changing nature of the Nation State, the former justification for systematization and rationalization has faded away. The new areas of regulatory private law cannot so easily be integrated into the foundations of national private law systems. The shift from the welfare logic to the market-State logic, from the national to the European level, shatters the historical foundations of the national private law systems.

The first example is consumer law. When it comes to systematization and rationalization, the academic and the political debate very much focuses on the relationship between traditional private law and consumer contract law, as one of the most visible parts of regulatory private law. There are Member States which have integrated consumer law into the private law system, such as the Netherlands after a long-lasting and burdensome public debate, and Germany via a technocratic act, and the European codification project via an academic drafting exercise. Right from the beginning, since the adoption of the Communication in 2001, consumer contract law has been regarded as an integral part, if not the trigger, of the whole European codification project. Somewhat exaggeratedly,

---

53   See fn. 2.
54   See Hans-Wolfgang Micklitz, 'The Principles of European Contract Law and the Protection of the Weaker Party', (2004) Journal of Consumer Law 339–356.

one might argue that the *Acquis* Group was formulating the consumer *acquis*, whereas the Study Group focused its activities on general contract law. When both groups were merged, consumer contract law issues became an integral part of the DCFR. As the EU has no competence in private law or contract/tort law as such, the competence in consumer law under Art. 114 (3) TFEU serves as a bridge to justify the harmonization of not only business-to-consumer but also of business-to-business relations.[55]

The deeper political question is whether or not consumer law should become part of a civil code and how the institutional decision of a potential or realized merger affects the deeper foundations of consumer law, its rationality and its values, as well as potential cross-overs between the two fields of law. With the exception of France,[56] no country around the world has ever made a serious effort to try and think about the question whether and to what extent consumer law and traditional private law are inter-related and what exactly the relationship between the two legal orders looks like. I have argued in my 2012 report before the *Deutsche Juristentag* (The Association of German Lawyers) that consumer law has to be kept separate from the German Civil Code and should be understood as a distinct legal order governed by its own rationality and its own values.[57] In line with others,[58] I would uphold the argument with regard to the relationship of European private law (business-to-business) and European consumer law (business-to-consumers).

Let me take as an example the rules on contract conclusion. In all private law systems, offer and acceptance, the moment of contract conclusion, the possibility of withdrawing an offer, the moment from which the party who makes the offer is bound and so on, are subject to sophisticated discussions in traditional private law

---

55 It is highly debatable whether and to what extent the European Union has competence at all to adopt the CESL, see Stephen Weatherill, 'European Private Law and the Constitutional Dimension', in Fabrizio Cafaggi (ed.), *The Institutional Framework of European Private Law* (Oxford University Press, 2006), 81, arguing that contract law does not come under the scope of Art. 114; Hans-Wolfgang Micklitz and Norbert Reich, 'The Commission Proposal for a 'Regulation on a Common European Sales Law (CESL)'– Too Broad or Not Broad Enough', in Luigi Moccia (ed.), *The Making of European Private Law: Why, How, What, Who* (Sellier, 2013), 21, claiming a violation of the proportionality principle.

56 Proposition pour un nouveau droit de la consommation, Rapport de la commission de la refonte du droit de la consommation au secrétaire d'État auprès du ministre de l'Économie, des Finances et du Budget chargé du Budget et de la Consommation, 1985.

57 Hans-Wolfgang Micklitz, 'Do Consumers and Business need a New Architecture for Consumer Law? A Thought Provoking Impulse', in Piet Eeckhout and Takis Tridimas (eds), fn. 32; see for the opposite Dutch position, Ewoud Hondius and Anne Keirse, 'Does Europe Go Dutch? The Impact of the Dutch Civil Law on Recodification in Europe', in Reiner Schulze and Fryderyk Zoll (eds), fn. 2, 303.

58 Norbert Reich, 'A European Contract Law, or an EU Contract Law Regulation for Consumers?', (2005) 28 JCP 383–407; Christian Twigg-Flesner, 'Time to do the Job Properly – the Case for a New Approach to EU Consumer Legislation', (2010) 33 Journal of Consumer Law 355.

systems, whether codified or not. In consumer law, most of the regulation affects the pre- and the post-contractual stage. If the moment matters in consumer relations, it is submitted to particular regulatory adjustments like in e-commerce.[59] This means that in today's standardized consumer transactions, the sophisticated rules on offer and acceptance, of contract conclusion, do not matter. What matters is the degree to which pre-contractual information requires particular remedies which provide rights to consumers in case of lacking or insufficient information. The same is true for the post contractual stage, for after sales services, for example, here traditional private law is usually of little help. So the question is the following: what remains for traditional private law rules on offer and acceptance in business-to-consumer relations if the offer and acceptance do not play a role in consumer transactions?

This does not mean that the rules on the conclusion of the contract are no longer important. However, deeper reflections are needed to understand why EU law is hollowing out national private law rules on offer and acceptance, and why their practical importance in standard business-to-business transactions turns to zero, and how this affects not only the relationship between the two legal orders but also the underlying rationalities.

The second example is services. In the field of services, the situation is even more dramatic – at least much more obvious than in consumer law. In the aftermath of the adoption of White Paper on the Completion of the Internal Market and the Single European Act, the EU has liberalized regulated markets with three generations of directives, the fourth generation already being prepared. The Member States had to amend their national sector-related acts and regulations, they had to open up markets, to establish regulatory agencies and to grant the necessary regulatory powers to them. The overall strategy was to integrate the private law rules governing sectorial markets on services (telecom, postal services, energy, telecom, transport, financial services) into special regulatory acts, outside the national private legal orders and quite often also outside consumer law, whether integrated into the national code or not.[60]

Therefore, the new law on services in regulated markets and the traditional law on services exist side-by side. The traditional law on the contract for services is first and foremost the one dating back to the early nineteenth century. The distinction between *obligations de moyen* and *obligations de résultat*, introduced in the French Code Civil, is a distinction which has been taken over by later codifications and which dominates until today the distinction between services contracts and

---

59   Articles 9-11 of Directive 2001/31/EC on e-commerce.

60   To my knowledge there is no information available on whether and to what extent the EU Member States have integrated regulatory private law on services into their national codified private law systems. What exists, if any, are sector related comparisons, which, however focus to a large extent on the public dimension of the regulation of energy, telecom or financial markets, see as a paradigmatic model, Peter Cameron, *Legal Aspects of EU Energy Regulation, Implementing the EU Directives on Energy and Gas*, (Oxford University Press, 2005).

contracts to manufacture.[61] It deserves respect that the Study Group tackled the issue. A group of researchers analysed five types of services after a common scheme (construction, processing, storage, design, information, treatment), using them as a starter for developing model rules for contracts on services.[62] These model rules did not find their way into the CESL. In the CESL, services are only covered if they are combined with the purchase of goods.[63]

However, the major shortcoming in the Study Group project is the result of the exclusion of all the major services for which the EU is regulating markets, such as energy, telecom, postal services, transport and, most of all, financial services. It is not too much overstated to argue that all modern economically relevant services were excluded from the analysis, which necessarily affected the search for forward-looking solutions. Another reading of the restricted approach would be to say that the Group was well-advised not to embark on services in regulated markets, as they follow their own distinct rationality. Whatever reading is correct, it remains to be emphasized that the working group on services missed a promising opportunity to study services as such and to come up with a proposal which explained why certain services may be submitted to systematization and rationalization whereas others may not. It goes without saying where the distinction has be drawn. Systematization and rationalization of services is limited to those which remain in a purely national environment. However, even this assumption has to be questioned as certain service providers have changed the type of services tremendously over the last hundred years. Just one example might suffice: the repair of cars comes under the category of the contract to manufacture – *obligation de résultat*. However, the contract to manufacture was modelled after the craftsman who produced a unique piece of craftsmanship in line with the mandate he had received from the supplier. A deeper study of the impact on technology and standardization would have made it much more difficult to uphold the nineteenth-century distinction.[64]

---

61 The distinction is no longer convincing. The standardization of services would in theory allow for treating established contracts of services as contracts to manufacture with far reaching effects on the available remedies. Contracts to manufacture, however, are artifically turned into contract for services to avoid the strict consequences of the obligation de résultat.

62 Maurits Barendrecht, Chris Jansen, Marco Loos, Andrea Pinna, Rui Cascao, Stéphanie v. Gulijk (eds), *Service Contracts (Principles of European Law)* (Sellier, 2007); as a follow-up the Society for Comparative Law organized a symposium in Cologne. The results are published by Reinhard Zimmermann (ed.), *Service Contracts* (Mohr Siebeck, 2010), with contributions on the principles developed by the Study Group and on the law on services in Italy, Switzerland, Austria and Germany, France, UK, US, Netherlands, Brazil and China.

63 Martin Illmer, 'Related Services in the Commission Proposal for a Common European Sales Law Com (2011) 635 Final: Much ado about Nothing?', (2013) 21 European Review of Private Law 131–204.

64 Karl-Heinz Ladeur, 'The Evolution of Global Administrative Law and the Emergence of the Modern Administrative State', Osgoode CLPE Research Paper No. 16/2011.

The debate on how the two branches of law, the new regulatory private law and the traditional private law, could be linked together has not even started yet. This is mainly due to the fact that the majority of civil lawyers are ignoring or downplaying the bifurcation between traditional and regulatory private law.

Unification in Order to Overcome Territorial Diversity

The European Civil Code project, linked to the idea of a European Constitution, would mean to create the *United States of Europe*, a project that seems further away than ever. In such a perspective, Europe appears as a territory, but with unclear boundaries. Today Europe has 28 Member States, the Western Balkan States (Albania, Bosnia-Herzegovina, FYROM (Former Yugoslavian Republic of Macedonia), Serbia), are standing ante portas, and Ukraine has also expressed its intention to join the EU. An established relation exists between the EU and the European Economic Area (Norway, Iceland, Liechtenstein). Where does Europe end? What about Turkey with which the negotiations have lasted for decades now, without any clear-cut perspective? What about Switzerland, which remained outside the European Economic Area and is only loosely connected to the EU despite all sorts of bilateral cooperation contracts? This all means that, even if the European Constitution had been adopted, the territorial question would have remained an open one, subject to constant revision and adjustment.

Broken down into the two categories of traditional private law and regulatory private law, we can see a strong preparedness by the potential candidates, the neighbouring States, the members of the European Economic Area and even by those with particular bilateral agreements, to adapt or to adopt the EU's regulatory private law, but to uphold the particularities of the respective private legal orders. There is a certain approximation of regulatory private law, even beyond the territory of the existing 28 Member States, in particular in the field of regulated markets, and to a lesser extent in consumer law, with, by way of example, Switzerland and Turkey resisting the political pressure to adopt major pieces of European consumer law.[65] The fragmentation of private law, meaning the bifurcation between national private legal orders and transnational regulatory silos on energy, telecom, postal services, financial services and transport, is even deepening.

I see the failure of the Constitution and the failure of the European codification project as an opportunity. The EU could and should be understood as a laboratory for the post-Nation State and the post-Nation State legal order. It was the World Bank which attributed to Europe exactly such a forward-looking and positive

---

65 On Swiss law: Luc Thévenoz and Norbert Reich, *Droit de la consommation /Konsumentenrecht /Consumer law: Liber amicorum Bernd Stauder* (Baden-Baden, 2006), 177–194. See also Yesim Atamer and Hans-Wolfgang Micklitz, 'The Implementation of EU Consumer Protection Directives in Turkey', (2009) 27 Penn State International Law Review 551–607.

task.⁶⁶ It deserves to be emphasized that the authors come from the Chicago School of Economics, which does not usually have a reputation for favouring the European path of regulating and shaping the economy.

So far, the laboratory is located mainly outside traditional private law, which means in the field of European regulatory private law. Here, the EU has turned into one of the key players, or more precisely a key regulator, which yields effects inside and outside the EU. My own research is focusing on the European regulatory private law, its internal rationality and its inter-relationship with the national private legal orders. The laboratory, however, yields effects beyond the territory of the EU. This is the argument behind the *Brussels effect*. However, the US-led discussion focuses too much on areas where the EU appears as the standard-setter, such as food safety or data protection. In financial services, the European Commission works as a catalyst, channelling internationally agreed standards via EU law-making to the establishment of a European capital market.⁶⁷ Much needs to be done to disclose the role and function of the EU in the different regulated markets on services, telecom, energy and transport.⁶⁸

In theory, the European codification project could have been seen as a laboratory. The then introduced terminology, on *Common Frame of Reference*, on *toolbox* and the like, could have paved the way for a new understanding or private law making beyond the State in the traditional or the new branches of private law. As is well-known, the whole exercise turned into a missed chance. The *Acquis* group and the Study Group, who took over the drafting process, were not ready to embark on a journey into the unknown, although the leeway granted by the European Commission would not have excluded this possibility. Instead, they focused on the drafting of a civil code which was largely and mainly inspired by the nineteenth-century codification idea, the one of Maillet. The European Commission, which monitored the overall process, was obviously not ready or willing to direct the project into new territory.

However, the move from the Academic DCFR to the Political DCFR gave the overall nineteenth-century project a new twist. It is not so much the academic substance of the Draft CESL which opens up new avenues but its politically imposed optional character which has attracted the attention of law and economics in Europe and across the Atlantic. It could be understood as a genuine contribution to the

---

66   Indermit Gill and Martin Raiser, *Golden Growth*, World Bank, <http://siteresources.worldbank.org/ECAEXT/Resources/258598-1284061150155/7383639-1323888814015/8319788-1326139457715/fulltext_cover.pdf>, last accessed on 30 October 2013.

67   Antonio Marcacci, *Protecting Investors in Financial Times – the Design and Functioning of the Legal Protection of Retail Investors*, PhD Thesis, EUI Florence, 2013.

68   The gap will partly be filled via a forthcoming publication by Marise Cremona and Hans-Wolfgang Micklitz (eds), *The External Dimension of European Private Law*, forthcoming (Oxford University Press, 2014), with contributions investigating the role and function of the European Commission/Union in private law regulation of the energy, telecom, health care and financial service sector.

search for a private law beyond the Nation State. The *Common Market Law Review* published a special issue in early 2013[69] which is entirely devoted to the perspectives of an optional instrument (OI) as an alternative to a codified system of private law rules embedded in a Nation State. Even if one considers its optional character as being a key element for the elaboration of new post-Nation State private legal order, the CESL suffers from three major shortcomings which limit its potential value considerably. First, it reflects the past (sales law) and not the future (the law on services). Secondly, it does not identify the bifurcation between traditional private law and regulatory private law. Thirdly, it contains no hints on how and by what means the bifurcation between the two branches of private law could be overcome.

Private Law Building as Nation State Building

It is a very sensitive question whether and to what extent private law building in the Nation State context enshrines and promotes an idea of nationalism.[70] It requires a clarification of what nationalism means, how it is linked to private law and whether the *Volksgeist* of private national legal orders, so adamantly discussed in the late eighteenth and nineteenth century, is still alive despite more than 50 years of European integration.[71] In the context of the European codification, the argument is made that a European Civil Code would endanger national legal traditions and national legal cultures. The Treaty of Lisbon introduced in Article 4 a reference to the preservation of the national identity, territorial integrity and respect of essential State functions:

> The Union shall respect the equality of Member States before the Treaties as well as their national identities, inherent in their fundamental structures, political and constitutional, inclusive of regional and local self-government. It shall respect their essential State functions, including ensuring the territorial integrity of the State, maintaining law and order and safeguarding national security. In particular, national security remains the sole responsibility of each Member State.

It is by no means clear whether the private law system of a Member State codified or not belongs to its national identity.[72] There are a number of ECJ judgments

---

69   This is the result of a conference held in Chicago meant to bring together law and economics lawyers from Europe and the US, see <http://www.law.leiden.edu/organisation/publiclaw/europainstitute/news/special-issue-on-common-european-sales-law.html>, last accessed on 30 October 2013.

70   Guido Comparato, *Nationalism and Private Law in Europe*, PhD Thesis, University of Amsterdam, 2012, forthcoming (Hart Publishing, 2014).

71   Guido Comparato, 'The Long Shadow of the Volksgeist Or: The Nationalist Dimension in European Private Law Discourse', (2012) European Review of Contract Law 245.

72   In its Lisbon judgment the German Constitutional Court came up with a set of criteria which must be regard as belonging to the essential functions of the German State.

on what could be understood as being part of national identity, but the reasoning is of little assistance to our context.[73] It does not contribute to demarcating the thin line between protection of the national identity, territorial integrity, essential State functions, national culture, national tradition and *nationalism*. In 2012 the University of Amsterdam organized a workshop on *legal nationalism and cosmopolitan thought* and its findings are published in a special issue of the *European Review of Contract Law*.[74]

However, what matters is that the European codification project triggered quite strong reactions in the Member States – first, in academia and later in seven national Parliaments, which questioned the competence of the European Commission after the publication of the Draft proposal on CESL.[75] It has been argued that in France the resistance is expressed through sentiment, while in the UK the resistance is expressed via politics and reason.[76] The German reactions remained astonishingly moderate.[77] I am not sure whether I would agree with the French/UK categorization. The French Civil Code should be understood as a political project, presenting ideas and values of the then Nation State in the making and the establishment of a market society, deeply rooted in French Rationalism. This remains true even if one takes into consideration that the French Civil Code has no or limited democratic origins, since it was developed by a small group of scholars under the direct responsibility of Napoleon himself. Therefore, the French reaction is deeply rooted in a political sediment (which can easily be politically activated). This dimension was largely excluded in the technocratic professorial debates for more than ten years leading to the present proposal on CESL. The deeper attitude of common lawyers and politicians in the UK is pragmatism, leading us back to utilitarianism. The point then is whether the codification project brings an added value to the existing law on contracts and whether it contributes to improve the positioning of the common law system and the businesses using it. Michaels goes

---

However, the GCC does not (yet?) mention the German Civil Code in that context, see Hans-Wolfgang Micklitz, 'German Constitutional Court (Bundesverfassungs-gericht BVerfG), 2 BvE 2/08, 30.6.2009 – Organstreit proceedings between members of the German Parliament and the Federal Government', (2011) European Review of Contract Law 528–546.

73 See, respectively, Case C-208/09. Sayn-Wittgenstein [2010] ECR I-13693, paras 88 and 92; Case C-391/09, Runevič-Wardyn [2011] ECR I-3787, para 85; and Case C-202/11, Anton Las [2013] nyr. para 26.

74 (2012) 3 European Review of Contract Law, see in particular the Editorial from Stefan Grundmann, 'CESL, Legal Nationalism or a Plea for Appropriate Governance', 241.

75 Reference in Hans-Wolfgang Micklitz and Norbert Reich, in Luigi Moccia (ed.) fn. 55.

76 See for the French/English comparison Ruth Sefton-Green, 'French and English crypto-nationalism and European private law. An exercise in sentiment and reason', (2012) European Review of Contract Law 260.

77 See the publication of the Deutsche Zivilrechtslehrervereinigung Archiv für Civilistische Praxis, 1992 (192).

as far as to compare the debate and the pros and cons of the European codification project as a form of religious war.[78]

It should not be forgotten that the first strong reactions were triggered by the Academic DCFR. The proposed optional character of the CESL takes some heat out of the debate, as it formally leaves the national private legal orders as they are. The competence question has not yet come back to the political agenda in the European Parliament and in the Council. At the time of writing it is by no means clear whether the CESL will ever be adopted. For the sake of the argument – the analysis of private law as part of the national identity – let us assume that the competence question can be 'solved' and that the European Commission succeeds in convincing the Member States in the Council – which does not mean that the European Commission will manage to convince the national Parliaments. Let us go even further and start from the premise that the ECJ would confirm Art. 114 TFEU as the appropriate legal basis for the CESL.

If the CESL turns into a success, the European OI might gradually suppress national private law systems. The preservation of the national private legal orders would then be conditional on the failure of the CESL. It seems as if European politics (and, to some extent, the European private law academia) is caught in the self-installed trap. If the CESL succeeds, it endangers the existence of the national private legal orders, which might lead to the *national identity defence*. If CESL fails, the national private legal orders – and their identity – can be preserved. Just to recall – none of the academics or the national Parliaments has yet referred to the national identity argument. And just to mention in passing – it would be an intellectual delicacy to discuss whether and to what extent an action for annulment under Art. 263 TFEU could be brought forward years after the adoption of CESL or whether the two-month period in paragraph 5 must be regarded as exclusionary.

One way out of the trap would have been to conceive of the European codification project as an open exercise where all researchers and politicians compete over the best ideas in an open democratic discourse.[79] The implicit guidance, as laid down in the 2001 document, strived for a harmonized European solution. This would have been a unified top-down solution, imposed by Europe on the Member States, which would have built on the two selected groups, the *Acquis* and Study Group. It would have excluded all those who did not form part of the club, but also other ideas and concepts of what European private law in the twenty-first century could look like. The European Commission did not seriously consider the reservations raised against using the general tool of harmonization in private law. The early critique voiced from the legal perspective was fully in line with the later analysis of the inherent authoritarian category of a *one size fits*

---

78 Ralf Michaels, 'Code vs. Code: Nationalist and Internationalist Images of the Code Civil in the French Resistance to a European Codification', (2012) European Review of Contract Law 277.

79 Stefan Grundmann, 'European Contract Law(s) of What Colour', (2005) European Review of Contract Law 184.

all approach.⁸⁰ From this perspective, the rising nationalism or, more cautiously worded, the potential risk of the identity defenced is the late vengeance of the failure to search for broader legitimacy.

However, the overall debate about nationalism and private law focuses only on one part of the private law, the traditional private law – the national codes which were mostly developed in the nineteenth century and the common law. What is at stake here is freedom of contract, private autonomy and *liberté de la volonté*. All those involved in the debate, from whatever side – academia or politics – defend the past – and are completely blind to regulatory private law – the bulk of rules which affect the regulation of services or, to put the rules in a different perspective, the *service society* and the *information society*. In regulatory private law, none of the protagonists, neither the Member States, nor their political organs, nor the academics, nor legal practitioners, are questioning the need for European, if not international rules. This is certainly true with regard to defining the rules of the game, but perhaps not with regard to the question of who is enforcing them. Here, a clear tension can be observed between the European Commission claiming ever stronger competences for European regulatory agencies operating in the various fields of services markets (telecom, energy, financial services, banking), whereas the Member States defend their competences. This is the case even if strong arguments can be made for a more centralized supervision of the European services markets.⁸¹

Turning the two fields of private law into the perspective of *nationalism* and setting the struggle over enforcement competences aside, we may identify two different worlds – the old world of traditional private law, which is static and ideological, and the new world of regulatory private law, which is dynamic and pragmatic. It might be overstated to argue that those who forcefully defend national private law as part of the national identity, culture and tradition are defending an 'empty shell'. However, from the perspective of regulatory private law it seems hard not to admit that more and more relevant economic activities (services) are taken away from traditional private law and are submitted to sector-related rules. In Europeanized regulatory private law, the ECJ is more and more involved in preliminary reference procedures. Out of more than 120 cases which the ECJ had to decide in consumer law alone, a body of law has emerged which lays down foundations for a genuine European understanding of regulatory private law

---

80 Christian Joerges, 'Der Europäisierungsprozess als Herausforderung des Privatrechts: Plädoyer für eine neue Rechts-Disziplin', in Andreas Furrer (ed.), *Europäisches Privatrecht im wissenschaftlichen Diskurs* (Bern, 2006), 133–188 and Fritz Scharpf, 'Legitimacy Intermediation in the Multilevel European Polity and Its Collapse in the Euro Crisis', MPIfG Discussion Paper 12/6.

81 Madalina Busuioc, *European Agencies, Law and Practices of Accountability* (Oxford University Press, 2013); Madalina Busuioc, Martijn Groenleer, Jari Trodal (eds), *The Agency Phenomenon in the European Union, Emergence, Institutionalisation and Everyday Decision-making* (Manchester University Press, 2012).

concepts.[82] In the regulated service markets, energy, telecom, financial services, it is much more administrative practice than litigation – in fact it is *administrative* enforcement of *private* law – which sets the tone and which deserves to be analysed, in order to get a clearer picture of European regulatory private law in action.

One of the more difficult questions to answer is how the two legal orders, the traditional private legal order and the regulatory order, could be linked together. It seems as if silently but steadily the ECJ is slipping into the role of a European regulator who points a way out of the dilemma. Commandé even argues that the ECJ is using preliminary reference procedures to promote a genuine European identity, if not a European society.[83] This does not mean that the ECJ provides an answer to how the two legal orders should be connected. Quite to the contrary, the ECJ is promoting the development of a genuine European legal order, now also in the field of private law. All that remains to connect the two legal orders is the distinction between norms (increasingly to be determined by the ECJ by using the proportionality principle)[84] and facts (to be analysed by the national courts). Less spectacular, but equally controversial, is the more recent 'invention' of *general principles of civil law* which points in a similar direction. The few judgments in which the notion appears in various forms have triggered a powerful debate throughout Europe.[85] Perhaps this is the reason why the ECJ has not come back to the notion of *general principles of private law* in its more recent judgments.

4 Conclusion

If one accepts the distinction between traditional private law and modern regulatory private law, as well as the changing nature of the Nation State, codification of private law becomes a difficult and challenging exercise. It is certainly not possible to continue Nation State thinking in the ongoing so-called modernization of national private law. If States are not ready to engage in an open debate about the future of their national private laws in the Market State era, there is a risk that 'their' national legal orders are losing ever more importance, at the very least economically, if not

---

82 See, for an overview of the case law of the ECJ, Betül Kas and Hans-Wolfgang Micklitz, 'Rechtsprechungsübersicht zum Europäischen Vertrags- und Deliktsrecht (2008–2013) – Teil I', Europäisches Wirtschafts- und Steuerrecht 2013, 314; Betül Kas and Hans-Wolfgang Micklitz, 'Rechtsprechungsübersicht zum Europäischen Vertrags- und Deliktsrecht (2008–2013) – Teil II', Europäisches Wirtschafts- und Steuerrecht 2013, 353. It is too early to reconstruct the genuine understanding in categories of systems and orders.

83 Hans-Wolfgang Micklitz (ed.), fn 43.

84 Norbert Reich, 'How Proportionate is the Proportionality Principle? Some Critical Remarks on the Use and Methodology of the Proportionality Principle in the Internal Market Case Law of the ECJ', in Hans-Wolfgang Micklitz and Bruno de Witte (eds), *The European Court of Justice and the Autonomy of the Member States* (Intersentia, 2012), 83.

85 Ulf Bernitz, Xavier Groussot, Felix Schulyok (eds), *General Principles of EU Law and European Private Law* (Ashgate, 2013).

politically. EU Law and European private law should be understood as a laboratory which could be used to break well-established national boundaries in private law building as Nation State building. Moreover, it could be used to initiate a debate on two questions: whether codification of European private law in categories of legal orders and legal systems is possible at all in the post-Nation State era, and, if the answer is in the affirmative, to consider the development of a new architecture for European private law codification, one which takes the changing nature of the Nation States to Market States into account, which explains the genuine logic and rationality of European regulatory private law, and which investigates how to connect the old and the new – traditional national private law and new European regulatory private law.

Chapter 6

Integrating Consumer Law into the Civil Code: A Japanese Attempt at Re-codification

Hiroo Sono

1 Introduction

The challenges of "codification" may have different meanings depending on whether one speaks of a common law country or of a civil code country. "Codification" under common law would mean Acts of the legislature, and one important issue that it raises is the conflict of power between the judiciary (judge-made-law) and the legislature. However, under the civil law system, the primary law making power is vested in the legislature; the role of the judiciary is to apply the laws that are enacted by the legislature. Thus the issue of the tension between the legislature and the judiciary has a much smaller weight in a civil law system than in a common law system.

The issue in a civil law system, of which Japan is one, instead will be whether legislation should take the form of rules in a complete and comprehensive "Code", or whether a provision should be created as a piece of special legislation. A "Civil Code" in this sense presupposes that every solution to a legal question regarding private law matters can be found within the Code, and without resort to outside legal sources.[1] Another aspect of the Civil Code that is metaphorically advocated by some academics, influenced by French legal scholarship, is that the Civil Code provides a "Constitution", not of the state, but of the society.[2] According to this view, the Civil Code provides the structural principles upon which Japanese society is built.

The ongoing reform of the Japanese Civil Code (*Minpo*) (JCC)[3] has been subject precisely to this kind of debate. Whether private law rules designed to

---

1 For example, the American "Uniform Commercial Code" (UCC) would not be considered a "Code" in this sense, because it is designed to be supplemented by other sources of law. Cf. U.C.C. Section 1–103(b) which provides "Unless displaced by the particular provisions of [the UCC], the principles of law and equity [...] supplement its provisions."

2 See generally, Eiichi Hoshino, *Minpo-no Susume [Recommendation of the Civil Code]* (Iwanami Shoten 1998).

3 For accounts of this reform project, see Akira Kamo, 'Crystallization, Unification, or Differentiation? The Japanese Civil Code (Law of Obligations) Reform Commission and Basic Reform Policy (Draft Proposals)' (2010) 24 Columbia Journal of Asian

protect or support consumers should be included in the JCC, or whether they should be placed in various special statutes such as the Consumer Contract Act (*Shohisha Keiyakuho*) (CCA) enacted in 2000, has caused a stir.

The purpose of this chapter is to analyze the process of the JCC reform from the perspective of consumer law, and to attempt to demonstrate that the old concept of the "Code" dies hard.

2 The Civil Code Reform

The Current State of Affairs

The official revision process began in October 2009, when the Minister of Justice requested the Legislative Council (*Hoseishingikai*) (LC) to prepare an "Outline Draft (*Kaiseiyoko*)" for the reform of the Civil Code.[4] The LC is an advisory organ to the Minister of Justice, and has traditionally been charged with providing advice and guidance to the Ministry of Justice (MOJ) regarding its legislative activities in the field of basic civil and criminal laws.[5] The mandate given to the LC, however, did not cover the entire Code. The scope of the revision is limited to the law of obligations except *negotiorum gestio,* unjust enrichment and tort law. Some provisions of the General Part of the JCC, such as the law on validity, agency and prescription periods (limitation periods), are also included. Thus, all in all, this is a reform of Contract Law (together with related "obligor and obligee" or "debtor and creditor" laws).

In response, the LC set up a Working Group (WG), which began its deliberation in November 2009, with the mandate to prepare an Outline Draft. After almost three and a half years of deliberation, the WG approved an Interim Proposal (*Chukanshian*) (IP)[6] on 26 February 2013. After some minor editing, the proposal was officially made public on 11 March 2013.

Following the 16 April 2013 publication of a commentary to the IP prepared by Ministry staffs, the proposal was opened for "public comments", which were

---

Law 171; Takashi Uchida, 'Contract Law Reform in Japan and the UNIDROIT Principles' (2011) 2011 Uniform Law Review 705; Hiroyasu Ishikawa, 'Codification, Decodification, and Recodification of the Japanese Civil Code' (2013) 10 University of Tokyo Journal of Law and Politics 61; Souichirou Kozuka and Luke Nottage, 'Policy and Politics in Contract Law Reform in Japan' in Maurice Adams and Dirk Heirbaut (eds), *The Method and Culture of Comparative Law* (Hart, 2014). This author would like to thank Professors Kozuka and Nottage for sharing with this author an unpublished longer version of their chapter just cited.

4 There is pre-history to this event described under the sub-heading 'The semi-official Draft Proposal (DP) (2009)' in Section 3 below.

5 Eiichi Hoshino, '*Hoseishingikai – Kono Shirarezaru Sonzai* [The Legislative Council: This unknown being]' (1996) 600 NBL 4.

6 <www.moj.go.jp/content/000112242.pdf> accessed 25 November 2013.

accepted until 17 June 2013. Taking into account the comments received from the public, especially lawyers, business firms, business associations and academics, the WG is currently continuing their deliberations to finalize the Outline Draft.

With respect to the future timetable, media reports that the LC will publish the Outline Draft by February 2015 "at the earliest".[7] Since it is customary that the MOJ will be drafting draft legislation (namely, the "Bill for Reform of the Civil Code") alongside the deliberations ongoing at the LG, a bill should be ready shortly thereafter. Thus, at the earliest, the bill will be sent to the Diet in the spring of 2015.[8] It is not clear how long the Diet will need for the deliberation of the bill, but even if enacted in 2015, it is likely that there will be a grace period of at least 18 months before the revised Civil Code will come into force. This means that the revised Civil Code will come into effect, at the earliest, sometime in 2017.

Reasons for Reform

What are the reasons for a reform? In requesting the LC to prepare an Outline Draft, the Minister of Justice explicitly gave two reasons: the need for modernization and transparency. Supporters of the reform often raise a third reason: the need to consider global harmonization or convergence of contract law.

Modernization

The current JCC was enacted in 1896, as a part of Japan's attempt to demonstrate its eligibility to join the international community as a "civilized" state.[9] The JCC has been in force for almost 120 years. The parts dealing with family law (Book 4) and succession law (Book 5) underwent a thorough reform in 1947, during the Allied Occupation. The purpose of that reform was to bring in new ideas, such as "respect of individuals" and "equality of sex", embodied in the new Constitution of Japan of 1946.

However, other parts of the JCC dealing with patrimonial law were largely left intact for over a century. These parts are: Book 1 (General Part) including provisions on "person" and "thing"; Book 2 (Property) including provisions on "ownership", "possession", and various types of secured transactions; Book 3 (Obligations) including rules on contracts, debtor and creditor law, torts, *negotiorum gestio*, and unjust enrichment. In 2004, there was a facelift revision of Books 1 through 3, which modernized the "language". This was because the century-old language had

---

7 For example, '*Hoteiriritsu-sage, Hendosei-ni* [Statutory interest rate to be lowered, and will become fluctuating rate]' *Nihon Keizai Shimbun* (Unsigned, Morning edn, Tokyo, 18 February 2013) 1 and 3.

8 Ibid.

9 For an account by one of the main drafters of the Civil Code, including why and how the codification took place, see Nobushige Hozumi, *Lectures on the New Civil Code: as Material for the Study of Comparative Jurisprudence* (2nd and Revised edn, Maruzen Kabushiki-kaisha 1912).

become extremely obsolete, deviating from everyday usage in the current time. However, this revision was not intended to change the substance of the JCC.

There also had been other minor or medium-scale piecemeal revisions. Provisions related to secured transactions went through medium-scale revisions twice: first in 1971, a reform which added rules on revolving mortgages (*ne-teitoken*), and secondly in 2003, which streamlined the rules on enforcement of security interests. In 2000, in response to the emerging aging society, the rules on adult guardianships were reformed.[10] In 2004, requirements for personal guarantee agreements were made more stringent by imposing a "writing" requirement for a personal guarantee to be effective.[11] Most recently in 2006, rules in the JCC on incorporation of associations and foundations were replaced by special legislation.[12] However, none of these revisions had a scale as large as the current reform project, and none of these concerned the basic rules pertaining to civil obligations.

In the meantime, the society and economy have changed drastically. The economy in the late nineteenth century was largely an agricultural economy and Japanese society was still at the verge of "industrialization". Priority was given therefore to the promotion of heavy industry; property with value was mostly land and buildings, and mass-produced goods were yet to come. Today, transactions in mass-produced movables, financial instruments, services and information have become a significant part of the economy. Mass production has also brought attention to the class of people known as "consumers". Also, the society has "aged". The increase in the population of the elderly, who in many instances need more protection and assistance than the "strong individual" which the JCC tends to presuppose, as well as the decrease in the birth rate, have brought about an "aged society". JCC's assumption of a "strong individual" has increasingly been questioned.

One rationale for the reform is to bring the Civil Code into conformity with these socio-economic changes.

Transparency

During the 120 years of the JCC, the judiciary has struggled to solve issues that are not clearly provided for in the Code. Today, the true state of the JCC cannot

---

10 Makoto Arai and Akira Homma, 'Guardianship for Adults in Japan: Legal Reforms and Advances in Practice' (2005) 24 (Supplement) Australasian Journal on Ageing S19.

11 One exception was a change in the provisions dealing with personal guarantees (Arts 446, 456-2 to 456-5 JCC). The purpose of this revision was to impose a strict condition on the enforceability of personal guarantees, which tended to cause tragic consequences in the guarantors life. This social problem still lingers and the LC's latest "Interim Proposal" includes a proposal for prohibition of certain types of personal guarantees by individuals (IP 17-6(1)).

12 Act on General Incorporated Associations and General Incorporated Foundations (*Ippan Shadanhojin oyobi Ippan Zaidanhojin-ni kansuru Horitsu*) (Act No. 48 of 2006).

be understood without consulting case law that supplements the JCC. This is a cause of concern because the rules actually applied in the courts do not reflect the Code itself. Similarly, the legislature has developed various special statutes that override or supplement the JCC. These include the Act on the Restriction of Interests (*Risokuseigenho*) enacted in 1954, Act on Land and Building Leases (*Shakuchishakuyaho*) enacted in 1991 which consolidated two earlier pieces of legislation of 1921, Product Liability Act (*Seizobutsusekininho*) enacted in 1994, and the CCA. It is often pointed out that these judicial and legislative activities have brought about the "hollowing out of the Civil Code". This obscures the current state of law, and it is felt that these scattered rules should be incorporated into the Civil Code itself. One purpose of the current reform is to bring substance back into the JCC, so that it will increase transparency in the state of the law.

Globalization

One characteristic in today's contract law is that an increasing trend toward global harmonization or convergence of contract law can be witnessed. Most importantly, the successful 1980 United Nations Convention on Contracts for the International Sale of Goods (CISG) has become a "prototype" for recent contract law reforms.[13] International and regional unification efforts such as the UNIDROIT Principles of International Commercial Contracts (1994, 2004, 2010), Principles of European Contract Law (PECL) (1995, 1997, 2000) and the European Draft Common Frame of Reference (DCFR) (2009) are most well-known. There are other efforts such as initiatives from the Organisation for the Harmonisation of Business Law in Africa (OHADA)[14] and Principles of Asian Contract Law (PACL).[15] Recent domestic law reforms are also heavily influenced by this trend of global convergence. Examples include law reforms in Nordic countries, Germany, China, Eastern and Middle

---

13   Peter Schlechtriem, 'Basic Structures and General Concepts of the CISG as Models for a Harmonization of the Law of Obligations' (2005) 10 Juridica International 27, 30–31; Franco Ferrari, 'The CISG and Its Impact on National Legal Systems – General Report' in Franco Ferrari (ed), *The CISG and Its Impact on National Legal Systems* (Sellier 2008); Ingeborg Schwenzer and Pascal Hachem, 'The CISG: The Success and Pitfalls' (2009) 57 American Journal of Comparative Law 457, 461–463.

14   The sales law rules in OHADA's *Acte Uniforme portant sur le Droit Commercial Général* [Uniform Act Relating to General Commercial Law] (AUDCG), adopted in 1997, is already heavily influenced by the CISG. There also was an attempt to bring OHADA's general contract law into harmony with the UNIDROIT Principles. See, Marcel Fontaine, 'The Draft OHADA Uniform Act on Contracts and the UNIDROIT Principles of International Commercial Contracts' (2004) 2004 Uniform Law Review 573; Marcel Fontaine, 'Law Harmonization and Local Specificities – A Case Study: OHADA and the Law of Contracts' (2013) 2013 Uniform Law Review 50.

15   See generally, Naoki Kanayama, 'PACL (Principles of Asian Civil Law)' in Benoît Moore (ed) *Mélanges Jean-Louis Baudouin* (in French, Éditions Y Blais 2012); Shiyuan Han, 'Principles of Asian Contract Law: An Endeavor of Regional Harmonization of Contract Law in East Asia' (2013) 58 Villanova Law Review 589.

European countries and Baltic nations.[16] Against this backdrop, it is considered that the revised JCC should be able to contribute toward the furtherance of this trend.[17]

3 Integrating Consumer Law into the Civil Code

Crossroads of Consumer Law and the Civil Code Reform

In the Civil Code reform, integration of consumer law was or is being considered along the following two dimensions.

"Consumer" as the norm?
The first dimension is the reconsideration of the concept of "person". When the need for "modernization" is mentioned as a reason for reform of the JCC, it follows that the concept of "person", which is a cornerstone of the JCC, must be reconsidered. The recognition of the existence of "consumers" and the "elderly" has raised doubts about the concept of "person" in the JCC. A "person", whether a natural person or a juristic person (such as a corporation), is supposed to be "rational" and "strong". It was questioned whether this assumption might not be too remote from reality and too fictitious. The same applies to small and medium size enterprises (SMEs). Thus, reconsideration of the "person", whereby "consumers" are no longer the exception but the norm, was supposed to be a major theme in the reform.[18] This is especially so from the viewpoint of some academics

---

16 See generally, Schlechtriem (n 13); Ferrari (n 13); Schwenzer and Hachem (n 13).

17 See for example, Takashi Uchida, *Saikenho-no Shinjhidai [The New Era of Obligations Law]* (Shojihomu 2009) 31–34; Takashi Uchida, *Minpo Kaisei [Revision of the Civil Code]* (Chikuma Shobo 2011) 71–78. Interestingly, Japan's accession to the CISG in 2008 roughly coincides with the beginning of the Civil Code reform project. On Japan's accession to the CISG, see Hiroo Sono 'Japan's Accession to and Implementation of the United Nations Convention on Contracts for the International Sale of Goods (CISG)' (2010) 53 Japanese Yearbook of International Law 410. For some aspects of the influence the global convergence of contract law had on the Civil Code reform, see Hiroo Sono, 'The Diversity of *Favor Contractus*: The Impact of the CISG on Japan's Civil Code and Its Reform' in Ingeborg Schwenzer and Lisa Spagnolo (eds), *Towards Uniformity: The 2d Annual MAA Schlechtriem CISG Conference* (Eleven International Publishing 2011).

18 See, *Minpo (Saikenkankei)-no Kaisei-ni Kansuru Chukantekina Rontenseiri* [Interim Issues Paper for the Revision of the Civil Code (Law of Obligations)], <www.moj.go.jp/content/000074989.pdf> accessed 25 November 2013, Issue No 62, 183–187; and the following proceedings of the LC's WG meetings (in Japanese): Proceedings of the 20th Meeting <www.moj.go.jp/content/000064611.pdf> accessed 25 November 2013, 25–50; Proceedings of the 24th Meeting <www.moj.go.jp/content/000072447.pdf> accessed 25 November 2013, 49–54; Proceedings of the 61st Meeting <www.moj.go.jp/content/000109166.pdf> accessed 25 November 2013, 1–19.

who consider the Civil Code as a "constitution of the society".[19] However, this attempt has quietly faded away and the LC no longer explicitly pursues this goal.[20]

Integrating consumer law

The second aspect was to incorporate already existing consumer law into the Civil Code. The most obvious candidate for integration into the Civil Code is the CCA (2000). "Integration" may either take the form of simply incorporating the rules in the CCA into the JCC without changing their scope of application (that is, applying those rules only to consumer contracts), or of transforming the rules into a more general rule applicable to all contracts (including "business-to-business" – B2B transactions).[21] The more interesting and important is the latter approach. The possibility of this integration has drawn wide attention. The sub-headings 'The development of the Consumer Contract Act (CCA)' and 'Integration of the CCA into the Civil Code: The shrinking ambition' in Section 3 will focus on this possibility. However, equally significant is the integration of the various rules established by the courts, through case law.[22] This aspect will be dealt with under the sub-heading 'Remnants of consumer law' in Section 3.

The Development of the Consumer Contract Act (CCA)[23]

The CCA was enacted in 2000. It includes very limited rules on "substantive control of unfair contract terms" and "procedural control" over contractual unfairness.[24]

---

19   See n 2 and accompanying text.

20   However, IP 26–4 may have, although limited, a similar effect of differentiating consumers under the Civil Code. See the sub-heading 'Remnants of consumer law' in Section 3.

21   On the two different approaches, see Kamo (n 3) 206–210.

22   The judiciary has been quite active and innovative in furthering the goal of consumer protection. See generally, Sôichirô Kozuka, 'Judicial Activism of the Japanese Supreme Court in Consumer Law: Juridification of Society through Case Law?' (2007) 27 Zeitschrift für Japanisches Recht/Journal of Japanese Law 81; Andrew Pardieck, 'Japan and the Moneylenders: Activist Courts and Substantive Justice' (2008) 17 Pacific Rim Law and Policy Journal 529; Hiroo Sono, 'Private Enforcement of Consumer Law: A Sketch of the Japanese Landscape' (2012) 16 Hokkaido Journal of New Global Law and Policy 63. However, for a more reserved view, see Luke Nottage, 'Form and Substance in US, English, New Zealand and Japanese Law: A Framework for Better Comparisons of Developments in the Law of Unfair Contracts' (1996) 26 Victoria University Wellington Law Review 247.

23   See generally, Tsuneo Matsumoto, 'Privatization of Consumer Law: Current Developments and Features of Consumer Law in Japan at the Turn of the Century' (2000) 30 Hitotsubashi Journal of Law and Politics 30; Masahiko Takizawa, 'Consumer Protection in Japanese Contract Law' (2009) 37 Hitotsubashi Journal of Law and Politics 31; Masami Okino, 'Recent Developments in Consumer Protection in Japan' (2012) 4 UT Soft Law Review 10; Sono, 'Private Enforcement' (n 22).

24   In 2006, another set of rules was added to allow certified consumer associations to bring injunction suits against businesses that violate the procedural control provisions of the

Substantive policing
Civil Code For substantive policing of contracts, one may rely on Article 90 JCC, which provides that contracts against public policy are void.[25] Contracts involving "excessive profiting" (*bori koi*) (or "gross disparity") are often regarded to be in violation of public policy.[26] Case law originally required both that:

i. one party has taken advantage of the other party's distress, thoughtlessness or inexperience; and
ii. the contract gives excessive profit to one party.

Recent trends deemphasize the second requirement, and this is now more a tool for procedural policing rather than substantive policing.[27] However, Article 90 JCC being an overarching "general clause", predictability is not guaranteed.

Consumer Contract Act (CCA) It was against this backdrop that the CCA was drafted. It includes a very limited "black list" of clauses it considers to be void (Article 8 CCA on business operators' exemption or limitation of liability clauses, and Article 9 CCA on liquidated damages clauses imposed on consumers).

CCA (Art 4). This part was expanded in 2008 to cover acts violating certain prohibitions in the "Act against Unjustifiable Premiums and Misleading Representations" (*Futokeihinrui oyobi Futohyoji Boshiho*) and the "Act for Specified Commercial Transactions" (*Tokuteishotorihiki-ni kansuru Horitsu*). This injunctive relief will allow prohibition of use of standard contract terms including unfair contract terms. There currently are 11 certified consumer associations nationwide. Okino (n 23) 14–17.

25 On Article 90 JCC, see generally, Nottage (n 22) 275–281.

26 This reasoning led to an important case law development (although these are not necessarily consumer law cases): it often happened that in monetary loan contracts, the lender would insert into the contract a clause providing that, in case of default, the lender has the option of receiving transfer of ownership of a specific immovable from the borrower, in lieu of repayment of the debt. That "option right" could be registered, and by registration it achieved a security agreement status with third party effect. However, since there tends to be disparity between the amount of outstanding debt and the value of the immovable, these contracts were considered to be highly problematic. Case law developed a "settlement duty" (*seisangimu*) which requires the lender to settle the difference. The legislature also followed up with this case law development by legislation in 1978 of the Act on Contract for Establishment of Security Interests by Use of Provisional Registration (*Karitokitanpokeiyaku-ni kansuru Horitsu*). See generally, John O Haley, 'The Preliminary Contract for Substitute Performance: A Reflection of the Japanese Judicial Approach' (1974) 7 Law in Japan 133; Frank Bennet Jr, 'Getting Property Right: "Informal Mortgages" in the Japanese Courts' (2009) 18 Pacific Rim Law and Policy Journal 463.

27 For example, in a case where an inexperienced 52-year-old housewife was lured into futures trading, the Supreme Court ruled that the contract was concluded in a grossly unfair manner, and thus is void as being against public policy. Supreme Court Judgment, 29 May 1986, 1196 Hanrei Jiho 102.

It also has a general clause that provides that any derogation from non-mandatory provisions of the Civil Code or Commercial Code is void under Article 10 CCA if:

i. the derogation unilaterally impairs the interest of consumers; and
ii. if the derogation was entered into in violation of the principle of good faith.

This innovation in the CCA, borrowed from German law, has the potential to become a powerful tool for consumers.

In fact, the Supreme Court recently applied Article 10 CCA in a series of decisions concerning the validity of an "automatic deduction clause" ("*shikibiki*" clause) in residential lease contracts.[28] It is customary in Japan that lessees will pay a security deposit (known as "*shikikin*") when entering into a lease contract. The security deposit will be returned to the lessee at the end of the lease after deducting all outstanding payments such as unpaid rents and restoration fees. However, in the Kansai region, there is a twist to this *shikikin* agreement. Usually, there is an agreement to automatically deduct a fixed sum even when there are no outstanding debts. With respect to such automatic deduction agreement, the Supreme Court ruled in effect that if the clause is expressly made available to the lessee at the time of contract, the clause is not in violation of good faith and is thus valid, unless the amount of deduction is excessively high in comparison to the rent etc. In the case before it, the Court therefore upheld the validity of the automatic deduction clause.

Procedural policing
Civil Code With respect to procedural control of the contracting process, we have already seen above that Article 90 JCC (the public policy provision) is one tool that consumers may invoke. In addition, there are traditional invalidating rules such as mistake, fraud and duress (Articles 95 and 96 Civil Code). However, the rigid requirements of these rules have made it difficult for consumers to rely on them. For procedural control, we have to turn to other legislative responses.

Pre-Consumer Contract Act (CCA) Interventions: Statutory "Cooling-off Periods" Starting in the 1970s there has been a series of statutes that provide a "cooling-off period" within which time consumers have a right to cancel the contract without showing any cause. The first of such legislation was the "Installment Sales Act" (*Kappu Hanbaiho*) of 1972, but consider the "Act on Specified Commercial Transactions" (*Tokuteishotorihi-ni kansuru Horitsu*), originally enacted in 1976 as the "Door-to-door Sales Act" (*Homonhanbai-ni kansuru Horitsu*), as an example. This Act allows, for example, consumers to cancel the contract in door-to-door sales in which a salesperson appears at a consumer's doorstep to propose a contract,

---

28 Supreme Court Judgment, 24 March 2011, 65-2 Minshu 903; Supreme Court Judgment, 12 July 2011, 2128 Hanrei Jiho 43. See also Supreme Court Judgment, 15 July 2011, 65-2 Minshu 2269 for a similar decision upholding the validity of a "renewal fee" clause in a residential lease contract. For an overview of these cases, see Okino (n 23) 12–13.

if the cancellation right is exercised within eight days from the day of receipt of a written contract. The Act provides similar rules for other types of contracts with different lengths of "cooling-off periods" ranging from 8 to 20 days. In 2008, the "Installment Sales Act" and the "Act on Specified Commercial Transactions" were amended to expand the scope of this cancellation right. Other Acts which provide for similar rules include the "Building Lots and Buildings Transaction Business Act" (*Takuchi Tatemono Torihikigyoho*), "Financial Instruments and Exchange Act" (*Kinyu Shohin Torihikiho*) and the "Insurance Business Act" (*Hokengyoho*). Although this cancellation right is a private law remedy, it is interesting that all of these statutes basically are administrative regulation.

Consumer Contract Act (CCA)   Article 4 CCA enacted in 2000 provides for consumers' rescission rights that expand the fraud and duress provisions of the JCC. However, the expansion is available only in limited situations. This makes Article 4 CCA an inconvenient tool for consumers. Expansion of rescission for fraud is allowed only when the consumer's mistake was caused:

i. by "misrepresentation of an important matter" (Art 4, para 1, subpara i);
ii. by "providing conclusive evaluation of an uncertain matter" (Art 4, para 1, subpara ii); or
iii. by "non-disclosure of an important matter that is unfavorable to the consumer" (Art 4, para 2).

Expansion of rescission right for duress is even more restrictive. It is allowed for example when the consumer's distress was caused by the business operator's "refusal to leave" or "prevention of the consumer from leaving" the negotiations (Article 4, para 3). Thus, CCA is rather weak in procedural policing of unfair contracts.

Integration of the CCA into the Civil Code: The Shrinking Ambition

The semi-official Draft Proposal (DP) (2009)
As a prelude to the current official reform process, there was a semi-official effort to produce a Draft Proposal (DP) for reform.[29] This task was undertaken during

---

29   See generally, Kamo (n 3). There were at least two other groups of academics that published a reform proposal. One was a proposal by a group led by Professor Masanobu Kato (then of Sophia University) which published a proposal covering Books 1 to 3 of the JCC. Minpokaiseikenkyukai (ed), *Minpokaisei-to Sekai-no Minpoten [Civil Law Reform and Civil Codes of the World]* (Shinzansha 2009). The other was a proposal by a group led by Professor Naoki Kanayama (of Keio University) on the law of prescription periods. Naoki Kanayama (ed) *Shometsujikoho-no Genjo-to Kaiseiteigen [The Current State of Extinctive Prescription Period Law and Reform Proposals]* (Shojihomu 2008). However, it is clear that the influence of the DP outweighs by far the others.

the period from 2006 to 2009 by a privately formed group of leading academics known as the Japanese Civil Code (Law of Obligations) Reform Commission.[30] Their work resulted in the DP, which was published in April 2009.[31] Although it is merely a proposal by a group of academics, it is generally considered to have set the groundwork for the subsequent official reform under the MOJ.

The DP started out with an ambitious proposal to integrate the procedural control provisions of the CCA into the JCC. To be more precise, the DP proposed:

1. Incorporation of the misrepresentation rules (Art 4, para 1, subpara i and Art 4, para 2 CCA) into the JCC, making it applicable to contracts in general: that is, not only to consumer contracts. (DP [1.5.15])
2. Incorporation of the rule on the provision of conclusive evaluations (Art 4, para 1, subpara ii) and the rule on distress (Art 4, para 3) into the JCC. However, the application of these rules was limited to consumer contracts. (DP [1.5.18] and [1.5.19])

In addition, the DP also proposed a rule that is not in the CCA:

3. Addition of a rule on "fraud by silence", which in essence imposes a "good faith duty of disclosure" in contracts in general. (DP [1.5.16] <2>)

As far as these proposals are concerned, the DP formed the basis of the deliberation in the LC.

The debate inside (and outside) the Legislative Council (LC)
However, these proposals were met with opposition that came from various camps.

Opposition from business interests[32]   The understandable and expected response from the business side was that consumer laws do not belong in the Civil Code.

---

30   The Japanese Civil Code (Law of Obligations) Reform Commission's website is available at <www.shojihomu.or.jp/saikenhou/English/index_e.html> accessed 25 November 2013.

31   Minpo (Saikenho) Kaisei Kento Iinkai [The Japanese Civil Code (Law of Obligations) Reform Commission] (ed), *Saikenho Kaisei no Kihon Hoshin [Draft Proposals of Obligations Law Reform]*, (Shojihomu 2009). An English translation of the Draft Proposal (black letter proposal only) is available at <www.shojihomu.or.jp/saikenhou/ English/index_e.html> accessed 25 November 2013. Some of the provisions are presented in the Appendix to this chapter.

32   The interventions by committee members representing Ministry of Economy, Trade, and Industry (METI) and Japan's largest business association *Keidanren* generally are blatantly in disfavor of inclusion of general rules on duty of disclosure, gross disparity, and misrepresentation rules currently in the CCA. See the following proceedings of the LC's WG meetings (in Japanese): Proceedings of the 9th Meeting <www.moj.go.jp/content/000048744.pdf> accessed 25 November 2013, 30–34 (duty

The point was that the Civil Code applies to "equal parties", and therefore each party should assume responsibility with respect to gathering information. The opponents objected that the proposed incorporation of rules would bring paternalistic regulation into the free market and that it will unduly burden business activities.

Opposition of consumer advocates On the other end of the spectrum were the advocates of consumer law who, surprisingly, argued that incorporation of these rules into the Civil Code would make it difficult for these rules to be adapted to the needs of consumers.[33] What they meant was that since the Civil Code is amended only rarely, it will become difficult to revise the provisions compared to revising provisions in the CCA.

However, this argument is not really convincing. It is true that the Civil Code was rarely revised in the past, but there is no reason to suppose that it will be the same after the current reform. More importantly, the incorporation into the Civil Code of the current CCA rules will not be an obstacle to enacting special legislation that adds protection to consumers. The DP only makes the consumers better off, because what used to be an exceptional rule for consumer contracts was to become the bench mark for general contract. In this sense, this opposition from the consumer advocates was perhaps misguided.

One possibly legitimate concern would have been the question of "reverse application" of the provisions. For example, if the misrepresentation rules were made applicable to contracts in general, it may happen that a consumer who purchases an insurance policy will be accused of committing misrepresentation and thus face a rescission of the contract, if they fail to disclose inadvertently or intentionally certain information relating to their health. It is understandable that the consumer advocates preferred to keep these CCA rules as "consumer protection" rules rather than allowing it to become a more general rule.

It should also be noted that there was also an aspect of a power struggle between the MOJ and the Consumer Affairs Agency (CAA) in this debate. CAA

---

of disclosure); Proceedings of the 10th Meeting <www.moj.go.jp/content/000050017.pdf> accessed 25 November 2013, 4–12 (gross disparity), 42–58 (misrepresentation); Proceedings of the 11th Meeting <www.moj.go.jp/content/000051605.pdf> accessed 25 November 2013, 2–25 (standard terms), 35–48 (unfair terms); Proceedings of the 23rd Meeting <www.moj.go.jp/content/000071629.pdf> accessed 25 November 2013, 1–3 (unfair terms); Proceedings of the 49th Meeting <www.moj.go.jp/content/000101937.pdf> accessed 25 November 2013, 1–16 (duty of disclosure); Proceedings of the 50th Meeting <www.moj.go.jp/content/000103198.pdf> accessed 25 November 2013, 13–55 (standard terms), 55–65 (unfair terms); Proceedings of the 51st Meeting <www.moj.go.jp/content/000103200.pdf> accessed 25 November 2013, 1–44; Proceedings of the 67th Meeting <www.moj.go.jp/content/000113292.pdf> accessed 25 November 2013, 24–28 (duty of disclosure), 32–47 (standard terms and unfair terms).

33 See the proceedings of the LC's WG meetings cited in n 32.

is the sponsoring government body of the CCA, but incorporation of the CCA rules into the Civil Code will mean a shift of responsibility and jurisdiction to the MOJ.[34]

The Interim Proposal (IP) (2013)

Let us now turn our attention to the comparison of the DP and the IP, and see how the proposals in the DP fared in the IP.

From the very beginning, proposal 2 was dropped from the deliberations of the LC. Perhaps it was considered that there would be little gain by moving these provisions from the CCA to the JCC, if the application is still limited to consumer contracts.

With respect to proposal 1, this remained in the deliberation materials of the LC, but it *disappeared* in the IP. The reason for this retreat is not made clear, but the arguments of the business interests seem to have prevailed. This perhaps was a realistic compromise on the side of the LC or MOJ, to move the reform process forward.

What remains in the IP is only proposal 3. It is to be seen whether it will remain in the revised JCC.

In this way, the IP is far less ambitious than the DP in integrating CCA provisions, and thereby transforming the JCC.

Remnants of Consumer Law

However, there still remain interesting proposals in the IP.

Disparity between businesses and consumers

The most intriguing proposal is IP 26-4, which suddenly appeared in the IP and proposes that "the disparity in the quality and quantity of information and negotiating power between consumers and business" should be taken into consideration when applying the Civil Code provisions on "good faith" (Art 1(2) JCC). The wording quoted is literally taken from Article 1 CCA, which declares the purpose of CCA. This proposal may be seen as a "comeback" of the reconceptualization of the "person", and it may function as a bridge between the CCA and the Civil Code.

Duty to disclose information (johoteikyogimu)

Although the parties are, in principle, under no obligation to disclose information to the other party in the contracting process, IP 27-2 makes an exception for cases where:

i. a party knew or could have known a certain information; and

---

34 Although this chapter focuses on the substantive legal arguments, an "interest group analysis" of this kind is also required. For such attempt, see Kozuka and Nottage (n 3).

ii. that party could have known that the other party would not have entered into the contract had it known the information; and
iii. it cannot be expected that the other party would be able to obtain the information on its own, in light of factors such as the nature of the contract, the knowledge and experience of the parties, the purpose of the contract, the course of negotiations; and
iv. it is not reasonable to impose the disadvantage of entering into that contract on the other party.

The breach of this duty will give rise to damages claims, rather than a right to rescind the contract. It is intended that this rule will apply to B2B transactions,[35] but it has its origin in consumer cases, and it is easy to see that the main application of this rule will be to consumer contracts.

Gross disparity (bori koi)
The IP also proposes a rule on "gross disparity" (IP 1-2(2)). This provides that if a party has taken advantage of the other party's condition under which that other party cannot make reasonable decisions due to distress, lack of experience or knowledge, and if the contract gives grossly excessive advantage to one party while giving grossly excessive disadvantage to the other, that contract is void. This proposal is based on case law developments under the existing JCC.[36]

Policing of standard terms
Lastly, the IP includes a set of rules on "standard terms" or "adhesion contracts" (IP 30). It provides for rules on incorporation of standard terms into the contract, exclusion of "surprising terms", and invalidity of terms that give excessive disadvantage on the other party. Surprisingly, the CCA does not regulate standard terms in general. Therefore, if these proposed rules are included in the revised JCC, that will be a major improvement, especially for consumers.

4 Assessment

Lack of Counterbalance to Contractualism/Consensualism

The shrinking ambition with respect to incorporation of consumer laws into the Civil Code is perhaps a realistic compromise, but seen from the underlying guiding

---

35 There is already some case law that holds that even in B2B transactions, a party owes a duty of disclosure to the other party. For example, Supreme Court Judgment, 27 November 2012, 2175 Hanrei Jiho 15 (The arranger of a syndicated loan agreement is under a duty, toward other participants, to disclose the financial state of the borrower).

36 See 'Substantive Policing, Civil Code' and 'Procedural Policy, Civil Code' above in Section 3.

policy or philosophy behind the reform, this is a cause for serious concern. That philosophy was "contractualism" or "consensualism": parties are governed and bound by their own contract, that is, what they have agreed. This is, in a sense, a simple application of the "party autonomy principle", but the current contract law regime under the JCC provides several excuses from a party being bound by its own agreement.

For example, the JCC adopts a "fault principle" which requires fault of the obligor in order to hold the obligor liable (Art 415 JCC). Even if the obligor breaches the contract it agreed to, it is not held liable unless the additional requirement of "fault" is satisfied.

Another example is the doctrine of "impossibility". According to this doctrine, a contract that is impossible to perform at the time of conclusion (that is, "initial impossibility") is void. The party who undertakes an obligation that turns out to have been impossible is not bound by that agreement. Likewise, in the case of "subsequent impossibility", instead of holding the obligor liable for breaking its contract, the impossible obligation is extinguished (unless it was due to the fault of the obligor, in which case the obligation will be converted into an obligation to pay damages).

The DP clearly proposed the abandonment of these "fault principles" and "impossibility" doctrine (DP [3.1.1.08], [3.1.1.62] and [3.1.1.63]). The IP is less clear with respect to abandonment of the "fault principle" (IP 10-1), but the "impossibility" doctrine is abandoned (IP 26-2). Under these rules, parties will be held liable for non-performance of "what they have agreed", whether they are at fault or not, or whether an obligation is impossible or not. This is a departure from the current contract law regime.[37]

Although this author is generally in favor of this shift to "consensualism", one condition is that there should be a countervailing mechanism that secures a true and meaningful "consensus".[38] The revised JCC needs a much richer rule on procedural policing of not only consumer contracts but also contracts in general. It is lamentable that the integration of the CCA into the JCC has been discarded. However, we can still hope that the incorporation of case law developments (See the sub-heading 'Remnants of consumer law' in Section 3 above) will go through, and that the courts will continue with active intervention in securing fair bargains.

---

37 This departure is influenced by the global convergence of contract law represented by the CISG. See 'Globalization' under the sub-heading 'Reasons for reform' in Section 2 and Sono, 'Diversity of *Favor Contractus*' (n 17).

38 This author has once argued the necessity of contract law in which contracts are fully upheld only when they result from "competitive choices". Hiroo Sono '*Kyosochitsujoto Keiyakuho* [Order of Competition and Contract Law]' (2007) 863 NBL 64.

Non-"Code" Developments of Consumer Law

It is also interesting that the Cabinet has now decided, in its "Consumer Basic Plan" (March 2010), that the CAA and MOJ will consider revisions of the CCA in conjunction with the ongoing Civil Code reform project. This has resulted in several efforts by various actors. For example, in August 2011 the Consumer Commission, which is an independent organization established in 2009 to monitor the government's engagement in consumer affairs and to make recommendations to the government regarding consumer affairs, urged the CAA to begin work on revision of the CCA; the Consumer Commission also published a lengthy report in August 2013 that analyzes points where the CCA may be improved. Thus, the retreat of consumer issues from the Civil Code reform does not immediately mean that consumer law reforms are stalled. Developments outside the Civil "Code" will continue.

Final Remark

Thus, what we see is a shrinking ambition with respect to the Civil Code reform. Although comprehensive "Codes" are powerful, their comprehensive nature is a drawback that can stifle devising of specific rules. On the other hand, consumer law most likely will continue to be vital and will thrive through special statutes and case law development. Proponents of integration of consumer law into the Civil Code dreamed a dream that will not be fulfilled in the context of the current Civil Code reform. However, hope is not shattered.

APPENDIX

1 Selected Provisions of the Civil Code (Act No. 89 of April 27, 1896)

(Excerpt from: <www.japaneselawtranslation.go.jp/law/detail/?id=2057&vm=04&re=01&new=1> accessed 25 November 2013)

(Fundamental Principles)
Article 1
(1) Private rights must conform to the public welfare.
(2) The exercise of rights and performance of duties must be done in good faith.
(3) No abuse of rights is permitted.

(Public Policy)
Article 90
A juristic act with any purpose which is against public policy is void.

(Mistake)
Article 95
Manifestation of intention has no effect when there is a mistake in any element of the juristic act in question; provided, however, that the person who made the manifestation of intention may not assert such nullity by himself/herself if he/she was grossly negligent.

(Fraud or Duress)
Article 96
(1) Manifestation of intention which is induced by any fraud or duress may be rescinded.
(2) In cases any third party commits any fraud inducing any person to make a manifestation of intention to the other party, such manifestation of intention may be rescinded only if the other party knew such fact.
(3) The rescission of the manifestation of intention induced by the fraud pursuant to the provision of the preceding two paragraphs may not be asserted against a third party without knowledge.

2 Selected Provisions of the Consumer Contract Act (CCA) (Act No. 61 of May 12, 2000)

(Excerpt from: <www.japaneselawtranslation.go.jp/law/detail/?id=2036&vm=03&re=01&new=1> accessed 25 November 2013)

(Purpose)
Article 1
The purpose of this Act is to protect the interests of Consumers, and thereby contribute to the stabilization and improvement of the general welfare and lives of the citizens and to the sound development of the national economy, in consideration of the disparity in the quality and quantity of information and negotiating power between Consumers and Business Operators, by permitting a Consumer to rescind the manifestation of his/her intention to offer or accept a contract when the Consumer has misunderstood or was distressed by certain acts of Business Operators, and by nullifying any clauses, in whole or in part, that exempt Business Operators from liability for damages or that otherwise unfairly harm the interests of Consumers, in addition to providing a Qualified Consumer Organization with the Right to Demand an Injunction against a Business Operator, etc. for the purpose of preventing the occurrence of, or the spreading of damage to, other Consumers.

(Rescission of the Manifestation of an Intention to Offer or Accept a Consumer Contract)
Article 4
 (1) A consumer may rescind the manifestation of his/her intention to offer or accept a Consumer Contract if either of the actions listed in the following items in which the Business Operator engaged when soliciting the Consumer to enter into such a Consumer Contract caused the Consumer to be under the mistaken belief listed in the relevant item, based on which the Consumer manifested the intention to offer or accept the relevant Consumer Contract:
  (i) Misrepresentation as to an Important Matter:
   Mistaken belief that said misrepresentation is true; or
  (ii) Providing conclusive evaluations of future prices, amounts of money that a Consumer should receive in the future and other uncertain items subject to future change with respect to goods, rights, services and other matters that are to be the subject of a Consumer Contract: Mistaken belief that the content of said conclusive evaluations is certain.
 (2) A Consumer may rescind the manifestation of his/her intention to offer or accept a Consumer Contract if a Business Operator, when soliciting said Consumer to enter into said contract, represents only the advantages of an Important Matter or a matter related thereto but intentionally omits disadvantageous facts (limited to facts that a Consumer would normally consider to be non-existent by such omission), about such Important Matter, causing said Consumer to mistakenly believe the non-existence of such facts. However, this shall not apply where said Business Operator has attempted to communicate such facts to said Consumer and said Consumer refused to hear such attempted communications.

(3) A Consumer may rescind the manifestation of his/her intention to offer or accept a Consumer Contract if he/she is distressed as a result of either of the following acts engaged in by a Business Operator when soliciting said Consumer to enter into said Consumer Contract:
   (i) Failure to leave a Consumer's residence or place of business in defiance of the Consumer's request that the Business Operator leave such place; or
   (ii) Preventing a Consumer from leaving a place where the Business Operator is soliciting the Consumer to enter into a Consumer Contract in defiance of the Consumer's request to leave.
(4) The term "Important Matter" as used in item (i) under paragraphs (1) and paragraph (2) means the following matters that, if included in a Consumer Contract, would normally affect a Consumer's decision as to whether to conclude such Consumer Contract:
   (i) Quality, purpose of use and other details of the objects of a Consumer Contract, such as goods, rights and services; and
   (ii) Price and other conditions of a transaction involving the objects of a Consumer Contract, such as goods, rights and services.
(5) The rescission of the manifestation of an intention to offer or accept a Consumer Contract under paragraphs (1) to (3) may not be asserted against a third party without such knowledge.

(Nullity of Clauses which Exempt a Business Operator from Liability for Damages)
Article 8
(1) The following Consumer Contract clauses are void:
   (i) Clauses which totally exempt a Business Operator from liability to compensate a Consumer for damages arising from default by the Business Operator;
   (ii) Clauses which partially exempt a Business Operator from liability for damages arising from default by the Business Operator (limited to default which arises due to an intentional act or gross negligence on the part of the Business Operator, the Business Operator's representative or employee);
   (iii) Clauses which totally exempt a Business Operator from liability for damages to a Consumer which arise from a tort pursuant to the provisions of the Civil Code committed during the Business Operator's performance of a Consumer Contract;
   (iv) Clauses which partially exempt a Business Operator from liability for damages to a Consumer arising from a tort (limited to cases in which the same arises due to an intentional act or gross negligence on the part of the Business Operator, the Business Operator's representative or employee) pursuant to the provisions of the Civil Code committed during the Business Operator's performance of a Consumer Contract; and

(v) Where a Consumer Contract is a contract for value, and there exists a latent defect in the subject matter of the Consumer Contract (including where a Consumer Contract is a contract for work, and there exists a defect in the subject matter of a Consumer Contract for work; the same shall apply in the following paragraph): Clauses which totally exclude a Business Operator from liability to compensate a Consumer for damages caused by such defect.

(2) The provisions of the preceding paragraph shall not apply to clauses as provided in item (v) of the preceding paragraph that fall under the cases enumerated in the following items:

(i) Where a Consumer Contract provides that a Business Operator is responsible to deliver substitute goods without defects or repair the subject where a latent defect exists in the subject matter of the Consumer Contract; and

(ii) Where a Consumer contract is concluded between a Consumer and a Business Operator simultaneously with or after another contract is concluded between the Consumer and another Business Operator entrusted by the Business Operator, or between the Business Operator and another Business Operator for the benefit of the Consumer, and said other contract provides that the other Business Operator is responsible to provide compensation for all or part of the damages caused by a defect, deliver substitute goods without defects or repair the defective subject where a latent defect exists in the subject matter of the Consumer Contract.

(Nullity of Clauses that Stipulate the Amount of Damages to be Paid by Consumers, etc.)

Article 9

The following Consumer Contract clauses are void to the extent provided in each respective item:

(i) a clause that stipulates an amount of liquidated damages and/or establishes a fixed penalty in the event of cancellation, wherein the total amount of damages and/ or penalty exceed the normal amount of damages that would be caused to a Business Operator by the cancellation of a contract of the same type in accordance with the reason for the cancellation, the time of the cancellation, etc.: The amount by which the total exceeds the normal amount; and

(ii) a clause in a Consumer Contract that stipulates an amount of liquidated damages and/or establishes a fixed penalty in the event of a total or partial default by the customer (if more than one payment is to be made, every delinquent payment is a default under this item), wherein the total amount of damages and/or penalty exceeds the amount calculated by deducting the amount actually paid from the amount which should have been paid on the due date and multiplying the result by 14.6% a year in accordance with the number of days from the due date to the day on which the money is actually paid: The amount by which the total amount exceeds the calculated amount.

(Nullity of Clauses that Impair the Interests of Consumers Unilaterally)
Article 10
Any Consumer Contract clause that restricts the rights or expands the duties of the Consumer more than the application of provisions unrelated to public order in the Civil Code, the Commercial Code (Act No. 48 of 1899) and any other laws and regulations, and that unilaterally impairs the interests of the Consumer, in violation of the fundamental principle provided in the second paragraph of Article 1 of the Civil Code, is void.

3 Selection from "Draft Proposal" by the "Japanese Civil Code (Law of Obligations) Reform Commission"

(Excerpt from <www.shojihomu.or.jp/saikenhou/English/index_e.html> accessed 25 November 2013)

DP [1.5.15] (Misrepresentation)
(1) With regard to a manifestation of intention made to the other party, in cases where the other party made a representation which differed from fact regarding matters which would ordinarily influence the decision of the person manifesting the intention as to whether or not to make the manifestation of intention, and such person manifested an intention based on an incorrect understanding of the facts, such manifestation of intention may be rescinded.
(2) With regard to the manifestation of intention made to the other party, in cases where a third party made a representation which differed from fact regarding matters which would ordinarily influence the decision of the person manifesting the intention as to whether or not to make the manifestation of intention, and such person manifested an intention based on an incorrect understanding of the facts, such manifestation of intention may be rescinded only when falling under one of the following items:
   (a) The third party serves as a representative for the other party or is some other person for whose act the other party should bear responsibility; or
   (b) At the time of the person manifesting the intention making the manifestation of intention, the other party knew or could have known that the third party had made a representation to the person manifesting the intention which differed from fact.
(3) The rescission of the manifestation of intention pursuant to (1) and (2) may not be asserted against a third party who is without knowledge or fault.

* Cases falling under Article 4, paragraph 2 of the Consumer Contract Act (failure of notification of a disadvantageous fact) would constitute the "misrepresentation" denoted here, and therefore rescission would be permitted in accordance with [1.5.15], but one view was also expressed that it would be preferable to explicitly confirm to such effect.

DP [1.5.16] (Fraud)
  (1) If the person manifesting the intention was induced to do so through fraud, it may rescind such manifestation of intention.
  (2) If through information, which should have been provided under the principle of good faith not being provided, or an explanation, which should have given under the principle of good faith not being given, the person manifesting the intention was deliberately made to make a mistake or the mistake of the person manifesting the intention was deliberately abused leading to the person making the manifestation of intention, it shall be deemed that the manifestation of intention was made through the fraud of (1).
  (3) If a third party committed fraud with regard to the manifestation of intention made to the other party, such manifestation of intention may be rescinded only when falling under one of the following:
      (a) The third party serves as a representative for the other party or is some other person for whose act the other party should bear responsibility; or
      (b) At the time of the person manifesting the intention making the manifestation of intention, the other party knew or could have known that such third party had committed fraud.
  (4) The rescission of the manifestation of intention pursuant to (1), (2) and (3) may not be asserted against a third party who is without knowledge or fault.

DP [1.5.18] (Special provisions on consumer contracts – misconception based on the provision of a conclusive evaluation)
  (1) At the time of the business operator soliciting for the conclusion of a consumer contract, if through providing the consumer with a conclusive evaluation on uncertain items with regard to the goods, rights, services or other things which were the object of such consumer contract, the consumer was under the misconception that the details of the conclusive evaluation so provided were definite and, through such misconception, manifested an intention to offer or accept the consumer contract, such manifestation of intention may be rescinded.
  (2) If a third party provided the consumer with the conclusive evaluation in (1), the manifestation of intention to offer or accept such consumer contract may be rescinded only when falling under one of the following items:
      (a) Such third party serves as the representative or some other person of such business operator and the business operator is the person who should bear responsibility for such act; or

(b) At the time of the consumer manifesting the intention to offer or accept the consumer contract, the business operator knew or could have known that the third party had provided a conclusive evaluation.
(3) A representative for the consumer pertaining to the conclusion of the consumer contract (including sub-agent (including those persons who are appointed as sub-agents through two or more layers)) is deemed to be the consumer with regard to the application of (1) and (2).
(4) The rescission of the manifestation of intention for the offer or acceptance of a consumer contract pursuant to (1), (2) and (3) may not be asserted against a third party without knowledge or fault.

DP [1.5.19] (Special provisions on consumer contracts – distress)
(1) At the time of the business operator soliciting for the conclusion of a consumer contract, aside from when falling under one of the following acts, if the business operator continued to solicit the consumer despite the consumer indicating a desire to the effect that continuation of the solicitation was unwanted, and through the business operator continuing the solicitation the consumer was distressed into manifesting the intention to offer or accept such consumer contract, such manifestation of intention may be rescinded:
   (a) The consumer indicated a desire to the business operator to the effect that the business operator leave the residence or the place where the business was being conducted but the business operator did not leave such place; or
   (b) The consumer indicated a desire to the effect that it wished to leave the place where such business operator was soliciting for conclusion of the consumer contract but the business operator did not allow the consumer to leave such place.
(2) [1.5.18] (2), (3), and (4) shall apply *mutatis mutandis* to (1).

Chapter 7

The Government's Proposed Review of Australia's Contract Law: An Interim Positive Response*

Luke Nottage

1 Introduction

This chapter outlines and responds to a thought-provoking 'Discussion Paper to Explore the Scope for Reforming Australian Contract Law' (DP). It focuses on eight sets of questions posed in the DP, addressed respectively in eight Parts below, followed by the general conclusion that the preliminary public consultation process has already uncovered sufficient evidence for the Australian government now to initiate a proper law reform project.

The DP was released on 22 March 2012 by the Australian Attorney-General's Department (AGD), as part of its project aimed at 'Improving Australia's Law and Justice Framework'. It has generated significant controversy among those more comfortable with existing domestic law, making it uncertain whether the government will proceed with any reforms whatsoever. By 7 September 2013, the date called for Australia's general election, the AGD had still not released any follow-up report or analysis of the 53 publically available Submissions and other responses to the DP, including an online survey and views expressed at invitation-only Forums held in Melbourne and Sydney over 2012.[1] The AGD has

---

* This chapter is an updated and expanded version of a Submission (finalised on 16 July 2012, available at <http://ssrn.com/abstract=2111826> accessed 1 September 2013) for the Australian government's consultation on contract law reform, elaborated after the workshop hosted by Griffith University (in Ubud, 1–2 May 2013). I am grateful for the helpful discussions and views expressed at that workshop as well as at three research events related to the government's consultation, held in Sydney over June–July 2012.

1 For readers outside Australia and the common law tradition: the AGD is similar to a Ministry of Justice found in other countries. The DP and related material (including most of the Submissions in response to the DP) can be found at: Attorney-General's Department, Australian Government, *Review of Australian Contract Law* (20 July 2012) available at <http://www.ag.gov.au/consultations/pages/ReviewofAustraliancontractlaw.aspx> accessed 1 September 2013. A numbered list of the Submissions, referred to accordingly throughout this chapter, is added as an Appendix to my original Submission (available at <http://ssrn.com/abstract=2111826>).

also meanwhile embarked, since December 2012, on a public consultation on reforming private international law in Australia – another area based primarily on a burgeoning corpus of case law.[2] The main background to both initiatives is the National Partnership Agreement to Deliver a Seamless National Economy, reached in 2009 by the federal, state and territory governments, which includes the aim of 'reducing costs incurred by business in complying with unnecessary and inconsistent regulation across jurisdictions'.[3]

Although contract law reform is unlikely ever to become a high priority in Australia, this chapter analyses the DP in light of the public Submissions to highlight especially:

a. additional problem areas and hence 'drivers for reform' for contract law reform in Australia (including consumers and some parts of the legal profession), as well as the ten helpfully identified by the DP;
b. the direct and opportunity costs incurred by complex domestic contract law, and their disproportionate impact on certain groups;
c. the growing disparities with the contract law regimes found in Australia's major trading partners nowadays (especially now that some are engaging in comprehensive contract law reforms of their own) or at the international level;
d. how best to conceptualise and address challenges involved even in a 'Restatement' approach to reforming Australian contract law.

Reform initiatives may indeed promise fewer directly-measurable benefits than in the European Union (EU, with significant divergences in contract law rules and broader legal culture across member states) and even the United States (US, because its highest court does not bind state courts on contract law issues – unlike the High Court of Australia). Yet contract law initiatives in Australia can also be carried out at lower cost, learning from the harmonisation processes as well as the results or legal norms generated by comprehensive national and international reform projects, particularly over the last decade. In addition, reform of Australian contract law highlights major questions of distributive justice and 'nation-building' in a broader sense, not just issues of aggregate economic

---

2   See Attorney-General's Department, Australian Government, *Private International Law Consultation* <http://consult.govspace.gov.au/pil/> accessed 1 September 2013; generally Keyes, in this volume.

3   This Agreement emerged through the Council of Australian Governments (COAG). The other two main goals of the 2009 Agreement are: 'enhancing Australia's longer-term growth, improving workforce participation and overall labour mobility' and 'expanding Australia's productive capacity over the medium-term through competition reform, enabling stronger economic growth'. See COAG Reform Council, *Competition and Regulation* <http://www.coagreformcouncil.gov.au/agenda/competition> accessed 1 September 2013.

efficiency which have figured prominently in the Australian government's reform agenda so far. On balance, therefore, it is high time for the Australian government to proceed with a more detailed inquiry into various means of addressing some significant problems with Australian contract law, under the leadership of the Australian Law Reform Commission (ALRC).

2 Problems and Drivers of Reform in Australian Contract Law

The DP begins by asking what the main problems are for 'users' (and non-users) of Australian Consumer Law (ACL), and hence what 'drivers of reform' are the most important for contract law.[4] The Paper lists the following ten drivers, which do indeed highlight most – but not all – of the challenges affecting Australian contract law:

- accessibility;
- certainty;
- simplification;
- setting acceptable standards of conduct;
- supporting innovation;
- compatibility for e-commerce;
- elasticity (that is, to support more 'relational contracts'[5]);
- suitability for small and medium-sized businesses (SMEs);
- harmonisation; and
- internationalisation.

Accessibility, Certainty and Simplification through Harmonisation

Most problematic is probably 'accessibility', and the related difficulty of a lack of 'certainty', generating a need for 'simplification' and better 'harmonisation' of contract law even within Australia. Even as an immigrant to Australia in 2001, from New Zealand (a country also still firmly within the English variant of the

---

4 See the DP: Attorney-General's Department (n 1) 3–6.

5 'Relational contracts' comprise longer-term or other more complex contractual relationships, lying at the other end of a spectrum from 'discrete' contracts (such as one-off sales of goods) characterised by a simpler set of norms. See, for example, Ian Macneil, 'Adjustment of Long-Term Economic Relations under Classical, Neoclassical and Relational Contract Law' (1978) 72 Northwest University Law Review 854. In its Submission in response to the DP (No 9), the Australian Newsagents Federation gives the example of the long-term contracts that its members conclude with large newspaper publishers. The Submission of Dr Jenny Buchan (No 13) highlights franchise contracts. Donald Robertson, 'The International Harmonisation of Australian Contract Law' (2012) 29 Journal of Contract Law 1 focuses on international contracts.

common law tradition)[6] and with a doctorate in comparative contract law,[7] it took me several years of researching and teaching Australian contract law to discern sufficiently many of the ways its case law-driven principles have evolved and apply in practice. Other academics in Australia also find its contract law to be unnecessarily complex and confusing in various significant respects.[8]

Problems are compounded for those who do not need to research Australian contract law principles on a regular basis, including many Australian solicitors (many of whom remain in sole practices or small firms, or work as in-house counsel) and even some barristers.[9] Local lawyers do mostly get by, of course, thanks largely to standardised contract forms (for example for residential property transactions or certain financial products). Yet the difficulty in keeping up with developments in the voluminous Australian case law limits their ability to negotiate and draft contracts more effectively, and causes extra costs and delays when disputes end up in court. This becomes particularly problematic when the amounts under the contract or claimable in damages are small, or involve cross-border transactions.[10]

Foreign lawyers encounter even more impediments in determining Australian contract law, when advising their clients overseas wishing to deal with Australian parties. This problem is exacerbated by an apparent tendency for local legal advisors generally to urge the exclusion of the United Nations Convention on Contracts for the International Sale of Goods (CISG) in cross-border sales contracts, partly due

---

6 See Bigwood, in this volume; Luke Nottage, 'Tracing Trajectories in Contract Law Theory: Form in Anglo-New Zealand Law, Substance in Japan and the United States' (2013) 4(2) Yonsei Law Journal 175–271, available at <http://ssrn.com/abstract=2270889> accessed 1 September 2013.

7 Luke Nottage, 'Form, Substance and Neo-Proceduralism in Comparative Contract Law: The Law in Books and the Law in Action in England, New Zealand, Japan and the US' (PhD thesis, Victoria University of Wellington Law Faculty, 2001) <http://hdl.handle.net/10063/778> accessed 1 September 2013.

8 See, for example, the Submissions by Prof Philip Clarke and Dr Julie Clark (No 18), Prof Andrew Stewart (No 50, appending his article, 'What's Wrong with the Australian Law of Contract?' (2012) 29 Journal of Contract Law 75, which focuses on uncertainties regarding principles of contract interpretation and the possible contours of a duty of good faith in Australian contract law) and Prof Dan Svantesson (No 52). See also the Submission by Dr May Fong Cheong and Dr Pei Meng Teng (No 16, focusing on contracts for the benefit of third parties).

9 See generally <http://www.lawcouncil.asn.au/lawcouncil/index.php/12-resources/231-how-many-lawyers-are-there-in-australia> accessed 1 September 2013. On legal education and the comparative ease of qualifying as a lawyer in Australia, see also James Douglas, Luke Nottage and Charles Tellier, 'The Role of Practice in Legal Education: National Report for Australia' (2012) 12/28 Sydney Law School Research Paper No 12/28 <http://ssrn.com/abstract=2041691> accessed 1 September 2013.

10 The Submission by the Australian Society of Authors (ASA, No 10), for example, highlights the practical problems in enforcing such contractual rights.

to persistent misunderstandings of the CISG.[11] They encourage clients instead to seek specification of a domestic law – including perhaps Australian contract law – to govern such relationships.[12] Yet reaching agreement on an acceptable governing law becomes more difficult without ready access to clear statements of Australian contract law principles.

Several submissions in response to the DP seem to acknowledge the challenges of accessing and interpreting Australian contract law, especially for SMEs. The Australian Copyright Council, for example, mentions that creators of copyrighted works often copy over terms seen elsewhere without understanding their meaning.[13] Presumably these can later give rise to disputes and the problem could be reduced – although probably never completely avoided – by making Australian contract law principles more understandable and readily available. The Australian Society of Authors complains about Amazon Kindle requiring Australian authors and publishers to agree that the law of a US state shall govern their contract, to the express exclusion of the CISG,[14] suggesting that 'multilateral or bilateral agreements on contract principles' may provide a useful alternative. So too, presumably, would be a more accessible and clearer statement of Australian contract law, as an alternative to US law – at least in contract negotiations with a smaller commercial entity than Amazon. The Civil Contractors Federation complains that its members (diverse firms often dealing with state and local governments) contract 'on the basis of what they understand to be the basis of the agreement only to find that later a different interpretation or view is taken of a clause in the contract'.[15] Consult Australia

---

11   For example, the submission in response to the DP from the Australian Corporate Lawyers Association (ACLA, No 7, 4) includes the remarkable assertion that under the CISG 'the ability to return goods not fit for purpose would be removed'. Compare, for example, CISG arts 35(2)(a) and 49 (although CISG art 25 does generally make it *harder* for a buyer to avoid the contract for minor breaches, compared to a seller under Australia sale of goods legislation relying on an implied 'condition' of fitness for purpose).

12   Luke Nottage, 'Who's Afraid of the Vienna Sales Convention (CISG)? A New Zealander's View from Australia and Japan' (2005) 36 Victoria University of Wellington Law Review 815; Lisa Spagnolo, 'The Last Outpost: Automatic CISG Opt Outs, Misapplications and the Costs of Ignoring the Vienna Sales Convention for Australian Lawyers' (2009) 10 Melbourne Journal of International Law 141. Even if the CISG is not excluded, its scope is expressly limited (for example in Art 4 as to matters of contractual validity). Another contract law regime needs to apply to govern such matters, preferably by express specification in the sales contract following diligent research and negotiation by the parties and their legal advisors. See also generally Schwenzer, in this volume.

13   Submission No 6, 3.

14   Submission No 10, 5. Curiously, the Society seems to assume that the CISG would otherwise apply, even though it would not – for such a contract of services, rather than a sale of goods. This therefore provides another example of a fundamental misunderstanding of the CISG among the Australian business community.

15   Submission No 17, 6. The Federation does acknowledge, however, that this is arguably 'an inherent feature of a common law system which relies heavily on the courts for

(a peak association for consultants in the building industry) specifically draws attention to the need for considering accessibility of contract law, remarking that:[16]

> Many smaller businesses don't have the means to obtain legal advice, and will read and analyse the contract without legal training, and therefore use the plain English meaning of terms within that contract.

Other Submissions highlighting the costs of accessing accurate legal information for drafting contracts and enforcing rights come from the Information Technology Contract and Recruitment Association Ltd, Dr Cyril Jankoff (the 'risk doctor' consultant on contracts), the Licencing Executives Society (Australia and New Zealand), the Hon Paul Lynch MP (on behalf of his constituents), the New South Wales (NSW) Small Business Commissioner, the Small Business Development Corporation (SMBC, within the Western Australian government – drawing on original survey evidence) and the SME Association of Australia.[17]

Submissions from the legal profession were generally more sanguine about the accessibility of Australia's contract law, but most conceded that there were areas of uncertainty where the law might usefully be simplified or harmonised. Australia's main association for in-house lawyers urged consideration of 'centralisation, so that contract law is accessible in one location', as well as removal of some ambiguity and in particular more uniformity among different legislative regimes impacting on domestic contract law.[18] The Submission from the Law Society of NSW – Young Lawyers highlighted several common misunderstandings, as well as overlapping doctrines and some inconsistencies among the states and territories that increase the costs of providing accurate legal advice – especially for general practitioners.[19] The Law Council of Australia (LCA) identified many more (in fact, 19) 'areas of contract law which ... potentially warrant some form of further attention', while cautioning that the basic principles were generally sound – with problems arising more from increasingly complicated factual scenarios and the impact of legislative

---

interpretation'. Contractual interpretation disputes are also presumably exacerbated because of another major concern raised by the Federation: the plethora of 'standard' contracts used by government procurers in Australia.

16 Submission No 21, 4, 23. This association also points to 'the quality of legal practitioners' purporting to advise on relevant contract law issues in the consulting industry (at 29).

17 Respectively, Submissions No 30, 32, 36, 40, 43, 47 and 48.

18 ACLA Submission (No 7) 2–3. ACLA identified ambiguity in the case law as to what material can be used when interpreting written contracts (as well as a duty of good faith), but highlighted the following areas of incomplete or inadequate legislative intervention: third-party rights, proportionate liability, writing requirements, capacity of minors, frustration, sale of goods, consumer protection legislation, and unfair terms.

19 Submission No 44, 3–4.

requirements (particularly consumer legislation). The LCA was also concerned that 'further legislation could, rather than simplifying contract law, potentially increase uncertainty and costs, particularly in the short term'.[20]

King & Wood Mallesons doubted whether accessibility would in practice be able to drive reform, given the arguably 'different needs of each contract party' as well as the pressures that underlie and generate specific legislative interventions. However, this major international law firm did suggest further evidence-gathering and consultation about simplifying existing legislation, and targeted intervention in seven areas arguably involving uncertain or outdated case law.[21] Freehills (now Herbert Smith Freehills) asserted more definitively that 'domestic contract law works well and is well understood', although international contracting needed enhanced support – primarily by Australia engaging better with existing and emerging international regimes.[22]

The Chief Justice of NSW went further by arguing that 'codification' – one option mooted briefly in the AGD's DP (as discussed in Part 6 below) – was 'a flawed proposal'. One argument presented was that codification would never make contract law accessible to the lay public and would not likely make it simpler even for the legal profession.[23] Chief Justice Bathurst also disagreed with many other Submissions regarding areas of ambiguity and reform in the case law. However, he did acknowledge that 'remedial legislation' might be conceivable in some areas, giving 'internet contracting' as a good example.[24] Another senior jurist emphasised that the proliferation of judgments freely available over the internet has made it difficult (absent clear authority from the High Court of Australia) 'to assess what precedential value is likely to be attributed to particular judgments in future proceedings'.[25]

---

20 Submission No 35, 4–5.

21 Submission No 34, 3–5. The specified areas include: frustration, privity, capacity, mistake, illegality, consideration, and formal requirements (writing requirements and deeds). King & Wood Mallesons objected however to reformers adopting such concepts as unconscionability or good faith, arguing that they 'add to uncertainty and costs and result in more disputation' (at 6).

22 Submission No 26, 1–2. See also, by a partner in charge of the firm's international dispute resolution group in Sydney, Robertson (n 5). He too urges better engagement with international contract law instruments, acknowledging the 'fundamental importance of the principle of good faith' (at 20) – but without venturing an opinion on that principle's applicability to domestic contract law.

23 Hon TF Bathurst, Submission No 11, 4–5.

24 By contrast, he argued that admissibility of extrinsic evidence for contractual construction was 'tolerably clear' and that the question of good faith has not 'created uncertainty or concern amongst the commercial community such as to provide an imperative for clarification for codification' (at 14–15). Cf, for example, Stewart (n 8) 82–87; generally Wilson, in this volume.

25 Hon Geoff Lindsay SC (sworn in as a Justice of the NSW Supreme Court on 6 August 2012), Submission No 38, 13.

Additional Drivers of Reform

Curiously, however, the DP left out another important driver for reform: 'consumers'. Admittedly, Australia largely completed in 2010 a re-harmonisation of consumer (contract) law nation-wide, clarifying and significantly improving standards of fair dealing with consumers. But the new ACL ended up with various (in fact *more*) definitions of 'consumer'.[26] Some are *more* expansive than the intuitive definition largely adopted in European law (viz individuals contracting for a non-business purpose) and therefore include business-to-business (B2B) transactions, between SMEs and even large firms. Examples include 'consumer' guarantees for many transactions up to A$40,000 – as well as the prohibitions on misleading conduct mentioned in the DP.[27] But some definitions are *less* extensive, with carve-outs for entire sectors (notably insurance contracts) or for other special-interest groups (engineers and architects regarding the 'fitness for purpose' statutory guarantee).[28] Consumers in such contractual relationships need to revert to background contract law for minimum standards of protection. As such, they too should be considered and consulted as part of the AGD's 'Review of Australian Contract Law'. The LCA's Submission, for example, also emphasises 'that a consideration of the rights of consumers is as important as the need to facilitate domestic and international trade and investment'.[29]

More generally, many concepts in the ACL will inevitably be interpreted in light of general contract law principles, even when (re)stated in legislative form. Jurists in Australia prefer to analogise to what they know rather than to reinvent the wheel – even when seemingly given statutory licence to do so, as evidenced by case law involving relief against unconscionable conduct provided by the

---

26 Schedule 2 of the *Competition and Consumer Law 2010* (Cth), the new name for the *Trade Practices Act 1974* (Cth) (TPA); applied in each state and territory pursuant to an Inter-Governmental Agreement reached in 2009. For more details of this recent 're-harmonisation' and the ACL regime's diverse definitions of 'consumers', see for example Luke Nottage, 'Consumer Law Reform in Australia: Contemporary and Comparative Constructive Criticism' (2009) 9 QUT Law and Justice Journal 111; Luke Nottage and Justin Malbon, 'Introduction' in Justin Malbon and Luke Nottage (eds), *Consumer Law and Policy in Australia and New Zealand* (Federation Press 2013); Justice Stephen Rares, 'Striking the Modern Balance Between Freedom of Contract and Consumer Rights' (14th International Association of Consumer Law Conference, University of Sydney, 2 July 2013) <http://www.fedcourt.gov.au/publications/judges-speeches/justice-rares> accessed 1 September 2013.

27 At para 3.9. See ACL, ss 3, 18.

28 See ACL, s 61, and (on the ongoing discussion to bring insurance contracts within the ACL framework) The Treasury, Australian Government, *Unfair Contract Terms for Contracts of General Insurance* (31 May 2013) <http://www.treasury.gov.au/ConsultationsandReviews/Submissions/2013/Contracts-of-general-insurance> accessed 1 September 2013.

29 Submission No 35, 5. See also Submission No 22 from the Consumer Action Law Centre.

predecessor to the ACL.³⁰ Further, from a comparative perspective, Australian contract law comes across as having a rather 'classical' (or nineteenth-century) 'vibe'.³¹ It still seems to take one-off transactions as the norm for a (largely implicit) theory of contract law that gives high priority to a particular and strong view of party autonomy. However, the 'Mason Court' did prod contract law towards a more 'neo-classical' model in various areas from the mid-1980s through to the late 1990s, for example regarding equitable doctrines of promissory estoppel or unconscionable bargains.³²

The Australian government's Review since 2012 provides an opportunity to move Australian contract law at least towards the more thoroughgoing neo-classical model characteristic of the *Restatement (Second) of Contracts* (1979) and, for example, the Uniform Commercial Code (UCC) Article 2 on Sales in the US.³³ It may even lead to Australian contract law adopting more flexible doctrines characteristic of a 'relational contract' model, which instead takes a complex contractual relationship (with many more norms that simply party autonomy or 'consent') as an empirical and normative starting point for contract law rules.³⁴ At least in part, such a shift away from classical contract law principles may benefit consumers and other vulnerable groups in contractual relationships.³⁵

This issue is highlighted also by the Submission on the DP made by the Redfern Legal Centre, a non-profit community-based legal advice centre. It notes that 'changes to contract law as a whole would have a significant impact' on its clientele, including consumers, vulnerable individuals and workers (independent contractors as well as employees). Their everyday contracts are often unwritten or conducted on the basis of adverse standard-form contracts which cannot be properly negotiated, which they usually cannot enforce properly anyway due to the high cost of litigation.³⁶ The Centre draws attention to a recent report by Community Law Australia entitled 'Unaffordable and Out of Reach: The Problem of Access

---

30 Nyuk Nin Nahan and Eileen Webb, 'Unconscionable Conduct in Consumer and Business Transactions' in Justin Malbon and Luke Nottage (eds), *Consumer Law and Policy in Australia and New Zealand* (Federation Press 2013). Another example is the persistent tendency of Australian courts to the interpret CISG in light of domestic sale of goods law principles: see Spagnolo (n 12) and Submission No 55 (Zeller).

31 For readers outside Australia: the 'vibe' is the punch-line from a well-known Australian comedy movie about a family that contests (ultimately through the courts) the government's attempted compulsory acquisition of their home. See <http://www.youtube.com/watch?v=ITUSZ6LRHrk> accessed 1 September 2013.

32 See generally Nahan and Webb (n 30); Wilson, in this volume.

33 See generally Hyland, in this volume.

34 See (n 5).

35 Generally, on vulnerable groups in contemporary Australian society, see Therese Wilson, 'Vulnerable and Disadvantaged Consumers' in Justin Malbon and Luke Nottage (eds), *Consumer Law and Policy in Australia and New Zealand* (Federation Press 2013).

36 Submission No 46. The Centre acknowledges (at 7) that sector-specific ombudsman schemes help alleviate access to justice, but they 'have their own issues to be monitored'.

to the Australian Legal System', which certainly contains some startling statistics relevant especially to everyday disputes.[37] The Centre adds that simplification of Australian laws has often been discussed without reform eventuating, and indeed acknowledges that:[38]

> The law in relation to formation of contracts, the enforcement of them, the remedies available where the contracts or the circumstances are unjust, and the enforcement of contracts, is complex, but this might be seen to be for good reason. Each time a set of rules to regulate behaviour is put in place, it is found that unscrupulous dealers will use these rules to the disadvantage of those they seek to exploit. In more innocent situations, the rules can still operate harshly. For instance, in the process of negotiation the parties may have recorded some things in writing but not all encompassing terms. The common law, equity, and consumer protection legislation, all attempt to provide mechanisms, to balance certainty and rules, with safety valves where those rules themselves become unjust.

In other words, greater certainty is not always a panacea for consumers. Yet providing better knowledge of clearer contractual rights (and therefore more capacity to incorporate them into contracts or otherwise enforce those rights) can assist consumers as well as SMEs in dealing with larger entities, which otherwise may use their greater commercial negotiating power to avoid legal obligations.[39] To my mind, the best compromise involves regulation (including statutory interventions) setting minimum standards of protection, where there exist informational and other market failures or serious violations of other community norms,[40] while clarifying the background law and therefore contractual stipulations so the latter can be properly negotiated and subsequently enforced.

As well as consumers, a second additional driver for reform should be those involved in promoting Australian *courts*, not just international commercial

---

See also Luke Nottage, 'The New Australian Consumer Law: What About Consumer ADR?' (2009) 9 QUT Law and Justice Journal 176.

37 Community Law Australia, 'Unaffordable and Out of Reach: The Problem of Access to the Australian Legal System' (July 2012) available at <http://drawthelineatrelocation. files.wordpress.com/2012/11/cla_report_final__.pdf> accessed 1 September 2013, noting (at 12) that one survey 'conservatively estimated that around 1.7 million Australians can expect to encounter a legal problem each year and 490,000 of those people will not receive legal advice due to financial reasons or lack of knowledge'. Lindsay J (Submission No 38) also identifies 'access to justice' as key backdrop to the AGD's present consultation on contract law reform.

38 Submission No 46, 7.

39 Cf Small Business Development Corporation (SBDC) Submission (No 47), under 'enforceability of contract'.

40 Even Australia's Productivity Commission acknowledges that consumer protection measures should be assessed in light of broader community expectations: see Nottage and Malbon (n 26) 17, Figure 1.

arbitration (ICA) venues as mentioned in the DP,[41] as a 'regional hub' for dispute resolution services. The 2010 amendments to the International Arbitration Act 1974 (Cth) (IAA) mark a significant step towards making Australia more competitive with the now well-established Asia–Pacific venues for ICA (namely Singapore and Hong Kong/China). But these reforms were somewhat conservative and belated, and case law is already revealing teething problems.[42]

Aligning our contract law more closely with international standards provides another way for Australia to signal commitment to 'trying harder' to attract not only ICA cases to our shores, but also to promote Australian courts as a preferred regional forum (rather than, say, London) if parties do not or cannot agree on submitting their contractual disputes to arbitration. Experience abroad (for example London and New York) suggests that a vibrant ICA culture goes alongside a court system that is also often selected as a forum for resolving cross-border disputes. It follows that those promoting Australian court services, as well as ICA services,[43] should also be engaged in this 'Review of Australian Contract Law'. However, the judiciary has not commented on this aspect of the AGD's DP.[44]

More generally, Australia's legal profession – especially the now numerous large and internationally competitive law firms – should be involved as a potentially significant driver for reform. This is particularly true in light of another wave of internationalisation in recent years. For example, Allens Arthur Robinson is now allied with Linklaters (a top-tier UK-based international law firm), Blake Dawson has merged into Ashurst (a somewhat smaller UK-based firm but also with a strong presence in some Asian markets), Mallesons has combined with King & Wood (a leading Chinese law firm) under a 'Verein' arrangement governed by Swiss law, and Freehills has merged fully with Herbert Smith. Various other international firms have recently established themselves (including Allen & Overy, Clifford Chance, Clyde & Co) or expanded (including Norton Rose Fulbright, K&L Gates) in the Australian market – partly to take advantage of Australia's mining boom, as well

---

41   At para 2.11. The DP does add (at para 5.11) the potential for a more internationalised Australian contract law to increase the regional attractiveness of Australia for court-based dispute resolution as well as ICA.

42   Richard Garnett and Luke Nottage, 'What Law (If Any) Applies to International Arbitration in Australia?' (2012) 35 UNSW Law Journal 953; Luke Nottage, 'International Commercial Arbitration in Australia: What's New and What's Next?'' (2013) 30(5) Journal of International Arbitration 465–494.

43   The Institute of Arbitrators and Mediators Australia (focused on domestic dispute resolution) did make a Submission (No 31), but requested the AGD to keep it confidential. Equally curiously, the Australian Centre for International Commercial Arbitration did not make any Submission.

44   Cf Submissions No 11 (Bathurst CJ, generally negative towards the AGD's proposal) and 38 (Lindsay J, more positive). A recently retired Federal Court judge, the Hon Kevin Lindgren AM QC, has added a brief Submission (No 37) focused on a narrow point about constitutional issues that would arise if that Court were to be given jurisdiction regarding certain contractual disputes: see Part 7 below.

as burgeoning economic and legal relations with Asia. These new international partners should create long-term incentives for thousands of Australian lawyers – and, indirectly, their clients – to reassess principles of contract law in Australia that have long been taken for granted, but which may be increasingly out-of-line with contract law abroad (as discussed further at Parts 4 and 5, below).

Diminishing their appetite for contract law reform, however, such large international law firms do tend to act for larger clients. The latter in turn will have stronger negotiating power when concluding contracts with counterparties, and may often therefore prefer to entrench such a commercial advantage through careful contract drafting. Thus, larger corporate clients – and their lawyers – may tend to dislike more open-ended contract law principles, such as good faith. These clients will also tend to be able to better afford the services of large international law firms, in negotiating, drafting and enforcing contracts. Admittedly, since the Global Financial Crisis of 2008 even larger corporate clients and international law firms are increasingly looking for ways to reduce legal fees,[45] and simplifying contract law rules may assist in that respect. In the short term, however, they will probably be quite concerned about the direct and indirect costs of transitioning from existing contract law (despite its flaws) to a new regime. It is therefore perhaps unsurprising that only two international law firms made (quite lukewarm) public Submissions in response to the AGD's DP.[46]

Nonetheless, even in 1994 a survey of NSW barristers identified several areas of law where practitioners had significant doubts about whether Australian contract law principles were as they should be. In particular, 77 per cent of respondents thought that the law should allow nominated third-party beneficiaries to claim under a contract, and 68 per cent thought that the law of mistake ought to reflect a more open-ended approach (allowing a significant creative role for judges) rather than concentrating on the 'will' or intentions of the parties. Around half considered that Australian contract law should imply a term when reasonable (rather than when the court believes the parties would have agreed to the term), and should allow for obligations to arise in contract from reliance or financial interdependence (rather than only where promises are exchanged for consideration) – even though significantly larger majorities did consider that these propositions did not reflect the law at the time.[47] It would be useful to

---

45 This is particularly true in the US, where the market for legal services (and legal education) has come under great stress: Steven Harper, *The Lawyer Bubble: A Profession in Crisis* (Basic Books 2013). But this in turn has led to US firms seeking overseas partners, including law firms in Australia.

46 No 26 (Herbert Smith Freehills) and No 34 (King & Wood Mallesons).

47 Cf John Gava and Peter Kincaid, 'Contract and Conventionalism: Professional Attitudes to Changes in Contract Law in Australia' (1996) 10 Journal of Contract Law 141, 154–55. However, those authors considered that these and other empirical results instead indicated considerable satisfaction for a more classical (will- or intention-based) model of contract, compared to the tendency of some influential Australian judges at that time.

conduct a similar empirical study, comparing practitioners' views nowadays as to what the law is and how it should be, also involving solicitors and in-house counsel (or indeed businesspeople more generally) and across different parts of Australia.

3 Costs or Difficulties for Businesses Arising from Domestic Contract Law

In response to the second question posed in the AGD's DP, considerable problems do appear to exist in accessing, understanding and especially in applying contract law, which remains one of increasingly few fields in Australia still dominated mostly by case law.[48] These problems increase out-of-pocket and other transaction costs for businesses – as well as consumers – although many agree that more systematic research is needed to gauge their extent and full implications.[49] Several difficulties are identified throughout the DP, and by subsequent public Submissions, but they can be usefully grouped into the following six categories:

1. differences even when all or most jurisdictions within Australia have contract law statutes (as with writing requirements for enforcing contracts);[50]
2. differences among jurisdictions where statutes apply (albeit usually with variation in drafting) and those where (almost) nothing has been enacted (as with contracts for the benefit of third parties – with legislation in effect only in Queensland, Western Australia and the Northern Territory);[51]
3. areas where statutes impacting on contracts may exhibit some differences, and/or be questionable in their policy rationale or practical application (as with recent legislation concerning proportionate liability claims);[52]
4. situations where the High Court has given a supposedly binding precedent for lower courts, but with different judgments, which make it hard to discern one ratio decidendi or to anticipate how the Court will rule in a different sub-category of cases (as with its decision on contracts for the

---

48 On the 'age of statute', another key feature of the contemporary legal landscape in Australia, see generally Submission No 38 (Lindsay J).

49 See for example Submissions No 54 (Sydney Law School academics) and No 26 (Herbert Smith Freehills).

50 See JW Carter, *Contract Law in Australia* (6th edn, LexisNexis 2012) paras 9.05–9.11.

51 See, for example, Cheong and Tan (Submission No 16). Curiously, moreover, the *Contracts (Review) Act 1980* (NSW) – mentioned in several Submissions (for example No 3) – remains on the statute book despite enactment of the ACL and the Inter-Governmental Agreement, which requires states to repeal inconsistent legislation.

52 See also for example Nick Seddon and Saul Fridman, 'Misleading Conduct and Contributory Fault – Inconsistency under the Uniform Australian Consumer Law' (2012) 20 Australian Journal of Competition and Consumer Law 87.

benefit of third parties,[53] in an insurance context now already covered by legislative amendments);
5. situations where the High Court has not attempted to rule definitively, including:
   – the extent to which there may be a general duty for parties to act in good faith even in the performance of contractual obligations;[54]
   – aspects of the doctrine of consideration, for example whether a 'practical benefit' overcomes the 'pre-existing duty rule', allowing enforcement of one party's promise to pay more to obtain the same performance originally promised by the other party; and
   – incorporation by conduct of terms from successive earlier oral contracts;[55]
6. situations where the High Court has provided a binding ratio or persuasive obiter dicta, but the rule seems to be outdated by international and comparative law standards, including refusals to allow:
   – subsequent conduct to be used to interpret what the parties originally intended; and
   – pure commercial impracticability to trigger 'frustration' of contract (and insistence that the only relief available is automatic termination of the contract);[56]
   – in contrast for example to the UNIDROIT Principles of International Commercial Contracts (UPICC).[57]

Admittedly, many of these problems can be minimised by careful advance planning and drafting (for example, by structuring the contract to bring in 'third' parties),

---

53 *Trident Insurance v McNiece* (1988) 80 *ALR* 573.

54 Stewart (n 8) 84–87. See also James Douglas, 'England as a Source of Australian Law: For How Long?' (2012) 86 Australian Law Journal 333, 347.

55 See Carter (n 50) paras 6–48, 10–18.

56 Luke Nottage, 'Changing Contract Lenses: Unexpected Supervening Events in English, New Zealand, U.S., Japanese, and International Sales Law and Practice' (2007) 14 Indiana Journal of Global Legal Studies 385. This refers (at 408–10) to survey-based research indicating a considerably more flexible attitude towards long-term contract renegotiation among both law and especially business students across 15 countries (including Australia), as well as businesspeople in New Zealand and Japan. On the latter see further for example Luke Nottage, 'Planning and Renegotiating Long-Term Contracts in New Zealand and Japan: An Interim Report on an Empirical Research Project' [1997] New Zealand Law Review 482.

57 See respectively art 4.3(c) and arts 6.2.1–6.2.3, available at <http://www.unidroit.org/english/principles/contracts/principles2010/blackletter2010-english.pdf> accessed 1 September 2013. Several Submissions (for example Nos 9, 35) indicate that 'hardship' rules may be a useful reform to the Australian law on frustration of contract (see also Robertson (n 5) 15, in relation to international contracts). However, the Chief Justice of NSW is opposed, arguing for example that on this point 'no crisis in Australian contract law or impetus among the commercial community exists to justify such a significant reform' (Submission No 11, 14).

albeit at the loss of some flexibility (for example, tax implications). However, not all fall in this category (for example, in some civil law tradition systems, good faith obligations cannot be completely contracted out). The uncertainties and complexity also favour large and/or repeat contractors, more likely to have cost-effective access to in-house counsel or outside lawyers, as well as large law firms (able to provide more authoritative initial advice and litigation support).

In other words, the costs actually or potentially imposed on some contracting parties (including those who do not contract or do so sub-optimally) are likely to be higher for SMEs and consumers, whereas the legal profession is likely to *benefit* from high or growing complexity in a contract law system. It is perhaps no coincidence that Australia's law firms and legal profession generally have expanded considerably since the 1980s,[58] along with growth for example of the internet and therefore hitherto completely unreported judgments in contract law. If the AGD's 'Review of Australian Contract Law' succeeds in diminishing uncertainties, this may significantly *reduce* the contribution of lawyers' legal services to the economy.[59] Some law firms, such as the large ones that have recently merged with international firms (mentioned in Part 1 above), might instead *benefit* from reforms prompted by this Review, if it brings Australian contract law into closer alignment with the regimes found or evolving abroad. Simplification and harmonisation should generate further advantages to other (non-law) firms and hence contributions to the economy in that way. However, the net aggregate economic effect will be difficult to ascertain precisely – making this sort of reform project hard to 'sell' to an electorate.

The government must also be aware that this project involves questions of 'distributive' justice, as well as a collective action problem that may impede reform: one group (the legal profession overall) may be more clearly disadvantaged, whereas a larger but more diffuse group (SMEs and so on) will likely benefit.[60] Perhaps one way forward is to involve the Productivity Commission (PC), associated with the federal Treasury. The PC was able to come up with a net economic benefit figure for ACL-like reforms for its 2008 Report that reviewed ACL and policy more generally. This amount (A$1.5–4.5 billion) was often highlighted in the subsequent political process.[61] However, the methodology and

---

58 Cf generally Bruce Aronson, 'The Growth of Corporate Law Firms and the Changing Role of Lawyers in Japan' (2008) 26 Journal of Japanese Law 33.

59 Even in 2007–08, legal services directly contributed A$11 billion to the economy and A$18 billion in income: see <http://www.abs.gov.au/AUSSTATS/abs@.nsf/Lookup/8667.0Main+Features12007-08?OpenDocument> accessed 1 September 2013. There are also indirect contributions for example through legal education through universities, which is now the main route into the legal profession, and where there is growing pressure to attract full fee paying students both locally and from abroad. See generally Douglas, Nottage and Tellier (n 9).

60 See also Spagnolo (n 12) 635.

61 See Productivity Commission, Australian Government, *Review of Australia's Consumer Policy Framework* (8 May 2008) <http://www.pc.gov.au/projects/inquiry/consumer/docs/finalreport/keypoints> accessed 1 September 2013.

estimates were very rough, and will be difficult to replicate given that contract law statutes are much less pervasive in the first place. Also desirable would be other quantitative (for example survey-based) studies and qualitative (interview-based) research – for which the PC is not as well qualified or staffed – regarding the likely 'winners' and 'losers' from various types of contract law reform.[62]

4 Adjusting Australian Contract Law to the Digital Economy

A traditionalist view on e-commerce has been that contract law, rooted in party autonomy, is able to invent new types of agreed solutions whatever the technological developments may be – just as it did in past eras. But a closer historical analysis shows how technological change (for example in the late nineteenth century) in fact significantly impacted on specific doctrines and the overall 'vibe' of contract law (viz a *more* laissez-faire 'classical' approach) in both England and the US.[63] As the DP suggests, we should approach today's explosion in e-commerce with the working hypothesis that internet-based technologies are already having, and will continue to have, significant reciprocal influences on contract law and practice.

For example, one reason behind enactment of the ACL is a proliferation in standard-form contract terms copied and pasted onto Australian supplier websites – probably from legal systems abroad with fewer mandatory consumer protections – as well as such terms being asserted via websites from suppliers abroad even when selling to Australian consumers.[64] Similar problems can arise in certain B2B situations, such as mandatory consumer guarantees provided by the ACL.

One response is to clarify when and how mandatory provisions of Australian contract law can apply even despite contrary choice of law by the parties. (The DP mentions this problem in the context of choice of courts,[65] but not regarding the ACL.) Section 67 requires an Australian court or tribunal to apply the ACL guarantees despite any election of non-Australian law, if the objective governing or proper law would otherwise have been Australian law pursuant to Australian

---

62 For an interest group analysis of different constituencies impacted by Japan's ongoing contract law reforms, see Souichirou Kozuka and Luke Nottage, 'Policy and Politics in Contract Law Reform in Japan' in Maurice Adams and Dirk Thilbaut (eds), *Methodology of Comparative Private Law* (Hart 2014).

63 PS Atiyah, *The Rise and Fall of Freedom of Contract* (Clarendon Press 1979); Morton Horwitz, *The Transformation of American Law, 1870-1960: The Crisis of Legal Orthodoxy* (Oxford University Press 1992).

64 See Submission No 6 and generally Lynden Griggs, 'E-Commerce' in Justin Malbon and Luke Nottage (eds), *Consumer Law and Policy in Australia and New Zealand* (Federation Press 2013).

65 At para 3.12.

private international law principles. Those principles also derive from case law and therefore have their own problems regarding accessibility and application, but in cross-border sales transactions they generally lead to application of the law of the supplier. Thus, if the contract is silent on the governing law or provides for the law of the overseas supplier, the latter usually applies and ACL protections are lost for the Australian party. If the contract also provides for a foreign court as the forum, then the Australian court may also have to stay its own proceedings. However, courts in practice quite often exercise jurisdiction if a claim of misleading or deceptive conduct is raised under ACL s 18 (or its predecessor, s 52 of the TPA), even in B2B contexts.[66]

The AGD's present 'Review of Australian Contract Law', in conjunction with its subsequently announced consultation on reforming private international law,[67] should consider whether this policy outcome is satisfactory, particularly in the e-commerce context, as well as potential alternatives. One reform option would be amend ACL s 67, at least for 'true' consumer transactions (that is, individuals purchasing for non-business purposes), to state that the Australian legislation governs in all cases and that only Australian courts (or perhaps arbitrators) ever have jurisdiction. Another possibility (or exception to this new rule) would be to allow overseas suppliers to instead opt-in to a separate regime when dealing with Australian 'consumers' (as outlined further in Parts 4 and 7 below).[68] Law reform should also specify what law applies regarding other parts of the ACL, such as s 18. In addition, this Review should take the opportunity to clarify the situation under the ACL (and other statutes raising issues of allegedly mandatory law) when parties have chosen international commercial arbitration (even abroad) in lieu of courts, to resolve their contract-related disputes.[69]

---

66   Richard Garnett, 'Jurisdiction Clauses since *Akai*' (2013) 87 Australian Law Journal 134.

67   See (n 2). See also Keyes, in this volume.

68   A further possibility is for legislation to direct the forum always to apply the substantive law 'most favourable to the consumer'. This alternative choice of law rule is contained in a Brazilian-Argentinean-Paraguayan proposal for a draft Organization of American States (OAS) Inter-American Convention (CIDIP VII-Part II). It is also now urged more generally by the International Law Association through its Committee for the International Protection of Consumers, namely in Resolution 4/2012 adopting the 'Sofia Statement on the Development of International Principles of Consumer Protection'. See further Luke Nottage, 'Reforming Private International Law – Finally 'Australia in the Asian Century'?' (21 November 2012) <http://blogs.usyd.edu.au/japaneselaw/2012/11/reforming_private_internationa.html> accessed 1 September 2013.

69   Unfortunately neither the IAA nor the ACL amendments in 2010 clarify this problem, which would also facilitate the task of arbitrators considering which laws to apply to the underlying contract dispute. Cf Luke Nottage and Richard Garnett, 'The Top 20 Things to Change In or Around Australia's International Arbitration Act' in Luke Nottage and Richard Garnett (eds), *International Arbitration in Australia* (Federation Press 2010) 152–56.

5 Costs and Difficulties for Businesses Due to Differences between Australian and Foreign Contract Law

Again, even for a body like the PC, comprised mainly of economists, this question posed in the DP regarding costs (from having a substantively different national contract law) is very difficult to quantify. The sort of study cited in the DP[70] regarding correlations between cross-border trade and similarities in legal systems, among developed countries, needs to allow for complex issues of causality. But care also needs to be taken with critical European studies,[71] which may well be reacting to over-generalisations from reformers like the European Commission that has traditionally invoked the intuition that differences in contract laws of trading partners significantly impede cross-border trade and investment flows. The Commission still draws on similar economic arguments, in proposing now an opt-in Common European Sales Law (CESL), although it now has more direct jurisdiction to promote such law reforms.[72]

However, compared especially now to the EU, Australia faces an extra difficulty in that its private international law rules are not clearly stated or readily accessible either. This makes it more unclear or costly to determine what country's contract law will apply in the first place. Law and Justice Ministers in Australia have now recognised this problem too, so the AGD has commenced a consultation to recommend ways of clarifying, restating or improving Australia's private international law principles.[73] Nonetheless, as now quite widely recognised in Europe, greater efficiencies are likely to arise if substantive contract law principles can be harmonised or unified anyway.

Australia should also take comfort that many of our major trading partners have embarked on large-scale reforms to contract law regimes over the last decade or so, usually appealing in part to that very intuition. The DP does not mention these reform initiatives abroad except in the context of recent European developments towards an opt-in CESL,[74] which some see as a stepping-stone towards a binding European Contract Law Code. These developments build not only on earlier

---

70   See DP: Attorney-General's Department (n 1) para 4.7 n 23.

71   See DP: Attorney-General's Department (n 1) para 4.7 n 24. Such arguments from the European Commission derive partly from earlier EU law that allowed 'positive harmonisation' of national laws if differences significantly impeded cross-border commerce among member states. See Luke Nottage, 'Convergence, Divergence, and the Middle Way in Unifying or Harmonising Private Law' (2004) 1 Annual of German and European Law 166.

72   European Commission, *Proposal for a Regulation of the European Parliament and of the Council on a Common European Sales Law* (COM 635 final, Brussels, 11 October 2011). See generally Gerhard Dannemann and Stefan Vogenauer, 'Introduction: The European Contract Law Initiative and the "CFR in Contexts" Project' in Gerhard Dannemann and Stefan Vogenauer (eds), *The Common European Sales Law in Context: Interactions with English and German Law* (Oxford University Press 2013).

73   See (n 2).

74   See the DP: Attorney-General's Department (n 1) para 5.8ff.

initiatives,[75] including specific consumer contract law protection measures, but also large-scale reforms to the Dutch Civil Code in 1992 and the German Law of Obligations in 2002.[76] Those, in turn, have helped prompt contract law reform projects in France[77] as well as Japan (from 2006, accelerating from 2009[78]) and Korea. The US also attempted a large-scale reform of UCC Article 2 on Sales, but this largely stalled a decade ago due partly to the sorts of distributive justice and collective action problems outlined above in Part 2.

Thus, Australian business is likely not only to be suffering from higher transaction costs from a contract law formulation and doctrinal structure differing significantly from those of its major trading partners, mainly now in the Asia–Pacific (not the UK).[79] In addition, Australian business is presently facing a growing challenge prompted by wide-ranging amendments to contract law principles within most of those jurisdictions. Now is therefore a particularly good opportunity to begin aligning Australia's contract law regime with those currently being reformed by many trading partners.

6 Costs and Benefits of Internationalising Australian Contract Law

Similar difficulties arise in identifying and especially quantifying costs and benefits from 'internationalising' Australian contract law, in the sense used in the DP – namely aligning it more closely with EU law (including also the semi-official opt-in Principles of European Contract Law (PECL)), as well as CISG and UPICC. Yet a key benefit is that the CISG, which inspired UPICC (which in turn inspired PECL and other EU contract law initiatives) have all played a major role already in reform discussions in countries such as Germany, Japan and Korea (as well as the US and China, to a lesser extent). Engaging more fully with these international instruments, in a process of reviewing Australian contract law, therefore has the further advantage of allowing easier access to contract law developments within our major trading partners.[80] It can reduce 'search costs' in

---

75 Nottage (n 71); Hector MacQueen, 'Europeanisation of Contract Law and the Proposed Common European Sales Law' in Larry DiMatteo, Qi Zhou and Severine Saintier (eds), *Commercial Contract Law: Transatlantic Perspectives* (Cambridge University Press 2013).

76 Jan Smits, 'The German *Schuldrechtsmodernisierung* and the New Dutch Civil Code: A Study in Parallel' in Oliver Remien (ed), *Schuldrechtsmodernisierung und Europaeisches Vertragsrecht [Modernisation of Obligations Law and European Contract Law]* (Mohr Siebeck 2008).

77 See, for example, Yves Picod, 'The French Projects Concerning the Law of Obligations' (2009) 4 InDret, available at <http://ssrn.com/abstract=1499134> accessed 2 September 2013.

78 Kozuka and Nottage (n 62).

79 As well illustrated by the DP: Attorney-General's Department (n 1) 3, Table 2.

80 This does not require Australia to abandon 'the mother country', namely England and its legal system. As pointed out by Douglas J (n 54) 349, due to a shared legal culture,

identifying and comparing provisions, and reduce the risks of selecting contract law rules based on inadequate policy considerations as well as risks of poor drafting when transposing the better rules into Australian law. Whatever route is taken by contract law reformers in Australia, it is important for the drafters not to 'fiddle' too much with tried-and-tested formulations abroad.[81]

Such international engagement would also have the benefit of arresting a disturbing tendency for some Australian law firms to routinely 'opt-out' of CISG, especially in the standard-form contracts provided to their clients as the basis for further commercial negotiations. Such blanket advice risks a claim of professional negligence, especially if the firm is advising a seller of goods rather than a buyer. It persists probably due to fear of the unknown and some rough intuition (perhaps more plausible for large commercial law firms and their client base) that Australia's domestic contract law remains more 'certain'.[82]

Yet, as an experienced Australian practitioner has pointed out in the context of the AGD's consultation, there has been 'an exponential growth in the number of reported cases involving the CISG'.[83] The Submission by Professor Bryan Horrigan, Dr Emmanuel Laryea and Dr Lisa Spagnolo argues that the CISG enjoys both substantive and procedural efficiencies, and that exclusion of the CISG is largely due to 'unfamiliarity, reluctance and learning costs, and a consequent interest in maintaining the status quo of selecting domestic law', underpinned

---

institutions and language, English law is likely to remain a major reference point – and it too exerts a major influence on European and international instruments. But Australian jurists need to appreciate that English law is already being exposed to greater internationalisation, and that this will affect Australian law both directly (through links to the UK) and indirectly.

81   There are many examples of Australian legislation based on foreign models where (even subtle) rewording has or is likely to cause confusion. One recent example can be found in the ACL's ss 23–28 on unfair terms in consumer contracts, which differ significantly from the 1993 EC Directive's wording. See generally Nyuk Nin Nahan and Eileen Webb, 'Unfair Contract Terms in Consumer Contracts' in Justin Malbon and Luke Nottage (eds), *Consumer Law and Policy in Australia and New Zealand* (Federation Press 2013). Another is s 18A of the IAA, which added a gloss to the 1985 United Nations Commission on International Trade Law (UNCITRAL) Model Law on International Commercial Arbitration, but failed to transpose directly a test from English case law regarding bias of judges or arbitrators. See Garnett and Nottage (n 42) 976. An older example is the slightly different wording of the 'development risks' defence to strict product liability (now found in ACL s 142(c)), compared to the 1985 EC Directive. See Luke Nottage and Jocelyn Kellam, 'Product Liability and Safety Regulation' in Justin Malbon and Luke Nottage (eds), *Consumer Law and Policy in Australia and New Zealand* (Federation Press 2013) 207.

82   Nottage (n 12).

83   Robertson (n 5) 13. He also agrees that a 'failure to understand the way in which CISG applies, and the practice of unthinkingly opting out of its provisions, may well lead to malpractice claims'. The expansion of case law (and commentaries) analysing the CISG was also important for Japan in acceding, somewhat belatedly, to the CISG: see Noboru Kashiwagi, 'Accession by Japan to the Vienna Sales Convention (CISG)' (2008) 25 Journal of Japanese Law 207.

by 'institutional behaviours entrenched within legal practice'. But these patterns are increasingly under threat as foreign counterparties (for example from China) become familiar with the CISG and insistent on maintaining it as the main governing law in international sales.[84] Their Submission also adds that lawyers abroad seem 'less likely to exclude CISG when it is similar to domestic contract law', pointing to the example of Germany (where exclusion is no longer standard practice, following reforms in 2002 to its domestic contract law).[85]

Nonetheless, the notion that the CISG remains too uncertain is still often heard from England, which refuses even to accede to the Convention partly on the hypothesis that English contract law (and therefore London as a dispute resolution forum) is selected precisely because it is more predictable – and that this is what parties overwhelmingly want in their contractual relationships. Yet there is little evidence for that argument.[86] The main reason why the Commercial Court is so active in cross-border disputes instead relates to procedural law aspects: English law allows ready assumption of jurisdiction along with world-wide freezing orders and anti-suit injunctions.[87] Anyway, the argument is difficult to advance in the Australian context because Australia's contract law is still largely based on English law (especially since some law firms routinely try to exclude the CISG), yet forums in Australia and its substantive law are infrequently chosen by parties to resolve cross-border contractual disputes. Aligning domestic contract law more closely – and not necessarily identically[88] – with such international instruments, as well as the laws of Australia's major contemporary trading partners, seems a more promising approach to promoting Australia as a venue for international dispute resolution.

---

84   Submission No 29, 4–7 (also noting moves in the US away from routinely rejecting CISG). See also Lisa Spagnolo, 'Green Eggs and Ham: The CISG, Path Dependence, and the Behavioural Economics of Lawyers' Choices of Law in International Sales Contracts' (2010) 6 Journal of Private International Law 417.

85   Submission No 29, 23.

86   Nottage (n 56). See also Stefan Vogenauer and Christopher Hodges (eds), *Civil Justice Systems in Europe: Implications for Choice of Forum and Choice of Contract Law* (Hart 2011), which surveyed European businesses and found they preferred, for cross-border contracting other than their own law, Swiss law (29 per cent) over English law (23 per cent), followed by US law (14 per cent). Compared to English law, Swiss law and even US law have some very different features – for example, recognising a general duty of good faith in the performance of contracts.

87   As emphasised by University of Cambridge Professor Richard Fentiman, 'International Commercial Litigation: the London Experience' (Presentation to the International Law Association – Australian Branch, Sydney, 9 July 2012). See also Submission No 25 (Doris) 4.

88   Cf the Submission by Herbert Smith Freehills (No 26) 2, arguing that: 'A wholesale re-write of a well understood common law contract regime would make Australia less attractive to international parties in terms of choice of law and forum and a less attractive place for international parties to do business'.

Scepticism and a lack of knowledge about CISG (and related international instruments), at the contract negotiation and drafting stages, also generate another Catch-22 situation. Few CISG cases are litigated in Australian courts and, when they are, the barristers and judges struggle to apply CISG principles in an internationalist spirit.[89] This further undercuts Australia's efforts to promote itself as a dispute resolution hub.

A comprehensive governmental 'Review of Australian Contract Law' has the benefit of possibly reversing these trends. For example, if an Australian trader currently proposes in contract negotiations to exclude the CISG in favour of Australian domestic contract law, the counterparty (say in China) is most likely to respond by proposing instead its own contract law (Chinese law) or by conceding this point in exchange for something else (such as agreement to arbitrate with the seat in China). Neither option may be objectively desirable for the Australian side, delays and transaction costs will escalate,[90] and in extreme circumstances the deal may even fall through. If Australian contract law becomes more closely aligned with international instruments like the CISG, such problems should diminish.

More generally, given the sophisticated contract law reform initiatives underway in countries like Japan and Korea, a more intangible benefit would be to reiterate commitment to 'Australia in the Asian Century'. The Australian government released a White Paper on this topic in November 2012 (six months after initiating the AGD's contract law consultation), prompted by the view that:[91]

> The scale and pace of Asia's transformation is unprecedented and the implications for Australia are profound. Australia's geographic proximity, depth of skills, stable institutions and forward-looking policy settings place it in a unique position to take advantage of the growing influence of the Asian region.

If Australia wants to be taken seriously in Asia, it would be helpful to demonstrate that it is no longer an antipodean outpost of the English common law tradition. A few Asian jurisdictions do follow that tradition (notably in South Asia, Singapore, Malaysia and Hong Kong – until it reverts fully to China), but most do not.[92] Australia's legal system is arguably already developing some hybrid features,[93] while its society is already thoroughly multicultural – with a large and growing proportion of residents of Asian origin.[94]

---

89 For a comprehensive analysis, see Spagnolo (n 84). See also Submission No 55 (Zeller).

90 See also, in EU cross-border contracting practice, MacQueen (n 75) 537.

91 See Australian Government, *About the Australia in the Asian Century White Paper* <http://asiancentury.dpmc.gov.au/about> accessed 2 September 2013.

92 As highlighted in the DP: Attorney-General's Department (n 1) Table 2, para 4.9.

93 Submission No 38 (Lindsay J).

94 Of permanent settlers arriving over 2004–5, 15 per cent were from the UK and 14 per cent from New Zealand, but 9 per cent were from China and 8 per cent from India.

In the EU, growing internal diversity (among now 28 member states) has underpinned the emergence of contract law reform as a socio-political issue, not just an economic problem.[95] This is scarcely surprising for legal historians, as one aim of the first major modern codification of private law (the Napoleonic Code of 1804) was to modify the existing law to build a nation-state.[96] By contrast, the DP focuses almost exclusively on economic or utilitarian considerations, except perhaps by remarking in the context of 'setting acceptable standards of conduct' (as one driver of reform) that they:[97]

> should be unambiguous, simple to understand and take particular account of the needs of people from different cultural backgrounds or experiencing disparate circumstances. Australia's cultural diversity demands that our contract law should be readily translatable into other languages to facilitate domestic and international trade and improve general public awareness of the law.

7 Costs and Benefits of Restatement, Simplification or Substantial Reform of Contract Law

The DP then asks for views on a spectrum of possible reform options, ranging from maintaining the status quo, through to:[98]

- a 'Restatement' of existing law (in more accessible format);
- 'Simplification' (to clarify specific areas of law); and even
- wide-ranging 'Reform' (making 'significant changes' to the content of Australian contract law – noting that this 'could be implemented without codification, but the more far-reaching the reform the lower the cost of combining it with a general codification of contract law as a whole').

The proportion of UK-born residents had fallen from 33 to 20 per cent of the population over the last 25 years. Almost 30 percent of residents were not born in Australia and more than a quarter of Australian-born residents have at least one parent born overseas. See Hugh Mackay, 'Untrue Blue: Myths Obscure a Beautiful Diversity' *Sun-Herald* (Sydney, 25 August 2013) 28.

95 See especially Hugh Collins, *The European Civil Code: The Way Forward* (Cambridge University Press 2008). The Commission and other EU policy-makers may also be driven by broader concerns about advancing a European identity in the face of rising nationalism within some EU member states. See Martijn Hesselink, 'The Case for a Common European Sales Law in an Age of Rising Nationalism' (2012) 8 European Review of Contract Law 342.

96 Jean Maillet, 'The Historical Significance of French Codification' (1969) 44 Tulane Law Review 681.

97 At para 2.5. Few Submissions raise this broader context either, although the Redfern Legal Centre (Submission No 46) 6 obliquely refers to consumers and other vulnerable groups not necessarily being able to communicate perfectly in English.

98 At paras 6.4–6.6.

The DP also acknowledges that the pace of change is another variable: reforms could be implemented in one legislative package or in several phases.

In my view, shared by many others making public Submissions in response to the DP,[99] a Restatement would be a useful first step. It would be much simpler (and therefore quicker and cheaper) to generate than in the US, thanks to the unifying influence of the High Court of Australia as well as (relatedly) the existence of widely-acknowledged authoritative commentaries.[100] In addition, costs can be minimised by learning from the modus operandi and outputs of other national and international bodies that have generated restatements of contract law, such as the American Law Institute (ALI) and International Institute for the Unification of Private Law (UNIDROIT).[101]

Further, to maximise net benefits a Restatement could be attempted on a regional or at least Trans-Tasman basis.[102] Indeed, previously I have proposed an Asia–Pacific analogue to the ALI to generate a regional 'Restatement of Product Liability Law', given that Australia and so many other economies in the region have now amended their civil liability rules for product defects based on similar (EU law-inspired) legislation.[103] For some years there has also been talk and some preliminary research towards developing 'Principles of Asian Contract Law'.[104] These would also help highlight important issues when attempting to restate 'Principles of Australian Contract Law' – or 'Principles of Antipodean Contract Law', if we take seriously the Memorandum of Understanding between Australia and New Zealand to try to harmonise business law in both countries, and provided we can interest law reformers in New Zealand to cooperate (and share in the costs involved) in this endeavour. If done on a Trans-Tasman or broader pan-Asian basis, we could end up with a Restatement that restates the common principles

---

99   See, for example, Submission No 7 (ACLA); No 23 (CPA Australia) 2 (suggesting that a Restatement would be a 'highly valuable education resource ... as there is an absence of a single authoritative source to which business professionals may refer even in such areas where the law is relatively settled'); No 36 (LESANZ); No 38 (Lindsay J); No 34 (King & Wood Mallesons); No 44 (Law Society of NSW Young Lawyers); No 47 (SBDC: albeit noting that SMEs will also incur costs in becoming familiar with any such new instrument); No 54 ('Sydney Law School academics': but including 5 from outside Sydney Law School).

100 See, for example, Carter (n 50), and indeed a much more succinct version for law students: JW Carter, *Carter's Guide to Australian Contract Law* (LexisNexis 2007).

101 Several eminent jurists in Australia have been or are involved in such organisations: see listings for example at <http://www.ali.org/> accessed 1 September 2013.

102 Compare also now the European Law Institute: Reinhard Zimmermann, 'Challenges for the European Law Institute' (2012) 16 Edinburgh Law Review 5.

103 Jocelyn Kellam and Luke Nottage, 'Happy 15th Birthday, TPA Part VA! Australia's Product Liability Morass' (2007) 15 Competition and Consumer Law Journal 26. Professor John Farrar had earlier proposed a similar initiative.

104 Shiyuan Han, 'Principles of Asian Contract Law: An Endeavor of Regional Harmonization of Contract Law in East Asia' (2013) 58 Villanova Law Review 589.

across jurisdictions, but which adds commentaries (as done carefully in the US Restatements) noting where there are still divergences in national case law or legislation (including New Zealand's distinctive contract law statutes).[105]

However, any Restatement project for Australia is still likely to be time-consuming. Further, it is likely to become quite political, if US experience is anything to go by – especially in the ALI,[106] but also the stalled attempt at a comprehensive reform of UCC Article 2 on Sales.[107] Part of the difficulty experienced in the US, and other jurisdictions reviewing contract law principles (like Japan and the EU),[108] arises precisely because the law subject to scrutiny is unclear and so cannot be easily or unambiguously 're-stated'. Political or ideological debates therefore tend to emerge, especially when traditionally mandatory contract law principles come to be investigated, such as contractual unfairness in situations involving parties of different types or with disparate bargaining power. Even the UPICC has been described as sometimes more of a 'pre-statement' (what the law *should* be),[109] rather than a simply a formulation of universally-accepted principles of international commercial contract law.

A Restatement project is also insufficient in situations where the law is clear, but out of line with international and foreign contract law principles (for example the use of subsequent conduct to interpret contracts, mentioned above in Part 2). A similar problem arises if the project instead or additionally focuses on Simplification (of technical language or concepts, or distilling principles from complex and lengthy judgments). Both types of project certainly remain very useful and should generally be pursued. But the Australian government should be prepared for – and not shy away from – engagement in some significant statutory Reform in contract law, even though this will mean incurring greater costs – through the legislative process – than (narrower) Simplification or (more comprehensive but possibly less controversial) Restatement initiatives.

However, it seems premature at this stage to propose codification, even though a few Submissions have done so in response to the DP.[110] As it is formally as well as often ideologically opposed to the common law tradition,[111] codification becomes an easy target for those (few) who seem essentially happy about the

---

105   See Bigwood, in this volume.

106   See, for example, the history of the *Restatement (Third) of Torts – Products Liability*, eventually published in 1998: Luke Nottage, *Product Safety and Liability Law in Japan: From Minamata to Mad Cows* (RoutledgeCurzon 2004) ch 2.

107   Richard Hyland, 'American Private Legislatures and the Process Discussion' in Arthur Hartkamp and others (eds), *Towards a European Civil Code* (Kluwer 2011).

108   See, for example, Collins (n 95); Hesselink (n 95); Kozuka and Nottage (n 62).

109   Klaus Peter Berger (ed), *The Practice of Transnational Law* (Kluwer 2001).

110   Notably Submission No 49 (Steinwall, presently an in-house counsel and a well-known expert on consumer and trade practices law), but also No 43 (NSW Small Business Commissioner, albeit more tentatively) and No 52 (Svantesson).

111   See generally Bigwood, in this volume.

status quo.¹¹² Instead, the most promising and feasible way forward in Australia is to assemble in one overarching Contract Law Act:

- harmonised versions of existing Australian statutory interventions (covering for example writing requirements, domestic sale of goods, international sale of goods, aspects of e-contracting, privity, frustration of contracts, and capacity of minors);
- targeted reforms where the case law remains persistently uncertain (for example, contract interpretation and good faith) or undeveloped (e-commerce, or perhaps unfair contract terms beyond the business-to-consumer (B2C) context);¹¹³ and
- an interpretive provision (along the lines of CISG Article 7) requiring the Act to be interpreted in light of its general principles.

The last-mentioned feature may be the most radical, as it bears parallels with how civil law tradition jurists are trained to approach a code – namely, on the assumption that it does or should not have 'gaps', so any apparent lacuna can be filled by abstracting more general principles from other parts of the code. The proposed interpretative provision might therefore be omitted initially, when the Contract Law Act still has fewer component parts. A separate interpretive principle might also need to be retained for the part on international sales (primarily incorporating CISG, and any future more comprehensive UN treaty on international contracts that Australia might accede to),¹¹⁴ as we can expect some different principles to apply in cross-border contexts.¹¹⁵

Additional parts could be gradually added to this Contract Law Act, beginning with less controversial aspects (such as rules on formation of contract),¹¹⁶ drawing also on parallel work elaborating a Restatement of Australian law.¹¹⁷ Eventually, the Act may in fact come to resemble a Contract Law Code, not just in its coverage but also in the way it is supposed to be interpreted. But it would not have to, in order to generate significant net benefits, and the process would anyway be a very protracted one. Various Submissions noted that even the Restatement projects in the US took a very long time,¹¹⁸ although it should not be forgotten that the first

---

112   Notably Submission No 11 (Bathurst CJ).

113   The latter issue is frequently raised in Submissions (for example Nos 2, 6, 8, 9, 13, 17, 21, 41, 43, 47 and 48) although some complaints over one-sided terms may simply reflect normal commercial imbalances in negotiating power.

114   See further Schwenzer, in this volume.

115   See generally Robertson (n 5); Submission No 29 (Hortigan and others); Luke Nottage, 'Afterthoughts: International Commercial Contracts and Arbitration' (2010) 17 Australian Journal of International Law 198.

116   See also for example Submission No 15 (Cheong) 2–7; No 39 (Lockwood).

117   For a quite similar dual-track proposal, see Submission 50 (Stewart (n 8)). Cf also the multi-pronged approach mentioned in Submission No 29 (Hortigan and others).

118   Submission No 53 (Swain and Gaskell) 6.

Restatement of the Law of Contracts (1932) also contributed to a major legislative codification in the form of the UCC.

Whatever approach or combination of approaches to reform may be adopted, Australia's contract law (re)formulations should take into account existing empirical studies,[119] and commission or encourage new ones, as to the real (and reasonable) expectations of contracting parties – not just as viewed through the eyes of the courts or doctrinal scholars commenting on their judgments. Also useful for this 'Review of Australian Contract Law', and on-going studies, is the survey-based research by Professors Fred Ellinghaus and Ted Wright. This suggested significant advantages for contract law problem-solving from more succinct formulations of rules, as under UPICC or even (albeit more controversially) the 1992 draft Contract Law Code mooted by the Victorian Law Reform Commission.[120]

8 Implementation of Any Reform of Australian Contract Law

In response to the DP's more specific questions as to how to implement amendments to Australian contract law, the largest technical impediment is that the Constitution does not give jurisdiction to the Commonwealth regarding general private law.[121] One possibility is that States and Territories expressly give up (or 'refer') their powers in this field, as they did for example recently regarding consumer credit, but this seems unlikely in a major area of private law. After all, major statutory 'tort reform' across Australia from 2002 did not proceed on that basis.[122]

If no referral is made, an innovative compromise is proposed by a recently retired Federal Court judge. The Hon Kevin Lindgren AM QC suggests drawing on the powers under the Constitution for the Commonwealth to regulate corporations and 'trade and commerce', to give partial jurisdiction to the Federal Court by enacting a provision along the lines that 'a corporation must not, in trade or commerce, engage in conduct that constitutes a breach or wrongful repudiation of a contract that is binding on the corporation within the meaning of the unwritten law from time to time'.[123] Such 'unwritten law' would remain the general contract law as elaborated by State and Territory courts. Remedies for a contravention of

---

119 In New Zealand (comparing Japan and so on), see for example Nottage (n 56).

120 Fred Ellinghaus and Ted Wright, 'The Common Law of Contracts: Are Broad Principles Better than Detailed Ones? An Empirical Investigation' (2005) 11 Texas Wesleyan Law Review, available at <http://ssrn.com/abstract=771204> accessed 2 September 2013.

121 See especially Submissions No 3 (Australian Academy of Law: comprising professors, (ex-)judges and senior practitioners); No 44 (Young Lawyers) 22–24; No 51 (Street SC).

122 See generally Kellam and Nottage (n 103), and (on consumer credit reforms) Justin Malbon and Luke Nottage (eds), *Consumer Law and Policy in Australia and New Zealand* (Federation Press 2013).

123 Submission No 37 (Lindgren), noting that a precedent can be found in ACL s 20 (formerly TPA s 51AA: see generally Nahan and Webb (n 30)).

this provision (namely, breach or repudiation of contract) could be added to this provision (perhaps inspired by the Contractual Remedies Act 1979 (New Zealand) and/or CISG[124]) and thus become regulated by federal law too, or that aspect could remain covered by State or Territory law. However, this provision would not generally cover other disputes such as mistake or frustration of contract, as the Constitution requires the Commonwealth to legislate a right or duty.[125]

Alternatively or in addition, an 'Application Legislation' model could be useful for significant statutory Reform (for example concerning third-party beneficiary contracts or a general principle of good faith), initiatives for Simplification (particularly of existing statutes), and potentially the overarching Contract Law Act project (proposed in Part 6 above). This model was adopted to harmonise the ACL nation-wide over 2010.[126] An inter-governmental agreement for each state or territory (including possibly New Zealand), to implement identical legislation to Australian federal law and any subsequent amendments, need not necessarily involve *all* jurisdictions committing to this procedure at the outset, even though this occurred for the consumer law reforms within Australia.

A Restatement project could proceed in parallel, under the auspices of an 'Australian [and New Zealand] Law Institute'.[127] As mentioned in Part 6 above, one advantage would be to help identify areas that might benefit from further legislative reform, providing policy or empirical foundations for law-makers. Secondly, a Restatement could add persuasive authority for Australian courts interpreting and applying contract law principles – especially where clear direction is lacking from superior courts. This is the primary motivation behind US Restatements generated by the ALI.

Thirdly, and most intriguingly, a suite of Restatements could be made available to contracting parties on an opt-in basis. Australia could enact conflict of laws statutes allowing parties the following options, perhaps initially only if they consent in writing, depending on whether the transaction is (a) domestic or international and (b) between businesses (B2B) or between a business and a consumer (B2C):

	Domestic contracts	**International contracts**
B2B	PACL	UPICC
B2C	n/a (ACL)	CESL (with minimal amendments)

124 See further Bigwood, in this volume.

125 *R v Court of Conciliation and Arbitration, ex p Barrett* (1945) 70 CLR 141. A similar constitutional problem arises concerning proposals to give the Federal Court exclusive jurisdiction to decide purely contractual matters under the IAA: Nottage and Garnett (n 69) 174–75.

126 Malbon and Nottage (n 122). See also Submission No 18 (Clarke and Clarke).

127 Membership could be drawn in part from the Australian Academy of Law (established in 2007): see generally <http://www.academyoflaw.org.au> accessed 1 September 2013.

For domestic B2B contracts, parties could choose 'Principles of Australian [or Antipodean] Contract Law' (PACL), a Restatement elaborated from Australia's general law of contract. The statute authorising this election should clearly state that such election excludes the application of any allegedly mandatory principles of domestic Australian common law or equity (but perhaps not, at least initially, domestic statutory requirements). If this seems initially too risky, the legislation might specify that parties could allow for the application of such mandatory rules (such as unconscionability) instead of comparable provisions in the Principles otherwise generally elected by the parties. For B2C transactions, however, an optional instrument such as PACL should not be allowed as consumer contract law has recently been reformed and harmonised through the ACL, following extensive consultation.[128]

For international B2B contracts, the conflict of laws statute should clearly authorise commercial parties to opt-in to UPICC, the primary international instrument designed precisely for this purpose. Again, the statute would need to clarify the role (if any) left for Australian domestic law principles (such as unconscionability).

By contrast, something like CESL is a preferable option to be made available in cross-border B2C contracts (especially for overseas suppliers to Australian consumers). It was designed in the EU primarily for cross-border B2C transactions,[129] and CESL therefore contains significantly more protective and flexible provisions compared to UPICC.[130] Due to the EU's incomplete harmonisation of mandatory consumer laws, various member states impose different provisions, creating uncertainties for suppliers as well as consumers in cross-border sales; these can be avoided by allowing the parties instead to opt-in to CESL, which includes adequate protections for consumers. The same approach can apply when it comes to international traders considering dealing with Australian consumers. However,

---

128 Nottage and Malbon (n 26). But see the Treasury's consultation (May–August 2014) on 'Extending Unfair Contract Terms Provisions to Small Business', available at <http://www.treasury.gov.au/ConsultationsandReviews/Consultations/2014/Small-Business-and-Unfair-Contract-Terms> (without reference to the Contract Law DP).

129 The English and Scottish Law Commissions have suggested making it available also for domestic sales: see Eric Clive, 'A General Perspective on the European Commission's Proposal for a Regulation on a Common European Sales Law' (2012) 19 Maastricht Journal of European and Comparative Law 120, 126. That seems inadvisable for Australia given that the ACL now provides a very comprehensive and familiar regime for consumers, which also includes protections in some B2B transactions. CESL is also available to B2B transactions, but only if at least one party is a (defined) SME.

130 Another advantage to allowing an opt-in to a CESL-like instrument is that it will familiarise Australian jurists and policy-makers with international rules regulating matters such as the validity of contracts, presently excluded (by Article 4) from CISG. This should make it easier for Australia to accede to any 'CISG+' treaty that may emerge from UNCITRAL (as discussed further by Schwenzer, in this volume, and in special issue (2013) 58(4) of the Villanova Law Review, available at <http://lawweb2009.law.villanova.edu/lawreview/?page_id=1879> accessed 2 September 2013). Cf Spagnolo (n 84) 637–41.

Australia's private international law statutes authorising such an option (to the exclusion of Australian domestic law, including the ACL) would need to include some amendments to CESL,[131] and should also consider adding rules not presently found in the instrument.[132]

At present, Australian private international law remains uncertain as to the extent to which parties can fully adopt UPICC or other *lex mercatoria* to exclusively govern their contracts. On the other hand, it is very plain that parties to arbitration agreements in Australia cannot elect the *lex mercatoria* to govern that sort of contract; a (national) law must be applied to determine questions as the validity and scope of arbitration agreements. Legislative amendment is certainly needed to expand party choice in this latter respect.[133]

Lastly, the government should consider supporting free or subsidised provision of standard-form terms and contracts. This option did not prove popular in the EU,[134] seemingly due to collective action problems among industry members and associations, but in Australia it might be possible to involve also for example the pro bono departments of large law firms. Some support for developing standard-form contracts has also been expressed in response to the DP, particularly on the part of SMEs.[135] However, many Submissions urge more ambitious reforms, including some legislative amendments and restatement projects. The latter can anyway assist in generating appropriate standard-form terms, particularly in light of any mandatory provisions of Australian contract law.

9 Next Steps

As outlined above, the DP and public responses to it already provide a prima facie case to proceed to the next stage. In particular, many Submissions agree that the ALRC is the most appropriate body to take charge now of the project of considering and recommending specific reforms of Australian contract law.[136]

---

131 In particular, for example, it will not be appropriate for Australia's version to require at least one of the parties to be from a state within the EU. Also deserving scrutiny are some particular problems regarding the drafting of certain CESL provisions: see for example Submission No 25 (subsequently published as Martin Doris, 'Promising Options, Dead Ends and the Reform of Australian Contract Law' (2014) 34(1) Legal Studies 24-46; MacQueen (n 75).

132 Such as expanding coverage to all services (CESL only includes those related to delivery of the goods, for example installation and maintenance), and perhaps stating rules on minors or capacity and illegal contracts.

133 Nottage (n 115). See also Robertson (n 5) 17–18 (and 6–8, on the *lex mercatoria* more generally).

134 Submission No 25 (Doris) 13.

135 See, for example, Submission No 14 (Caroll).

136 See, for example, Submissions No 12 (Bowrey: noting overlaps anyway with the ALRC's project on copyright law issues), No 34 (King & Wood Mallesons:

The ALRC can draw for example on its early work on 'legal risk in international transactions',[137] as well as the Victorian Law Reform Commission's 1992 Discussion Paper outlining a draft Australian Contract Code.[138] The ALRC can also coordinate with other state or territory law reform bodies,[139] perhaps allowing them to take the lead on certain reform topics.

The New Zealand Law Commission has also published significant reports on aspects of contract law reform, and so should be closely consulted. These reports include a review of the operation of New Zealand's statutory interventions made already especially over the 1970s–80s (for example on contractual remedies, and to allow third-party beneficiaries to enforce contracts) as well as a proposal to liberalise writing requirements for enforcing various types of contracts.[140] Ideally, there should be a joint reference to both Law Commissions – as occurred recently with the Productivity Commissions in both countries – for a joint study into new ways of 'Strengthening Economic Relations Between Australia and New Zealand'.[141]

In addition, as mentioned above in Part 3, Australia's PC (or PCs jointly) might provide valuable input on quantitative estimations of costs and benefits of various types of contract law reforms. However, Law Commissions should take the lead as they are better placed to conduct or coordinate other types of empirical work, as well as of course the difficult doctrinal research required in any sustained review

---

albeit recommending an incremental approach focusing on discrete problems requiring Simplification), and No 35 (LCA). See also Paul Finn, 'Internationalisation or Isolation: The Australian Cul De Sac? The Case of Contract Law' in Elise Bant and Matthew Harding (eds), *Exploring Private Law* (Cambridge University Press 2010).

137 See <http://www.austlii.edu.au/au/other/alrc/publications/reports/80/ALRC80.html> accessed 1 September 2013 (albeit mostly focused on procedural rather than substantive law topics).

138 It can be accessed via a website by Professors Ellinghaus and Wright for their 'Global Law of Contract' Project, which also provides a 'Concordance' of contract law rules from PECL, the US *Restatement* (Second), Chinese and Russian law codifications: <http://www.newcastle.edu.au/school/law/research/global-law-of-contract/> accessed 1 September 2013.

139 Submission No 54 (Sydney Law School academics).

140 See New Zealand Law Commission, *A New Act for Incorporated Societies* (NZLC R129, 21 August 2013) <http://www.lawcom.govt.nz/publications> accessed 1 September 2013; further Bigwood, in this volume.

141 See Productivity Commission, Australian Government and New Zealand Productivity Commission, *Strengthening Economic Relations Between Australia and New Zealand: A Joint Study* (13 December 2013) <http://transtasman-review.pc.gov.au/> accessed 1 September 2013. Law Commissions and similar law reform bodies in other jurisdictions, particularly within the common law tradition, should also be consulted. An example is the British Columbia Law Institute, which released in 2011 a proposal to reform the law generally concerning unfair contracts: see Bigwood, in this volume.

of this area of law.¹⁴² They are also better placed to investigate and assess also the socio-political dimensions to law reform, even in this field, including implications of multiculturalism and Australia's engagement with Asia more broadly (as mentioned in Part 5 above).

The fact that the Commonwealth has no direct and express power to legislate on contract law generally, under the Australian Constitution, is no impediment to the ALRC now taking the lead in considering specific reforms in this field. After all, as mentioned in Part 7 above, the DP has already generated an interesting proposal to enact Commonwealth legislation impacting on contractual remedies and giving jurisdiction (exclusively or concurrently) to the Federal Court.¹⁴³ Anyway, there already exists some federal legislation dealing with specific aspects of contract law, such as the Insurance Contracts Act 1984 (Cth). Most importantly, the federal AGD has already initiated a preliminary consultation, pursuant to a mandate from the Council of Australian Government (COAG). It is time now to acknowledge simply that the AGD's consultation has generated sufficient feedback to justify proceeding to the next stage, and that the ALRC is the more appropriate specialist body to consider now more detailed reforms. That is precisely why the ALRC was set up.¹⁴⁴

Unfortunately, there has been a growing tendency to sideline the ALRC in recent years, as evident from reforms to consumer law (directed primarily by the federal Treasury) and international arbitration (by the federal AGD). Some say that this is because the ALRC's recommendations are not (or not quickly) implemented, but there is little hard evidence of this (in comparison, for example, with the PC). A more important reason may be that politicians are increasingly wary of losing control by referring matters from line ministries (or offshoots like the PC) to a body like the ALRC that is independent of the executive branch and instead advises Parliament. Yet such independence is a valued feature, particularly for a long-term project like contract law reform.

With more than two years after releasing the DP, it is high time for the federal Attorney-General to let go and refer the matter into the primary charge of the ALRC, which should be given sufficient time and resources to conduct a proper inquiry in consultation with other relevant bodies. In addition, as part of its broader responsibility for the justice system nation-wide, COAG should provide resources to establish an 'Australian [and New Zealand] Law Institute', with the initial task of working with the ALRC on this particular Restatement project.¹⁴⁵

---

142 Cf, for example, Submission No 41 (MBA: proposing a referral to the ALRC only after the PC); Robertson (n 5) 24 (suggesting a joint reference to the ALRC and the PC).

143 Submission No 37 (Lindgren).

144 See Australian Law Reform Commission, *About* (20 May 2010) <http://www.alrc.gov.au/about> accessed 1 September 2013.

145 Cf Submission No 50 (Stewart (n 8)), suggesting that all aspects of contract law reform should proceed under the aegis of COAG. See also Submission No 5 (ACCI), one of very few Submissions generally negative about any form of reform, suggesting that if

10 Conclusion

Many public responses to the AGD's DP have pointed out that further research is needed into the pros and cons, as well as the format, of various possible reforms to Australian contract law; but almost all agree that more detailed investigation is worthwhile. Admittedly, one commentator has emphasised that generally change 'should only occur if the benefits of change clearly outweigh the costs', and that 'any regulatory response should be proportionate to the issue addressed'.[146] The point is elaborated in one Submission made by that commentator jointly with full-time legal academics (including myself) as well as another by his law firm,[147] by reference to the Australian government's *Best Practice Regulation Handbook*.[148]

However, the framing of the AGD's DP and its consultation process so far seem to have complied with such 'best practice', at least to the extent of now allowing the contract law reform project to proceed to the next stage, namely a detailed inquiry led by the ALRC along the parallel lines outlined above (especially in Parts 6–8). Anyway, as mentioned in Part 5 above, contract law reform in Australia – as elsewhere – is not just matter of economic efficiency, implicating a narrower view of 'cost-benefit'; it is also deeply entwined with the existing legal system, and involves broader socio-political issues implicating other non-economic values.[149] Legislative amendment will implicate 'nation-building' (and now international relations), not just efficiency gains from 'clarifying' existing law and from 'unifying' or harmonising it nationally (or now internationally).[150] History also suggests that 'legal values' and doctrines peculiar to the legal system will and should not be simply displaced by either economics or politics.[151]

---

however 'matters are to be progressed beyond this point, they should be progressed through the existing COAG structure and its various select councils'.

146 Robertson (n 5) 24.

147 See, respectively, Submission No 54 (Sydney Law School academics) and No 26 (Herbert Smith Freehills).

148 See Department of Finance and Deregulation, Australian Government, *Australia's Best Practice Regulation Requirements* <http://www.finance.gov.au/obpr/proposal/gov-requirements.html> accessed 1 September 2013. Note that there are somewhat different 'best practice' requirements for regulatory impact assessments by COAG, or state and territory governments or agencies.

149 See also generally Michael Sandel, *What Money Can't Buy: The Moral Limits of Markets* (Farrar, Straus and Giroux 2012).

150 Cf Maillet (n 96) in relation to codification in France; and the quite similar three goals of Japan's present reforms of its Civil Code, outlined in Kozuka and Nottage (n 62) and by Sono, in this volume, chapter 6.

151 Cf Nils Jansen, 'The Authority of an Academic "Draft Common Frame of Reference"' in Hans-W Micklitz and Fabrizio Caffagi (eds), *European Private Law After the Common Frame of Reference* (Elgar 2010); John Gava, 'How Should Judges Decide Commercial Contract Cases?' (2013) 30 Journal of Contract Law 133.

Admittedly, the case for reforming Australian contract law should not be overstated or idealised. First, globalisation does create challenges as well as opportunities for national law reform projects nowadays, exacerbating a tendency already for contract law and practice to fragment into specific sub-fields.[152] Yet this should not be over-emphasised or necessarily acclaimed, even in cross-border contexts.[153] Second, empirical studies continue to show how the impact of contract law norms is not as direct as jurists tend to assume, thus lessening the purported benefits from reform. Other factors, including institutional and procedural law mechanisms for resolving disputes, are also very important.[154] However, improvements in these mechanisms (including access justice for consumers and another round of commercial arbitration law reforms) can be addressed in tandem with contract law reform, particularly in the contemporary Australian context.

Another key point is not to let any one group hijack the reform agenda. This includes legal academics, either those with a propensity towards overly 'elegant solutions' (which may not work well in practice)[155] or those with very strong political views (as some perceive in the EU setting).[156] However, strong leadership by key professors appears to have been crucial in advancing contract law reform in Europe (nationally and at the EU level), Japan and in international forums (such as UNCITRAL, and especially UNIDROIT). By contrast, the over-politicisation of the law reform process in the US resulted in the failed attempt to revise comprehensively the UCC's provisions on sales law.[157]

Australia is well placed to find a good balance, if it now proceeds to examine contract law reforms more closely under the leadership of the ALRC. After all, its Commissioners usually comprise senior professors (often with practical experience) as well as judges and other senior legal practitioners, and the ALRC has well-established and effective mechanisms for consultations with both expert groups and the general public. So far, however, no one (professor or otherwise) has publically stepped out as willing to take up the challenge of exploring specific ways to ensure Australian contract law meets the economic and socio-political needs of the twenty-first century.[158]

---

152 See Micklitz, in this volume.

153 Robertson (n 5) 20.

154 Submission No 25 (Doris) 24. See also generally Gava (n 151); Nottage (n 56), with further references.

155 Submission No 25 (Doris) 5.

156 Submission No 53 (Swain and Gaskell).

157 Compare Hyland (n 107) with Kozuka and Nottage (n 62) and Nottage (n 71), with further references.

158 But see, more generally, MP Ellinghaus, Ted Wright and D StJ Kelly, 'A Draft Australian Law of Contract' (2 March, 2014), available at <http://ssrn.com/abstract=2403603> (accessed 8 September 2014).

Chapter 8

The Partial Codification of Contract Law: Lessons from New Zealand

Rick Bigwood

1 Introduction

One of the primary impulses for this collection of chapters is the Commonwealth Attorney-General's recent Discussion Paper to explore the scope for reforming Australian contract law.[1] The production of a national, mandatory, potentially highly prescriptive, contract-law code is one[2] option on the table for consideration.[3] Such a code might restate and clarify existing law, as well as effectuate significant changes – perceived improvements – to the law as currently understood. The professed aim of the Discussion Paper, however, is merely 'to stimulate discussion among businesses, legal practitioners, academics and other stakeholders about whether Australian law is fit for its purpose and prepared for the challenges of the future'.[4] Nothing concrete is certain, or perhaps even likely, to eventuate from the anticipated discussions on the subject. But it might, if not in the short-to-medium term, then at some distant point in the future.

Now, few, if any, would argue that Australian contract law is perfect as it stands. Indeed, the perceived deficiencies of the current system are well documented.[5] Australian contract law, it has been pressed, has too many diverse sources (which

---

1 Australian Attorney-General's Department, Improving Australia's Law and Justice Framework: A discussion paper to explore the scope for reforming Australian contract law (2012) (hereinafter 'Discussion Paper').

2 To be sure, the Discussion Paper recognises a wide spectrum of 'possible options lying in between "no action" and "radical overhaul" and, even then, ranging from less to more far-reaching change' (ibid 18–19). The basic reform options are restatement of the current law in a new form, simplification of the current law in certain areas, and substantial reform of contract law (ibid 18 [6.2]).

3 See Infolet 4 ('Should contract law be codified?'). Of course, calls for an Australian contract code (or similar) are hardly novel; see Joseph G Starke, 'A Restatement of the Australian Law of Contract as a First Step Towards an Australian Uniform Contract Code' (1978) 49 Australian Law Journal 234.

4 Discussion Paper (n 1) 2.

5 Many of these are mentioned in the Discussion Paper and separately published 'Infolets'. Generally see Andrew Stewart, 'What's Wrong with the Australian Law of Contract?' (2012) 29 Journal of Contract Law 74.

'is a recipe both for incoherence and for inertia in legal developments[6]);[7] it is unnecessarily complex, overly technical, uncommercial and/or out of date;[8] it is unclear, unsettled and/or underdetermined in a number of important respects or areas (for example, the modern High Court has been criticised for being too taciturn on various issues in contract law, such as the interpretation principles relating to formal contracts and the place and role of 'good faith'[9]);[10] it is unnecessarily fragmented and non-uniform across various States and Territories (which breeds complexity);[11] it is insufficiently sensitive to the digital economy (technological changes and increased online transactions),[12] and under-responsive to the globalisation of markets or discordant with international commercial and/ or legal trends (which might repel major trading partners whose business laws are incompatible with Australia's);[13] it is insufficiently elastic in relation to long-term or 'relational' contracts;[14] and so on.[15] Recently, Justice Paul Finn (as he then was)

---

6   Justice Paul Finn, 'Symposium Paper: The *UNIDROIT* Principles: An Australian Perspective' (2010) 17 Australian International Law Journal 193, 193. Justice Finn regards this as unhelpful and identifies (ibid) six potential sources of Australian domestic contract law: the common law, equity, Commonwealth statute, State or Territory Statute, international instruments such as the Vienna Convention on the International Sale of Goods, and the terms of contracts themselves.

7   Discussion Paper (n 1) [3.4]–[3.10].

8   Finn (n 6).

9   Generally see Stewart (n 5) 81ff. Stewart describes this quite scathingly as 'an abrogation of the court's responsibility to act as a custodian of the common law' (ibid 84). See also, to similar effect, Andrew Stewart and John W Carter, 'The High Court and Contract Law in the New Millennium' (2003) 6 Flinders Journal of Law Reform 185, 213.

10   Justice Paul Finn also identifies 'the whole area of suspension and renunciation of rights dealt with variously by waiver, estoppel, variation and election' as in need of attention; see Finn (n 6) 193. I could not agree more; see Rick Bigwood, 'Fine-Tuning Affirmation of Contract by Election' [2010] New Zealand Law Review 37 (Part 1), 617 (Part 2); 'Circumscribing Election: Reflections on the Taxonomization and Mental Componentry of Affirmation of a Contract by Election' (2012) 30 University of Queensland Law Journal 235.

11   Stewart, for example, has recently complained of the 'patchwork framework' and 'fragmented nature' of the legislation that governs contracting in Australia, especially when one takes a cross-jurisdictional approach: Stewart (n 5) 87. See also the Discussion Paper (n 1) 5 [2.10]; Infolet 5 ('Should contract law be harmonised?').

12   See generally Raymond T. Nimmer, 'The Legal Landscape of E-commerce: Redefining Contract Law in an Information Era' (2007) 23 Journal of Contract Law 10; Discussion Paper (n 1) [2.7], [3.13]–[3.15]; Infolet 2, 2 ('Small business and e-commerce').

13   Generally see Justice Paul Finn, 'Internationalisation or isolation: The Australian cul de sac? The case of contract' in Mary Hiscock and William Van Caenegem (eds), *The Internationalisation of Law: Legislating, Decision-Making, Practice and Education* (Edward Elgar, 2010) 145, especially at 150ff; Discussion Paper (n 1) 11–14; Infloet 6 ('Should contract law be internationalised?').

14   Finn (n 6) 193; Infolet 8 ('Long-term contracts and good faith').

15   For further discussion, see Stewart (n 5).

denounced Australian contract law as 'a little tired, a little inadequate to the world in which it now finds itself. It needs regeneration.'[16]

All that may well be conceded. But the *extent* to which a nation's domestic contract law might be perceived to be deficient at any particular moment is bound to remain experiential and perspectival. It is relative and contingent. There will inevitably be as many views on whether Australian contract law is 'fit for its purpose and prepared for the challenges of the future' as there are 'businesses, legal practitioners, academics and other stakeholders' willing to proffer a view on the subject. The 'KPIs' of contract law are matters about which reasonable minds might certainly differ, and their attainment seems to be something that is very hard, if not impossible, to scientifically measure.[17] In some instances the contrariant viewpoints may be formulated on evidence that is either not readily available or, if it is, not conclusive in its purport.[18] Moreover, some of the evidence that exists, at least within particular industries or contexts, tends to suggest that substantive contract law might not be as important to end-users in the real world of commerce as might otherwise be assumed.[19]

All of this, and more, renders the problematics of contract law vulnerable to significant exaggeration, for special-pleading purposes or otherwise. My own sense is that the current laws relating to contracting in Australia are not *fundamentally* defective, but rather merely impoverished or deficient in isolated and relatively minor respects.[20] There is certainly no ironclad evidence that the common law of contract routinely dispenses intolerable miscarriages of justice or causes the sky of commerce to crumble to the ground. Still, there can be no denying that the

---

16 Finn (n 6) 193. To similar effect is Finn (n 13).

17 Compare Martin Doris, 'Promising Options, Dead Ends and the Reform of Australian Contract Law' (2013) 34 Legal Studies 24, 29: '"coherence" in the law of contract, and private law generally, is not easily benchmarked'. Even senior contract-law scholars such as Stephen Waddams are sceptical of any modern assumption that 'problems in the existing law can be accurately identified, and that knowledgeable experts can, after directing their minds to the question, agree on appropriate reforms and put them efficiently into legislative form', through a wise and supportive legislature, for the betterment of everyone: Stephen M. Waddams, 'Codification, Law reform and Judicial Development' (1996) 9 Journal of Contract Law 192, 192.

18 For example, there is to my knowledge no compelling evidence that Australian businesses are disadvantaged by the current system of contract law (in contrast, perhaps, to other economic factors).

19 See, for example, John Gava, 'How Should Judges Decide Commercial Contract Cases?' (2013) 30 Journal of Contract Law 133, 134–9.

20 Take, for example, the problem of the lack of disharmony in various statutes affecting contract law across different States and Territories. The main examples mentioned (see n 11) are the laws governing the legal capacity of minors, the consequences of frustration, and privity. These areas of contract law are hardly the mainstays of commerce and contractual planning! Although privity issues can be important in certain areas, lawyers are well familiar with the drafting techniques around them.

Discussion Paper has afforded an interesting, and potentially salient, opportunity for Australian lawyers, judges and jurists (as well as all other interested parties) to reflect on the merits of the traditions and methods of the common law, and on the potential advantages of a new way of doing things, for example via codification. It is an opportunity not merely to restate and clarify the law, but also to reform and harmonise it, whether in radical, moderate or minor ways.

Of course, the advantages and disadvantages of codifying contract law have been so well recorded and debated that they hardly need repeating here.[21] But if history has taught us anything, it is that one can never underestimate the risks, politics, pragmatics, time investment, labour intensiveness, expense and other extraordinary barriers to the successful development and implementation of substantial law-reform initiatives, including codes, and perhaps contract-law codes in particular.[22] There will, no doubt, be massive inertia in the system to overcome; 'heroic acts of cooperative federalism or the Commonwealth's use of its legislative powers ... [will be required] to effect significant changes to contract law across the nation';[23] and significant costs will be imposed on the business and legal communities in preparing and implementing a major reform of Australian contract law.

---

21   The main advantages are presented in a famous article by Aubrey L Diamond, 'Codification of the Law of Contract' (1968) 31 Modern Law Review 361. See also John Farrar, 'The codification of commercial law' in Jeremy Finn and Stephen Todd (eds), *Law, Liberty, Legislation* (LexisNexis, 2008) 56–7 (Farrar concludes that the arguments for and against codification 'are of such a high level of generality that they cannot be established or refuted scientifically' (ibid 57); Francis MB Reynolds, 'Contract: Codification, Legislation and Judicial Development' (1995) 9 Journal of Contract Law 11, 16–17; Law Reform Commission of Victoria, Discussion Paper No 27, *An Australian Contract Code* (1992) 3–4; Dame Mary Arden, 'Time for an English Commercial Code?' (1997) 56 Cambridge Law Journal 516, 530–4.

22   See generally Warren Swain, 'Codification of Contract Law: Some Lessons from History' (2012) 31 University of Queensland Law Journal 39 ('Swain (2012)'). See also Warren Swain, 'Contract codification and the English: Some observations from the Indian Contract Act 1872' in James Devenney and Mel Kenny (eds), *The Transformation of European Private Law* (Cambridge University Press 2013) , 172. ('Swain (2013)'); Warren Swain, 'Contract Codification in Australia: Is It Necessary, Desirable and Possible?' (2014) 36 Sydney Law Review 131. There is a wonderful discussion of codification in both English and American legal history in Gunter A Weiss, 'The Enchantment of Codification in the Common-Law World' (2000) 25 Yale Journal of International Law 436, 470ff (England), 498ff (America). The practical and political obstacles to codification are also well noted by Alexander E Anton, 'Obstacles to Codification' (1982) 15 Juridicial Review 15, Peter M North, 'Problems of Codification in a Common Law System' (1982) 46 Rabels Zeitschrift 490, Bruce Donald, 'Codification in Common Law Systems' (1973) 47 Australian Law Journal 160, 172–7, and Diamond (n 21) 375–84.

23   Finn (n 6) 194. Constitutional heads-of-power considerations are discussed in the Discussion Paper (n 1) 5 [2.10], 21 [7.9], and in Infolet 5.

This is to mention just a few of the barriers to the radical reform of contract law in Australia (and many of them, notice, apply equally to less drastic reform options such as 'restatement' and 'simplification').[24] Without question, the comprehensive (or anything approximating a comprehensive) codification of Australian contract law would present a mission of absolutely Herculean proportions. And for what return? Scant empirical data exists to suggest that the future benefits of codification will demonstrably outweigh the present costs of enacting such a reform.[25] Comparisons with other common-law countries (especially trading partners) that have codified their contract laws are weakened by the fact that the circumstances of, and reasons for, codification in those other countries are typically unique to them.[26] The advocates of codification, it has been urged,[27] tend to downplay the differences between legal systems (although the reality is that the virtues and vices of codification can be exaggerated equally on both sides of the debate for special-pleading purposes).[28] Moreover, the harmonisation process can force compromises and hence produce, potentially, inferior law.[29] Suboptimal law can also result from the fact that a 'committee' of some sort will almost certainly be entrusted with drafting any contract-law code for Australia, and with this will likely come the compromises that tend to accompany many-hands-and-minds solutions to problems.[30] Even the goal of 'simplifying' contract law is not self-evidently unproblematic. To some extent the law must acknowledge and respond to the complexity of the relationships, transactions and subject matters that an official regulatory order must govern and serve. Relatedly, ensuring that contract law is more accessible (and perhaps even more 'user-friendly') to the public is potentially a rather vain goal given the poor

---

24 As Stewart also points out (n 5) 88, the Australian Consumer Law presents a major problem for a global contracts code, because it cuts across so much of legal contractual activity.

25 Even in Europe, '[p]ractical or economic arguments favouring a unified European code are not yet decisive one way or another': Swain (2012) (n 22) 47. Generally see also Doris (n 17).

26 See, for example, Swain (2013) (n 22); Arden (n 21) 522–3; Weiss (n 22) 484–6 (India); Finn (n 13) 153 (quoting Wei Luo) (China). On the flip side, failed attempts at codification in common-law legal systems tend similarly to be unique to those legal systems that have tried it and failed. Generally see Weiss (n 22).

27 Swain (2013) (n 22) 21–2.

28 Compare Hein Kötz, 'Taking Civil Codes Less Seriously' (1987) 50 Modern Law Review 1, 10.

29 Compare Reynolds (n 21) 15; Swain (2012) (n 22) 48: 'One of the strongest arguments for codification, namely the harmonisation of contract law across Australia, may also be one of the most difficult objects to achieve.' Australian codifiers, of course, will not be taxed by having to reconcile many heterogeneous legal systems, such as exists in Europe.

30 Swain (2012) (n 22) 49; Farrar (n 21) 60, quoting Sir Frederick Pollock (assisted by DF Mulla), *The Indian Contracts Act* (2nd edn, 1909), preface to the first edition.

literacy skills of a significant portion of the Australian adult population,[31] and given the fact, too, that many litigated commercial disputes turn on the resolution of complex *factual* matters (or on what evidence can be received, or on what inferences can be drawn from the admissible evidence), or on a court's exercise of *judgement* in relation to qualifying normative thresholds or standards: for example, did X act 'honestly' and/or 'reasonably' and/or 'in good conscience'? It strikes me as extremely difficult to increase the law's usability to those governed by its dictates, if not in relation to the substantive content of the rules and guiding principles, then certainly apropos the *conventions* of their application to individual relations or disputes.[32]

Obviously, comprehensive codification (or similarly ambitious law-reform) projects cannot be driven by zeal, blanket assumptions, speculation, blind faith or idealism alone. Unless reliable empirical data and sound analysis of those data are forthcoming in relation to the key drivers of the initiative at hand, the safest option is for the Government to adopt a minimalist attitude toward contract-law reform in Australia. Indeed, one of the reported reasons the English Law Commission eventually demitted its project to comprehensively codify contract law in the 1960s and early 1970s is that the draft code[33] sought to do too much before all the 'logically anterior' work had been done.[34] One way forward, of course, would be to *partially* codify domestic contract law, prioritising those areas perceived to be in the greatest need of reform. That approach might well deliver many of the perceived advantages of codification without quite the same level of ambition and cost; hence, it might be easier sold to the legal and business communities. Certainly the Discussion Paper contemplates partway measures short of comprehensive codification, such as a non-binding US-style restatement or targeted interstitial reform of specific pockets of contract law in need of improvement. Only if Australian contract law were truly in need of *wholesale* reform would a comprehensive code (or similar) be necessary; otherwise, one should think, less drastic, partial codification (or similar) ought to suffice, at least for the short-to-medium term.

Now, although the concept of 'codification' in general 'is both unclear and polysemous',[35] no overly restrictive conceptualisation of 'partial codification'

---

31 For the statistics, see Swain (2012) (n 22) 44, fn 64. Also, it is likely (but not inevitable) that a comprehensive code will be so large and detailed as to offset the intended benefits of public accessibility.

32 For a contrary view, see Manfred Ellinghaus and Edmund Wright, *Models of Contract Law* (Themis Press, 2005).

33 Harvey McGregor, *Contract Code Drawn Up on Behalf of the English Law Commission* (Guilffré, 1993).

34 See Reynolds (n 21) 14–15. The draft code also fell victim to disagreements between the English and Scottish Law Commissions; see Arden (n 21) 527; Weiss (n 22) 495.

35 Weiss (n 22) 451.

(within a common-law legal system[36]) is here intended. The general understanding[37] of 'code' applies equally to the part as to the whole, *mutatis mutandis*.[38] So if we were to take, for example, Farrar's characterisation of a code as 'a species of statute which attempts to sum up the existing legislation and common law and equity on a particular topic',[39] the 'particular topic' might be wide or narrow. Or if we were to adopt Donald's conceptualisation of the same – '[i]n its most general sense, codification is the systematic collection or formulation of the law, reducing it from a disparate mass into an accessible statement which is given legislative rather than merely judicial or academic authority'[40] – 'the law' to which Donald refers might similarly be wide or narrow. Suffice it to say, the key characteristic of a code in a common-law legal system, whether partial or comprehensive, is that it is an authoritative[41] statement of the law, announced by Parliament, which is intended to take effect *in place of* the former rules, whether common-law, equitable or legislative, governing the subject matter of the statute enacting the code. *Pace* the Victorian Law Commission, however, that statement of the law need not function *entirely* as a 'clean slate' or a 'self-contained statement of the law'.[42] A code need not break wholly with the past; nor must it be completely gap-free.[43] On the

---

36 It is possible that no conception of 'codification' within a common-law legal system will ever satisfy a civilian's strict understanding of a 'code' based on his or her own personal experience or preconceptions. See, for example, the remarks in the introduction to Hiroo Sono's chapter in this collection: Chapter 6.

37 To the extent that there can be a 'general understanding' of codification! See Weiss (n 22) 449–52, discussing the various meanings of 'codification', and concluding (ibid 451) 'that it is impossible to find a single uniform notion of codification'.

38 The most obvious examples of partial (or 'limited') codification are the nineteenth-century commercial-law statutes relating to sales of goods, bills of exchange and partnership. As Reynolds points out, these are 'mini-codes' that are in their own respective areas of operation similar in effect to more general codes: Reynolds (n 21) 17. Reynolds distinguishes these from law-reform statutes that 'change the law in limited ways only', and which might be regarded as mere 'excrescences on the law' (ibid 18), such frustrated contracts legislation, misrepresentation Acts, unfair contract terms legislation, or the Contracts Review Act 1980 (NSW). Whether or not these sorts of statutes can fairly be described as 'partial codes' may be partly a matter of degree, although mostly it must be a matter of Parliamentary intention, and whether the legislation satisfies the core definitional elements of a 'code' in the text to nn 36–48. Clearly some of the New Zealand statutes regulating discrete parts of contract law satisfy that definition, even though they are short and very limited in scope. Some of them are even expressed to be codes, although statutes are not necessarily codes just because they adopt the 'code' label. They must also demonstrate and be treated consistently with the 'core elements' of codification. See (n 48).

39 Farrar (n 21) 51.

40 Donald (n 22) 161.

41 cf Weiss (n 22) 456.

42 Law Reform Commission of Victoria (n 21), 4.

43 Nor should it be thought that a code must be 'formally complete' in the sense that only those sources explicitly referred to in the code can be accepted as sources of law.

contrary, courts may still look to previous law when, for example, ambiguity or uncertainty appears in the words of the code, or the words used formerly had a technical meaning but have remained undefined in the code.[44] Indeed, Farrar goes so far as to suggest that 'even if the code expressly forbade resort to the prior law, lawyers would still in practice resort to it for guidance'![45]

It follows, then, that codification may be 'partial' in either or both of two senses (with shades on a spectrum in between). 'Partial' might signify 'non-comprehensive but exclusive', in the sense that the area of law covered by the code is a mere subset of a core field, but the code is intended to displace virtually altogether the prior law relating to that subset.[46] Obvious examples here are the substantial commercial-law codes of nineteenth-century England (codifying, separately, the prior laws relating to bills of exchange, partnership and sales of goods), and, on an even grander scale, the American Uniform Commercial Code of 1962.[47] The partiality, in other words, here relates to the *scope* of the codifying statute, not necessarily to the concept, nature or definitional consequences of 'codification' itself.[48] However, codification, whether comprehensive or non-comprehensive,

---

As Weiss (n 22) 523, points out, '[t]he only claim a theory of codification can honestly make is that the codification has to be the primary source of law.'

44 The classic judicial statement of how courts are to interpret codifying statutes is Lord Herschell's in *Vagliano Brothers v Bank of England* [1981] AC 107 (HL), a case concerning the interpretation of the Bills of Exchange Act 1882 (UK): 'I think the proper course is in the first instance to examine the language of the statute and to ask what is its natural meaning, uninfluenced by any considerations derived from the previous state of the law, and not to start with inquiring how the law previously stood, and then, assuming it was probably intended to leave it unaltered, to see if the words of the enactments will bear an interpretation in conformity with this view.'

45 Farrar (n 21) 55. Compare also Kötz (n 28) 11: 'It is unrealistic to expect that lawyers trained under pre-code law can be prevented from going back to it if the code is silent, if the language is not clear or if the words used in it had previously acquired a technical meaning.'

46 Generally see Donald (n 22) 168–9 (on 'partial comprehensive codes').

47 For the history and operation of the UCC, see generally Weiss (n 22) 52–7. Again, some civilians will object that the UCC does not qualify as a 'code', because it is not comprehensive (see, for example, Hiroo Sono's chapter in this collection, Chapter 6, fn 1). As to whether comprehensiveness is a precondition of a code, see the following footnote (n 48).

48 There are issues as to what extent *completeness* (including exclusivity and comprehensiveness), for example, are definitional preconditions of a 'code'. Suffice it to say for present purposes that codes do not have to be *fully* exclusive or *fully* comprehensive in order to qualify as 'codes'. Generally see Weiss (n 22) 456ff. There are stronger and weaker forms of codification, and no bright-line test exists, or can exist, in relation to what qualifies as 'a code' and what does not. Weiss (ibid 470) presents a useful conceptualisation of codification based on a summary of its *core elements*: 'Codification is a conception of the law that is centred upon a code. Such a code is authoritative rather than merely persuasive. It is complete in the sense that it is the primary source of the law with respect to the exclusion of other sources in the field of law that it covers. It requires a theory of

may be 'partial' in another, quite different sense. That is to say, the legislative objective might be to codify (comprehensively or non-comprehensively) the subject area, but the codification is 'not fully exclusive' in the sense that the considered intention of the framers of the code is not to abrogate entirely the prior law in that subject area.[49] So, although the reform initiative is expressed to be an exercise in 'codification' *stricto sensu*, the resultant 'code' self-consciously assumes some (and indeed possibly significant components) of the infrastructure of the pre-code common law. Hence, the application of the code depends upon unstated common-law concepts and principles that must be incorporated into the development and application of the code in order to give meaning and content to some (many, all) of its provisions. Partial codes of this nature tend to be short instruments, comprising, typically, quite simple and general rules or principles. This, as we shall see in the following section, characterises the contract-law codes of New Zealand. They are 'partial codes' in both of the two senses above: non-comprehensive *and* non-exclusive.

2 The New Zealand Contract-Law Codes (Partial)

Like Australia (or individual States or Territories of Australia), New Zealand adopted the nineteenth-century English commercial codes dealing with bills of exchange, sales of goods and partnership. It also, through a series of (relatively short) statutes, significantly reformed distinct parts of general[50] contract law. The statutes began with the Minors' Contracts Act 1969,[51] followed by the Illegal Contracts Act 1970, the Contractual Mistakes Act 1977, the Contractual Remedies Act 1979, and the Contracts (Privity) Act 1982.[52] Three of those Acts are

---

adjudication that binds the judge to a code, yet gives the judge the power to fill in gaps and develop the law. The code aims at presenting a clearly structured and consistent whole of legal rules and principles ("outer" system), promoting the internal coherence of the law ("inner" system), and providing a conceptual framework for further doctrinal, judicial, or legislative development. It often serves to promote both legal and political unification.'

49 To be clear, I am speaking here mostly in terms of degree, for even the significant partial codes relating to bills of exchange, sales of goods and partnership preserve the rules of common law to the extent that they are not inconsistent with the express provisions of the legislation codifying those sub-fields of commercial law. See, for example, Bills of Exchange Act 1909 (Cth), s 5; Partnerships Act 1891 (Qld), s 121; Sale of Goods Act 1923 (NSW), s 4(a).

50 There are, of course, other important statutes affecting specific kinds of contract (for example, insurance, hire purchase, credit contracts, employment) that are beyond the scope of this chapter. They are not 'codes' in the sense defined in this chapter.

51 The structure of the Act was significantly amended in 2005: Minors' Contracts Amendment Act 2005.

52 Generally see Francis Dawson, 'The New Zealand Contract Statutes' [1985] Lloyd's Maritime and Commercial Law Quarterly 42; David W McLauchlan, 'Contract and

intended to function as 'partial codes' in the senses earlier defined,[53] and all five of them, among other things, confer upon the courts broad discretionary powers to grant relief, or to authorise variations or discharges of the contract, in specified circumstances. The legislative raft was not informed by any overarching theory of or approach to contract law as such; rather, each statute was a piecemeal response to an area of the law that was proving unsatisfactory in practice. Professor Coote, a long-serving member of the Contracts and Commercial Law Reform Committee that was the primary framer of the last four of the aforementioned statutes, has documented that the underlying purpose of the Committee's work was 'not to weaken but rather to strengthen the institution of contract by liberalising the effect of the law in a limited number of areas where it could operate unfairly'.[54] Writing in 1983, Professor Burrows opined that the new statutes were superior to the law they had replaced.[55] He also pointed out that a comprehensive contract-law code for New Zealand would have been too challenging to draft and much less likely to win Parliament's and the profession's approval.[56] Some of the statutes are completely novel (for example, the Illegal Contracts Act, Contractual Mistakes Act and Contractual Remedies Act), while the Contracts (Privity) Act was informed by statutory developments that had occurred elsewhere within the British Commonwealth.[57]

Right from the start the statutes attracted significant academic and professional criticism, much of it directed at the feared consequences of Parliament conferring so much discretion upon the courts in the contractual arena.[58] However, the New Zealand Law Commission reviewed the statutes in 1993 and made very few

---

Commercial Law Reform in New Zealand' (1984) 11 New Zealand Universities Law Review 36; Brian Coote, 'The Contracts and Commercial Law Reform Committee and the Contract Statutes' (1988) 13 New Zealand Universities Law Review 160.

53 Two of the Acts, the Minors' Contracts Act and Contractual Mistakes Act are expressed to be codes (s 15 and s 5, respectively). Section 7 of the Contractual Remedies Act signifies that a significant portion of that Act is intended effectively to function as a code as well – of which more below.

54 Coote (n 52) 188.

55 John F Burrows, 'Contract Statutes: The New Zealand Experience' (1983) Statute Law Review 76, 97.

56 ibid. For an argument that the New Zealand contract statutes should be brought together under a single Act — a 'Contracts (Consolidation) Act' — see Thomas Gibbons, 'A Contracts (Consolidation) Act for New Zealand' (2003) 11 Waikato Law Review 13.

57 The Contracts (Privity) Act 1982 is different from the other statutes. It is less about liberating the courts to dispense discretionary justice than about abrogation of a rule considered to be defective.

58 See, for example, Dawson (n 52), especially at 43 (criticism that broad discretion alters the fundamental nature of contractual justice as residing in the state giving effect to the parties' intentions, rather than altering them); George P Barton, 'Wither Contract?' [1981] New Zealand Law Journal 369, 379 (fearing 'the rise of palm tree justice administered by the Cadi who sat at the city gate in eastern countries'). See also McLauchlan (n 52);

recommendations for change.[59] The Commission observed that 'not only have the statutes by and large achieved their purpose, but also ... any fears which might have been entertained for "sanctity of contract" because discretions were conferred on the courts have proved to have little if any foundation'.[60] The statutes were described as having 'taken on a life of their own', which was seen as 'a positive feature of the legislation and of the jurisdiction of the courts under it'.[61]

In the interests of space, I shall consider just two of the New Zealand contract-law codes: the Contractual Mistakes Act and the Contractual Remedies Act. I shall also briefly consider a recent private law-reform proposal in Canada: a 'Contract Fairness Act' for British Columbia. All three reform initiatives, as we shall eventually see, contain valuable lessons for any common-law legal system, such as Australia, that is considering the option of codifying all or parts of its domestic contract law.

The Contractual Mistakes Act 1977 (NZ)

Section 5(1) of the Contractual Mistakes Act 1977 expressly declares that the Act is to function as a code:

5. ACT TO BE A CODE –
(1) Except as otherwise expressly provided in this Act, this Act shall have effect in place of the rules of the common law and of equity governing the circumstances in which relief may be granted, on the grounds of mistake, to a party to a contract or to a person claiming through or under any such party.[62]

The Contracts and Commercial Law Reform Committee of the (then) Ministry of Justice, which drafted the Bill that, after some amendment during the legislative process,[63] became the Contractual Mistakes Act, was primarily motivated by a

---

George Barton, 'The Effect of the Contract Statutes in New Zealand' (2000) 16 Journal of Contract Law 233.

59 New Zealand Law Commission, *Contracts Statutes Review* (NZLC: R 25) (1993). Those recommendations that survived the legislative process were not enacted until 2001, through various amending Acts.

60 ibid 2 [4].

61 ibid 2 [5].

62 There are various exclusions from the regime in s 5(2), such as non est factum, rectification, the law relating to undue influence, fraud, breach of fiduciary duty, or misrepresentation, and the Frustrated Contracts Act 1944.

63 These are summarised by David McLauchlan, 'Mistake as to Contractual terms under the Contractual Mistakes Act 1977' (1986) 12 New Zealand Universities Law Review 123, 149–51. The amendments were made apparently to restrict the availability for relief in order to preserve contractual certainty.

perceived need to remove artificial legal obstacles to the achievement of justice in cases of contractual mistake.

Many (but certainly not all)[64] consider the Contractual Mistakes Act to be the most problematic of New Zealand's contract-law statutes. Some have been absolutely scathing in their criticism. Professor McLauchlan, for example, whose work I have very much admired in this field, has complained that so numerous are the interpretation and conceptual problems with the Act that it has become virtually impossible to provide a coherent account of the law on the subject.[65] He has condemned the statute as 'conceptually and philosophically bankrupt'.[66] Another scholar has decried that 'the potential of this Act for the destruction of the law of contract as generally understood is unsurpassed'.[67] Professor Reynolds, too, has deemed the legislation 'misguided', opining that allowing the equitable principles relating to mistake to develop on a case-by-case basis would have been a better approach.[68]

To be sure, although it has been more than a quarter-century since the Contractual Mistakes Act was passed, and despite numerous judicial elucidations of a number of the Act's provisions, local textbook writers have been forced to concede that some of those provisions 'remain obscure or contentious and the proper interpretation of them remains a matter of speculation and debate'.[69] The same textbook writers have rightly opined that '[i]t is a measure of the intrinsic difficulty of the law of mistake and of the controversies over the application of that Act that 25 years after its passage there could be such spirited debates over the ambit, meaning and application of its provisions'.[70]

The self-declared aim of the Contractual Mistakes Act is to 'mitigate the arbitrary effects of mistakes on contracts',[71] which it seeks to do primarily by widening considerably the range of relief available to courts and arbitrators when

---

64 In their review of the Contractual Mistakes Act, Beck and Sutton opine that 'the Act has, to a large extent, been successful in achieving its aim of providing for a more extensive and systematic approach to relief for mistake'; see Andrew Beck and Richard Sutton, 'Contractual Mistakes Act 1977' in New Zealand Law Commission, *Contracts Statutes Review* (NZLC: R 25) (1993) 127, 164 [2.97].

65 David W McLauchlan, 'Analysing Mistake' (1997) 3 New Zealand Business Law Quarterly 194.

66 ibid 194. See also Jeremy Finn, 'The Contractual Mistakes Act 1977' (1977) 8 New Zealand Universities Law Review 312, 320 (Act is 'well-intentioned but ill-executed').

67 Dawson (n 52) 48.

68 Reynolds (n 21) 22. Ironically, though, since 2000 when Reynolds expressed his views, *Solle v Butcher* [1950] 1 KB 671 (EWCA) has been overruled, at least for the United Kingdom; see *Great Peace Shipping Ltd v Tsavliris (International) Ltd* [2003] QB 679 (EWCA).

69 John Burrows, Jeremy Finn, and Stephen Todd, *Law of Contract in New Zealand* (2nd edn, LexisNexis, 2002) 270.

70 ibid 270, fn 16.

71 Contractual Mistakes Act 1977, s 4(1)

the conditions triggering the powers to grant such relief are satisfied. Those conditions are enumerated in s 6(1)(a)–(c) of the Act, of which more shortly. Essentially, by codifying this area of the law, the New Zealand Parliament sought to strike (what at the time was perceived to be) an appropriate balance between 'fairness' for mistaken parties on the one hand, and 'security' for those who may well rely on the validity of an apparent contract on the other.[72] Hence, s 4(2) of the Act instructs courts not to exercise their powers under the Act 'in such a way as to prejudice the general security of contractual relationships', and s 8(1) protects good-faith purchasers for value without notice.

Surprisingly, given the centrality of the mistake concept to the operation of the code, no substantial definition of 'mistake' is to be found anywhere in the Contractual Mistakes Act. We are told, rather obviously, that there is no 'mistake' where a party 'becomes aware' of the mistake but enters into the contract nonetheless (s 6(2)(b)), and that although a 'mistake of law' includes a mistake in the interpretation of a document (s 2(2)), that document cannot be the contract itself (s 6(2)(a)). Apart from that, all we have is the tautological definition of mistake in s 2(1): '"Mistake" – Means a mistake, whether of law or of fact.'[73] Although the absence of a more meaningful definition has certainly created some problems – and doubtless afforded counsel and the courts significant wiggle room to frame a mistake conveniently to fit or to evade the Act as suits them – those problems have more or less been resolved by the courts as they arise (albeit not to the satisfaction of everyone[74]).[75]

---

72 See Contracts and Commercial Law Reform Committee, *Report on the Effects of Mistakes on Contracts* (1976) [5].

73 In its draft Bill the Contracts and Commercial Law Reform Committee had proffered the following definition of 'mistake':
'Mistake' —
(a) Means a mistake, whether of law or of fact; and
(b) Includes —
    (i) An erroneous opinion; and
    (ii) An erroneous calculation; and
    (iii) An error in the manner in which a document is expressed; but
(c) Does not include any matter of expectation which concerns, or is dependent on, an event occurring or failing to occur after a particular contract is entered into.

The Statutes Revision Committee, however, considered this definition too wide (see (1977) 413 New Zealand Parliamentary Debates 2804), and so it was amended to its present form in the Act.

74 See generally McLauchlan (n 65).

75 The absence of a substantive definition of mistake has, for example, allowed the courts to exclude from the ambit of the legislative scheme cases of 'mere ignorance' in contrast to 'positive mistake'. Hence, where a party has not actually turned his or her mind to the matter at hand, there can be no mistake for the purposes of the Act; conscious consideration must have been given to the matter and a erroneous conclusion based on it. See *New Zealand Refining Co Ltd v Attorney-General* (1993) 7 NZBLC 103, 996;

In order to establish a qualifying mistake that enlivens the court's discretionary powers under s 7 of the Act, the applicant must satisfy each limb of a tripartite test set out in s 6(1):[76]

- there must be a mistake falling within the definitions contained in s 6(1)(a): a (known) unilateral mistake, a common mistake, or a mutual mistake;
- the mistake(s) shown must have resulted, at the time of contract formation, in either a substantially unequal exchange of values, or a benefit or burden that is substantially disproportionate to the consideration therefor (s 6(1)(b)); and
- there was no term in the contract expressly or impliedly allocating to the relief-seeking party the risk of the particular mistake that occurred (s 6(1)(c)).

Also, whatever the mistake pleaded, it must have 'influenced' the mistaken party's decision to enter into the contract in question.

If the s 6 criteria are satisfied, s 7 of the Contractual Mistakes Act confers upon the courts a very broad power to grant a wide range of relief to any party to the contract (not merely the mistaken party), as well as to any person claiming through or under that party. Basically, s 7(3) declares that a court may make any order that it thinks just, upon and subject to such terms and conditions as it thinks fit. The orders include, but are not limited to, declaring the contract to be valid and subsisting in whole or in part or for any particular purpose, cancelling the contract, varying the

---

Ladstone Holdings Ltd v Leonora Holdings Ltd [2006] 1 NZLR 211, 226–9. A contrary view is expressed in *Slater Wilmshurst Ltd v Crown Group Custodian Ltd* [1990] 1 NZLR 344, 356–7, and it might plausibly be argued that ignorance is capable, conceptually, of constituting a tacit mistake. See David W McLauchlan and Charles EF Rickett, 'Mistake and Ignorance under the New Zealand Contractual Mistakes Act 1977' (1995) 8 Journal of Contract Law 193. This problem can be avoided by the way the possible mistake is framed (see Burrows, Finn and Todd (n 69) 275), which again underscores the laxity of the definition of mistake in the Act. Regarding the question of whether 'mistake' can extend to matters of expectation as to future events or contingencies, the court in *Compcorp Ltd v Force Entertainment Ltd* (2003) 7 NZBLC 103,996 held not. Contracting in the expectation of a course of events does not produce a qualifying mistake if matters do not turn out as expected, although this, too, seems open to manipulation in the way the mistake is formulated on the facts. Compare *Ware v Johnson* [1984] 2 NZLR 518, 537 (Pritchard J), a misrepresentation case (although the orchard being sold in that case did not produce a crop in the future as represented (unknown to both parties at the time of sale, the vines had been poisoned and were dying), the representation was not construed as being one as to the future; 'the real nature of the representation, which was that the vines in their then condition were of such quality that they would produce a crop in May 1982. It was ... a representation as to the present state of the orchard').

76 McLauchlan (n 65), 195, has described the criteria for relief in s 6 as proving 'to be somewhat of an unhappy compromise between old and new ideas'.

contract, and granting relief by way of restitution or compensation. Section 7(2) also provides that, in considering whether to grant relief under s 7, the court must consider the 'extent to which the party seeking relief, or the party through or under whom relief is sought, as the case may require, caused the mistake'.

Doubtless the most perilous problem with the Contractual Mistakes Act was exposed well within the first decade of its enactment. The majority judgments in the New Zealand Court of Appeal case of *Conlon v Ozolins*[77] threw serious doubt on whether the common law's objective approach to contract formation, exemplified perhaps most famously by Blackburn J's judgment in *Smith v Hughes*,[78] had survived the Act's passing into law. Of course, under the objective approach to contract formation, a contracting party is generally bound if he or she leads the other party reasonably to believe that that party's terms or understanding of the transaction was being agreed to, regardless of what the first party's subjective belief or understanding of the transaction happened to be. If, unknown to the other party, the first party was subjectively mistaken about some fact material to his or her decision to enter into the contract in question, that mistake is simply a legally irrelevant consideration. The first party is bound despite his or her mistake.[79] The law's policy behind the objective approach to establishing contractual consensus is self-evident and pellucid;[80] and given Parliament's obvious concern that the court's powers under the Act not be 'exercised in such a way as to prejudice the general security of contractual relationships' (s 4(2)), in addition to the exclusion of mistakes in the interpretation of the contract itself (s 6(2)(a)), one might be forgiven for thinking that if Parliament had intended to affect the law's objective approach in connection with the screening of pre-contractual errors, it would have done so explicitly in the Act.[81]

In *Conlon v Ozolins*, the defendant, Mrs Ozolins, was an elderly widow with poor English skills. She owned a house, together with property, which comprised four sections on a separate title: Lots 1, 2, 3 and 4. Lot 4 adjoined the defendant's house and was her garden. It was separated from the other lots by a high fence, so that visually the house and its garden appeared to form one coherent site, whereas the lots beyond the fence had the appearance of a grass paddock.

---

77 *Conlon v Ozolins* [1984] 1 NZLR 489.

78 *Smith v Hughes* (1871) LR 6 QB 579, 607.

79 Generally, David W McLauchlan, 'Objectivity in Contract' (2005) 24 University of Queensland Law Journal 479.

80 The policy is nicely expressed, for example, in the various judgments in *Tamplin v James* (1880) 15 Ch D 215 (CA).

81 There is a well-known presumption in New Zealand that Parliament does not intend any alteration in the existing law beyond that which it expressly declares. See, for example, *CIR v West-Walker* [1954] NZLR 191; J Evans, *Statutory Interpretation* (OUP, 1988) 299–300. There are opposing views on the treatment of the *Smith v Hughes* principle in *Conlon v Ozolins*; see Francis Dawson, 'The Contractual Mistakes Act 1977: *Conlon v. Ozolins*' (1985) 11 New Zealand Universities Law Review 285, and McLauchlan (n 63) 129–36.

Mrs Ozolins, through her solicitor, entered into negotiations with the plaintiff, a property developer. She eventually agreed to sell 'the land out the back', which in her mind comprised Lots 1, 2 and 3; but the plaintiff believed, in part because of a misunderstanding of Mrs Ozolins' solicitor who prepared the formal contract, that Mrs Ozolins was selling Lots 1, 2, 3 and 4. The parties signed a contract describing a sale and purchase of all four lots, but when Mrs Ozolins discovered this she refused to complete the conveyance. The plaintiff sought specific performance of the contract and Mrs Ozolins pleaded, inter alia, the Contractual Mistakes Act. She relied, in particular, on s 6(1)(a)(iii) of the Act, the provision governing so-called 'mutual' mistake: that the plaintiff and defendant 'were each influenced in their respective decisions to enter into the contract by a different mistake about the same matter of fact or of law'.

In the Court of Appeal the majority judgments differed in their detail, but nevertheless each of Woodhouse P and McMullin J held that Mrs Ozolins' mistake fell within the provisions of Act. Woodhouse P classified the 'mistake' that occurred as follows: P thought that D intended to sell four lots, and D thought that P intended to purchase three lots, and these are different mistakes about the size of the land to be bought and sold.[82] McMullin J, however, said nothing about the nature of the mistake. He simply said that what happened was that P thought that D intended to sell four lots, and that D thought she was selling three lots.[83] However, while these may well be different mistakes (as required by s 6(1)(a)(iii)), they clearly are not about the *same* matter of fact (as is also required by s 6(1)(a)(iii)). McMullin J's analysis of the mistake, it would appear, simply does not satisfy the wording of s 6(1)(a)(iii).

This problem was identified by the third judge in the case, Somers J, in a perspicacious dissenting judgment. His Honour agreed with both Woodhouse P and McMullin J that P thought that D intended to sell four lots, and he agreed with McMullin J that D was mistaken about the amount of land she was selling. However, he pointed out that the parties were not mistaken about the same thing: P's mistake was about D's intention, but D's mistake was about the subject matter of the sale (how much land was being sold). The case therefore did not fall within the plain words of s 6(1)(a)(iii). But Somers J went further, effectively dealing with Woodhouse P's problematic analysis, by holding that the plaintiff was *not mistaken* in any event: he intended to purchase four lots and that was exactly what the contract provided. Mrs Ozolins' mistake was of the 'pure unilateral' variety (that is, it was unknown to the non-mistaken party), and such mistakes are not caught by the Act.[84] Somers J averted to the obvious mischief that follows from the majority's interpretation of s 6(1)(a)(iii):

---

82 [1984] 1 NZLR 489, 498–99.
83 ibid 505.
84 Section 6(1)(a)(i) of the Contractual Mistakes Act requires unilateral mistakes to be 'known to' the non-mistaken party.

If the purchaser's postulated mistake – namely that he erroneously thought the vendor intended to sell him all four lots – is sufficient to bring the case within subpara (iii), there will be few, if any, cases of mistaken intent not falling within the Act. For as often as one party is mistaken in intention the other party will be taken to be relevantly differently mistaken about the same matter of fact so as to bring the case within subpara (iii). I do not consider this can have been the legislative purpose.[85]

It seems clear that the consequence of the majority's decision in *Conlon v Ozolins* was that the traditional objective approach of *Smith v Hughes* could no longer operate to prevent reliance upon a pre-contractual mistake for the purposes of the Act. Needless to say, there was in the wake of the decision no shortage of vociferous condemnation of the majority's reasoning.[86] Partly the problem lay in the drafting of s 6(1)(a)(iii). The only situation where parties can sensically be found to have made *different* mistakes about the *same* thing is where some third fact exists to demonstrate that each party is indeed differently mistaken: A believes X, B believes Y, but the true position is Z. This is an extremely rare eventuality. But the Committee behind the Act thought the words of s 6(1)(a)(iii) also took in cross-purposes mistakes, such as the one that occurred in the famous case of *Raffles v Wichelhaus*.[87] But as McLauchlan has rightly exposed,[88] the words of s 6(1)(a)(iii) are unlikely to catch that scenario. In cross-purposes situations the parties are mistaken, but not about the same fact; rather, it is as to each other's intentions, which are *different* facts. It is of course impossible for *both* parties to be mistaken where the words they have used to express their bargain permit of two possible meanings only. One party must be right, and the *Smith v Hughes* objective approach usually tells us which party that is. Where the objective approach is unable to produce an answer – as it failed to do in *Raffles v Wichelhaus*, for example – the contract must fail for non-correspondence of offer and acceptance, or perhaps for fatal uncertainty (an insoluble latent ambiguity), rather than for 'mistake' per se.

It was four years before the Court of Appeal was able to recapture (to some extent) the rabbit it had set running in *Conlon v Ozolins*. In *Paulger v Butland Industries Ltd*[89] the defendant, Mr Paulger, had sent a letter to the creditors of a

---

85 [1984] 1 NZLR 489, 508.

86 See, for example, McLauchlan (nn 63 and 65); Dawson (n 81). The Act has been defended by Richard Sutton, 'The Code of Contractual Mistake: What Went Wrong?' (2003) 9 New Zealand Business Law Quarterly 234 (soundly criticised by David McLauchlan, 'The Contractual Mistakes "Code": Professor Sutton's Solutions' (2003) 9 New Zealand Business Law Quarterly 261).

87 *Raffles v Wichelhaus* (1864) 2 H & C 906; 159 ER 375. See Contracts and Commercial Law Reform Committee, *Report on the Effect of Mistakes on Contracts* (1976) 15–16 [19].

88 McLauchlan (n 63) 151–3.

89 *Paulger v Butland Industries Ltd* [1989] 3 NZLR 549. See generally David W McLauchlan, 'The Demise of *Conlon v Ozolins*: "Mistake in Interpretation" or Another Case of Mistaken Interpretation?' (1991) 14 New Zealand Business Law Quarterly 229.

company of which he was the founder and former managing director. The letter stated that Mr Paulger 'personally guarantees that all due payments will be made [good within 90 days]' if the creditors would forbear from pursuing their debts against the company for that period. The company went into receivership and its unsecured creditors, including the plaintiff, remained unpaid. The plaintiff sought to recover from Mr Paulger personally, relying on his letter. The Master held that, objectively, the letter demonstrated an intention to be bound: it was a legal offer that had been accepted by the plaintiff forbearing from suing the debtor-company at Mr Paulger's request. On appeal, Mr Paulger pleaded the Contractual Mistakes Act, arguing both a common and a mutual mistake as to the effect of the letter (the common subject matter being said to be the source of funds for payment of the company's creditors).

As for common mistake under s 6(1)(a)(ii) of the Act, the Court focused on s 6(2)(a) – mistakes as to the interpretation of the relevant contract do not qualify – which indicated that the traditional objective test was to prevail.[90] Mr Paulger's mistake as to the effect of his letter was a mistake in interpretation, and so he could not plead as a mistake an understanding that was different from the plain and ordinary meaning of his letter. Moreover, consistently with what Somers J had said of Mrs Ozolins' mistake in *Conlon v Ozolins*, for there to be a 'common mistake' both parties must have made the same mistake, but here it was only Mr Paulger who was mistaken. The plaintiff was not legally mistaken, because it had understood the letter in precisely the way that an objective bystander would understand it.

As for mutual mistake under s 6(1)(a)(iii) of the Act, Mr Paulger's counsel naturally relied on *Conlon v Ozolins*. However, this time the Court of Appeal held that the plaintiff had made no legally relevant mistake at all. It is no 'mistake', the Court pronounced, simply to believe that the contract meant what it said. Mr Paulger, like Mrs Ozolins before him, was effectively arguing that he did not intend his letter to mean what it plainly did mean, and this was a non-qualifying mistake in the interpretation of the document that ultimately became the contract. The Court distinguished *Conlon v Ozolins* as 'a decision on its particular facts. It is not authority for invoking the Act where one party misunderstood the clearly expressed intention of the other, or where one party meant something different from the plain meaning of his own words.'[91]

It is, with respect, difficult to accept the sincerity of this sidelining of *Conlon v Ozolins* in *Paulger*. Although *Conlon* of course turned on its own facts, as will all 'mistake' cases, it mostly purported to be an exercise in the correct interpretation of s 6(1)(a)(iii) of the Contractual Mistakes Act, to which interpretation the facts

---

90 In their review of the Contractual Mistakes Act, Andrew Beck and Richard Sutton suggested that s 6(2)(a) be repealed, and that the making of an interpretative mistake be a discretionary factor in the exercise of the Court's discretion under s 7; see Beck and Sutton (n 64). The Law Commission declined to adopt that recommendation.

91 [1989] 3 NZLR 549, 554.

of the case were then applied.[92] Nonetheless, it now seems that the objective, 'Smith v Hughes' approach has been judicially reinstated for determining whether a relief-seeking party has made a 'mistake' for the purposes of s 6(1)(a) of the Act.[93]

The Contractual Remedies Act 1979 (NZ)

In my view the most interesting and important of the New Zealand contract-law reform statutes is the (somewhat inaptly named)[94] Contractual Remedies Act. That Act significantly alters the prior law relating to breach of contract and misrepresentation, which law was considered by the framers of the legislation, the Contracts and Commercial Law Reform Committee, to be plagued by complexity and riddled with anomalies. The explanatory note to the Contractual Remedies Bill 1978 disclosed the hope that the Act would rationalise and simplify the law, primarily 'by giving substantially the same remedies for misrepresentation inducing the making of a contract and for the repudiation or breach of a contract'.[95]

At the time of its enactment the Contractual Remedies Act in general aimed to:

- provide new remedies for parties induced to enter into a contract by the misrepresentation of the other party, whether innocent, fraudulent or negligent;
- define when an innocent party may 'cancel' (that is, 'terminate') the contract because of repudiation or a serious misrepresentation or a serious breach by the other party; and
- provide for discretionary remedies or the adjustment of the parties' interests in the event of cancellation of a contract under the Act.

---

92 *Conlon v Ozolins* should rightly have been overturned, but this would have required a Full Court of the Court of Appeal or a higher court. That option was therefore not available to the Court in *Paulger*.

93 Burrows, Finn and Todd (n 69) 272, consider that, despite *Paulger*, *Conlon v Ozolins* remains authoritative on the point that the *Smith v Hughes* objective test has not survived the Contractual Mistakes Act. I do not read *Paulger* in that way. *Conlon* has been marginalised beyond any real precedential value. In *Chatfield v Jones* [1990] 3 NZLR 285, 288, Cooke P indicated that *Conlon v Ozolins* was not 'a standing invitation to any defendant to a contract claim to give evidence that he or she intended a different bargain and misunderstood the document that was signed'. He said he was confident that the members of the *Conlon* Court 'would not have intended to extend any such invitation and that it is important in applying that Act not to overlook that the mistakes covered by it do not include mistakes as to interpretation. Moreover, relief under the Act is discretionary; in administering the Act the integrity of written contracts, particularly in commercial dealings, must be a cardinal consideration.'

94 The Act is not really about 'contractual' *remedies* at all!

95 See generally John Burrows, 'The Contractual Remedies Act 1979' (1980) Canterbury Law Review 82; David McLauchlan, 'Contract Law Reform in New Zealand: the Contractual Remedies Act 1979' (1981) 1 Oxford Journal of Legal Studies 284.

Although in contrast to s 5 of the Contractual Mistakes Act, above, the heading to s 7 of the Contractual Remedies Act does not use the word 'code', s 7(1) nevertheless states that except as otherwise expressly provided by the Act, 'this section shall have effect in place of the rules of the common law and of equity governing the circumstances in which a party to a contract may rescind it, or treat it as discharged, for misrepresentation or repudiation or breach'. It thus constitutes a code, in the sense earlier defined, governing the circumstances in which a party to a contract may determine the contract for pre-contractual misrepresentation, repudiation or breach. The Act's core provisions are not, however, mandatory, for s 5 allows the contracting parties to expressly provide for remedies in relation to those legal liability events otherwise covered by ss 6–10 of the Act. When such express provision has been made, those sections will operate subject to that provision.

Damages (the primary remedy) for pre-contractual misrepresentation, whether innocent or fraudulent, made by or on behalf of the other party to the contract are governed by s 6 of the Act. Under the pre-Act law, damages were only available for *tortious* misrepresentation (that is, deceit or negligent misstatement), and not for purely innocent misrepresentation. Section 6(1)(b), however, provides that no tort action for misrepresentation is available by the misrepresentee against the other party to the contract (although non-party misrepresentors such as agents may still be sued in tort if fraud or negligence exists on their part); and s 6(1)(a) provides that the misrepresentee's damages are to be assessed 'in the same manner and to the same extent as if the representation were a term of the contract that has been broken', even for purely innocent misrepresentation. The misrepresentee's claim is thus governed by the *contract* measure of damages, including the contract test for remoteness.

Needless to say, this is a radical inversion of the wrongdoer's normal legal responsibility for false statements inducing contract, and one that creates a serious disjunctive relationship between the wrong inflicted and the law's response to that wrong. The relationship between wrong and corresponding remedy is thus no longer purely correlative, for the wrong that triggers s 6 is the making of a false causative statement, whereas the remedy under s 6 would suggest that it lies instead in failing to honour it. Rather than prohibiting conduct, therefore, s 6(1) essentially renders a representation binding in the absence of an intention (even an objective intention), on the part of the representor, to assume a legal promissory commitment in relation to the statement. The reason for this transposal of the law's normal responsibility practices is that the Contracts and Commercial Law Reform Committee, on whose 1978 Report and annexed draft bill the Contractual Remedies Act was based,[96] was strongly opposed to the introduction of legal fault criteria as a precondition to liability for misrepresentation under the Act: 'It seems to us that the proper as well as the traditional approach is to look not at whether

---

[96] See Contracts and Commercial Law Reform Committee, *Misrepresentation and Breach of Contract: Report* (1978).

there was any fault on the part of the representor but [rather] at the expectations of the representee that naturally arise from the undertaking.'[97]

Personally I am not a fan of this innovation under the Act, for as Holmes once famously remarked, 'even a dog distinguishes between being stumbled over and being kicked'.[98] The unwavering strict-liability regime of s 6 seems unnecessarily harsh (or at least unresponsive to normatively sensitive dimensions of human responsibility and moral objection),[99] especially in relation to purely innocent misrepresentation. It is also easy to portend situations where outright fraudsters might achieve an undeserved windfall of reduced liability under s 6's mandatory damages model.[100] At least there ought perhaps to be an option within s 6 for the misrepresentee to elect for the tort measure of damages in cases where the contract measure produces an unjust result.[101]

Cancellation for misrepresentation is governed by s 7 of the Contractual Remedies Act, and in that regard the Act subjects misrepresentation to the same rules that apply to breach and repudiation. The old rules of 'rescission' for misrepresentation are thus replaced by a new remedy of 'cancellation', which operates prospectively and not retrospectively.[102] Although the damages regime

---

97 See Contracts and Commercial Law Reform Committee, *Misrepresentation and Breach of Contract: Report* (1967) [9.4.3] (incorporated into the 1978 Report, ibid).

98 Oliver Wendell Holmes, *The Common Law* (Boston, Macmillan, 1882) 3.

99 The common law's differential treatment of innocent and fraudulent misrepresentors, although perhaps messy, did capture well normatively sensitive dimensions of human responsibility and moral objection. Certainly, outside the Contractual Remedies Act, whether the law recognises strict liability for conduct usually depends, at least in part, on the *consequences* of imposing strict liability for conduct. Where the stigma or sanctions are serious, for example deprivation of liberty (under, say, the criminal law) or liability in substantial damages (under, say, tort law), the law ordinarily requires proof of agent-focused fault on the part of the accused or defendant, respectively. Where the consequence of imposing liability is merely State-assisted transaction avoidance or imposition of an enforcement disability, however, it is more palatable (other things being equal) to recognise strict liability for conduct. Generally, see Peter Cane, *Responsibility in Law and Morality* (Hart Publishing, 2002) 82–5 passim, 99, 197–202.

100 The 'bad bargain' situation is obvious one. P agrees to buy goods for $1000 on the strength of D's fraudulent misrepresentation as to their quality. The goods received are worth $500 only. Had D's statement been true, the market value of the goods would only have been $750. Under s 6, P recovers $250 (the amount required to put P in the position she would have been in had D's representation been true), whereas before the Act P would have recovered $500 in tort: the amount required to restore P to her pre-contract position. See also the example given by Francis Dawson and David McLauchlan, *The Contractual Remedies Act 1979* (Sweet & Maxwell, 1981) 31, based on the *Restatement (2d) of Torts*, § 549.

101 Compare the sentiments of Francis Dawson, 'Contractual Remedies Act 1979: Commentary' in New Zealand Law Commission, *Contracts Statutes Review* (NZLC: R 25) (1993) 101, 103 [1.132], 109 [1.150].

102 Section 8(3) provides that, 'Subject to this Act, when a contract is cancelled the following provisions shall apply:

for misrepresentation applies across all contractual contexts, including sales of goods,[103] the cancellation rules do not apply to contracts for the sale of goods,[104] or to contracts for the supply of consumer goods or services.[105] Nothing in the Act affects a party's right to recover damages for breach of contract or repudiation,[106] or the law relating to specific performance or injunction, so the main *remedies* associated with contractual liability are not actually governed by the Act, despite, perhaps, the impression created by its title.

The reader will appreciate the preconditions for cancellation of a contract covered by the Contractual Remedies Act if ss 7(2)–(4) of the Act are reproduced in full:

> (2) Subject to this Act, a party to a contract may cancel it if, by words or conduct, another party repudiates the contract by making it clear that he does not intend to perform his obligations under it or, as the case may be, to complete such performance.
>
> (3) Subject to this Act, but without prejudice to subsection (2) of this section, a party to a contract may cancel it if–
>   (a) He has been induced to enter into it by a misrepresentation, whether innocent or fraudulent, made by or on behalf of another party to that contract; or
>   (b) A term in the contract is broken by another party to that contract; or
>   (c) It is clear that a term in the contract will be broken by another party to that contract.
>
> (4) Where subsection (3)(a) or subsection (3)(b) or subsection (3)(c) of this section applies, a party may exercise the right to cancel if, and only if,–
>   (a) The parties have expressly or impliedly agreed that the truth of the representation or, as the case may require, the performance of the term is essential to him; or

> (a) So far as the contract remains unperformed at the time of the cancellation, no party shall be obliged or entitled to perform it further:
> (b) So far as the contract has been performed at the time of the cancellation, no party shall, by reason only of the cancellation, be divested of any property transferred or money paid pursuant to the contract.'

A party wanting to recover property or money passing under the contract must apply for an order for relief under s 9; it does not happen automatically.

103 Contractual Remedies Act 1979 (NZ), s 6(2).
104 Contractual Remedies Act 1979 (NZ), s 15(d). The rules are governed instead by the Sale of Goods Act 1908 (NZ)
105 Contractual Remedies Act 1979 (NZ), s 15(ga). The rules are governed instead by the Consumer Guarantees Act 1993 (NZ). This underscores the highly fragmented nature of the law relating to the termination of contracts for serious breach or repudiation in New Zealand.
106 Contractual Remedies Act 1979 (NZ), s 10(2).

(b) The effect of the misrepresentation or breach is, or, in the case of an anticipated breach, will be,–
  (i) Substantially to reduce the benefit of the contract to the cancelling party; or
  (ii) Substantially to increase the burden of the cancelling party under the contract; or
  (iii) In relation to the cancelling party, to make the benefit or burden of the contract substantially different from that represented or contracted for.

The main effect of s 7(4) is, within its field of operation, and in contrast to the approach of the majority of the High Court of Australia in *Koompahtoo Local Aboriginal Land Council v Sanpine Pty Ltd*,[107] to dispense with the need for an analysis and classification of contractual provisions as 'conditions', 'intermediate terms' or 'warranties', although the subsection generally absorbs and codifies what was understood to be the general-law position on repudiation and breach before the Act. Obviously, regarding misrepresentation, s 7 significantly alters the prior law relating to 'rescission' of a contract for misrepresentation. It has been conceded that the tests in ss 7(3) and (4) 'are not easy to apply',[108] which, as every antipodean contract lawyer will know, is no different than the common-law tests that preceded them and which continue to govern today in Australia.

If a contract is cancelled under s 7 of the Contractual Remedies Act, s 9 confers upon the court extensive powers to grant, upon application, relief to either party affected by the cancellation 'if it is just and practicable to do so'. Under s 9(2), a relief order may:

(a) Vest in any party to the proceedings, or direct any such party to transfer or assign to any other such party or to deliver to him the possession of, the whole or any part of any real or personal property that was the subject of the contract or was the whole or part of the consideration for it:
(b) Subject to section 6 of this Act, direct any party to the proceedings to pay to any other such party such sum as the Court thinks just:
(c) Direct any party to the proceedings to do or refrain from doing in relation to any other party any act or thing as the Court thinks just.

Subject to s 5 'contracting out' (above), and various bona-fide-purchaser and change-of-position protections in ss 9(5) and (6) of the Act, relief under s 9 is

---

107 *Koompahtoo Local Aboriginal Land Council v Sanpine Pty Ltd* (2007) 233 CLR 115 (HCA) (Gleeson CJ, Gummow, Heydon and Crennan JJ). Kirby J dissented and proposed a classification of terms that is consistent with s 7 of the Contractual Remedies Act.

108 John F Burrows, 'Contractual Remedies Act 1979' in New Zealand Law Commission, *Contracts Statutes Review* (NZLC: R 25) (1993) 61, 71 [1.33].

entirely a matter for the court's discretion. In exercising that discretion, s 9(4) mandates that the court must have regard to:

(a) The terms of the contract; and
(b) The extent to which any party to the contract was or would have been able to perform it in whole or in part; and
(c) Any expenditure incurred by a party in or for the purpose of the performance of the contract; and
(d) The value, in its opinion, of any work or services performed by a party in or for the purpose of the performance of the contract; and
(e) Any benefit or advantage obtained by a party by reason of anything done by another party in or for the purpose of the performance of the contract; and
(f) Such other matters as it thinks proper.

Mention might finally be made of s 4 of the Contractual Remedies Act ('Statements during negotiations for a contract'), which limits the effectiveness of acknowledgement clauses, entire-agreement clauses, integration clauses, and the like.[109] Such clauses routinely feature as boilerplate in formal contracts. Section 4 renders such clauses automatically ineffective unless the enforcing party can satisfy the court that, having regard to such matters as the subject matter and value of the transaction, the relative bargaining strengths of the parties, the presence or otherwise of legal advice or representation, the manner of drafting (negotiated or boilerplate), it is 'fair and reasonable' that the clause should be conclusive as between the parties. In my view s 4 is quite a neat solution to the problem of boilerplate 'entire agreement' (and so on) clauses in signed contracts, which in Australia[110] and the United Kingdom[111] are generally considered binding and

---

[109] Section 4 applies only to statements made during negotiations for a contract where a term in the contract purports to deny that any pre-contractual statements were made, or, if they were, that they were terms of the contract, or that they were relied on by the other party. It does not catch contractual provisions that simply purport to exclude liability for misrepresentation or breach of contract. See generally David W McLauchlan, 'Merger and Acknowledgment Clauses under the Contractual Remedies Act 1979' (1988) 19 Victoria University of Wellington Law Review 311.

[110] *Johnson Matthey Ltd v AC Rochester Overseas Corp* (1990) 23 NSWLR 190, 196 (McLelland J, reviewing the authorities). See generally Elisabeth Peden and John W Carter, 'Entire Agreement — and Similar — Clauses' (2006) 22 Journal of Contract Law 1.

[111] *AXA Sun Life Services Plc v Campbell Martin Ltd* [2011] EWCA Civ 133, [2011] CLC 312 [34], following *Springwell Navigation Corp v J P Morgan Chase Bank* [2010] EWCA Civ 12, [2010] CLC 705. This ignores the English Law Commission's preference against the conclusiveness of such clauses: English Law Commission, *The Parol Evidence Rule* (Law Com No 154, 1986) [2.15]. See generally David McLauchlan, 'The Entire Agreement Clause: Conclusive or a Question of Weight?' (2012) 128 Law Quarterly Review 521; Matthew Barber, 'The Limits of Entire Agreement Clauses' [2012] Journal of Business Law 486.

effective in accordance with their terms. It avoids unnecessary resort by counsel and the courts to artificial circumventing machinations such as conventional[112] and promissory[113] estoppel, although there has been a lessening of the need for such avoidance devices in connection with standard-form 'consumer' contracts in Australia since the Australian Consumer Law came into operation in 2011.[114]

The Contractual Remedies Act has not been without its critics. Reynolds, for example, has opined that 'the Act seems an interesting experiment, but not necessarily one to emulate'.[115] However, for the most part it seems to have worked fairly well – especially if the Contractual Mistakes Act is the comparator![116] Still, some unexpected consequences have followed from individual judicial interpretations of the Act's provisions. For sometimes the courts have used Parliament's prefatory statement in the Contractual Remedies Act – that it is 'An Act to *reform* the law relating to remedies for misrepresentation and breach of contract'[117] – to 'resist attempts to reintroduce into a reforming statute limitations associated with earlier principles of common law and equity'.[118] On other occasions, however, the courts have resisted applying the apparently clear words of the Act because, '[i]f Parliament had intended to change the common law in [an] important respect, a clear statement to that effect could have been expected in the legislation'.[119]

---

112 *Whittet v State Bank of New South Wales* (1991) 24 NSWLR 146.

113 *Franklins Pty Ltd v Metcash Trading Ltd* (2009) 264 ALR 15 [34] (Allsop P), [554] (Campbell JA); *Saleh v Romanous* [2010] NSWCA 274 [57] (Handley AJA, Giles JA and Sackville AJA agreeing).

114 Under the Australian Consumer Law ('ACL'), which is Schedule 2 to the Competition and Consumer Act 2010 (Cth), unfair contract terms in standard-form consumer contracts are declared void (s 23). Section 25 of the ACL contains a non-exhaustive, indicative 'grey-list' of examples of types of terms that may be unfair, including '(l) a term that limits, or has the effect of limiting, the evidence one party can adduce in proceedings relating to the contract'.

115 Reynolds (n 21) 22.

116 In his paper on the Act appended to the New Zealand Law Commission 1993 Report, Professor Burrows pointed out that the Act has 'attracted a fair amount of criticism, on the ground that [its] rules were far too simple, indeed crude, to adequately replace the subtlety and complexity of the common law. Some feared that the law of breach of contract would be distorted by forcing it into such a simplistic framework. There were also fears that some of the Act's rules were based on a misunderstanding of common law principle; and that the Act gave too much discretion in an area where certainty and predictability are important values.' See Burrows (n 108) 61 [1.01]. However, Professor Burrows went on immediately to conclude that '10 years of litigation have not thrown up as many problems as some have feared': ibid 61 [1.02].

117 Emphasis supplied.

118 *Newmans Tours Ltd v Ranier Investments Ltd* [1992] 2 NZLR 68 (HC), 90 (Fisher J).

119 *Garratt v Ikeda* [2002] 1 NZLR 577 (CA), 582 [15] (Tipping J).

An example of the first kind of interpretation is *Newmans Tours Ltd v Ranier Investments Ltd*,[120] where Fisher J used s 9 of the Act ('Power of court to grant relief') to make an award in the nature of *damages*,[121] when the framers of the Act (the Contracts and Commercial Law Reform Committee) had in mind restitution of money or reimbursement of services – that is, an adjustment of the parties' interests after cancellation – rather than conferral of the benefit promised by the terms of the contract.[122] One of the former members of the Contracts and Commercial Law Reform Committee, Professor Coote,[123] has cogently criticised Fisher J's reasoning in *Newmans Tours*. He points out[124] that the intention of s 9 was to enable the granting of *relief* – that is, *releasing* a party either from the consequences that would ordinarily follow from enforcement or from some incident of the contract itself or the general law – rather than providing a new form of primary remedy for the *enforcement* of a contract (that is, damages or debt).[125] It scarcely makes sense that Parliament would have intended the courts to have a discretion to award damages at large under s 9(2)(b) of the Act when it was at such pains, in s 10(1) of the Act, to preserve damages at common law, which are recoverable as of right.[126] Despite that logic, though, the Court of Appeal has subsequently endorsed Fisher J's views,[127] producing what can only best be described as an 'illustration of [the New Zealand courts'] ... use of the contract statutes for the purpose of what might be characterised as judicial reform by a sidewind'.[128]

An example of the second kind of interpretation is *Garratt v Ikeda*.[129] There, Mr Garratt had agreed unconditionally to purchase Mr Ikeda's residential property for $1.83 million. A 10 per cent deposit was payable under the agreement by way of three instalments. Garratt paid the first two instalments (totalling $50,000) but

---

120   *Newmans Tours Ltd v Ranier Investments Ltd* [1992] 2 NZLR 68.

121   And one that is guided, but not necessarily constrained, by the strict common law principles applying to the award of damages for breach of contract!

122   See Contracts and Commercial Law Reform Committee, *Misrepresentation and Breach of Contract: Report* (1978) 22.

123   Brian Coote, 'Remedy and Relief under the Contractual Remedies Act 1979 (NZ)' (1993) 6 Journal of Contract Law 141.

124   ibid 147. Compare also Brian Coote, 'The Changing New Zealand Law of Damages in Contract' (1996) 9 Journal of Contract Law 159, 161: 'From a relief provision designed to be of modest scope, the courts have fashioned a completely new discretionary remedy for enforcement, occupying the whole ground previously covered only by the common law of damages, but untrammelled by the constraints of the common law.'

125   See also Coote (n 52) 186.

126   Coote (n 123) 148. Space does not permit mention of the other arguments Coote provides to show why, within the scheme of the Act, Fisher J's interpretation of s 9 is problematic: generally see ibid 146–8.

127   See *Thomson v Ranier* [1993] 1 NZLR 408, 410 (Cooke P) and *Coxhead v Newmans Tours Ltd* (1993) 6 TCLR 1.

128   Coote (n 123) 156.

129   *Garratt v Ikeda* [2002] 1 NZLR 577 (CA).

defaulted on the third of $130,000. Ikeda eventually cancelled the contract under s 7 of the Contractual Remedies Act and forfeited the $50,000 that had already been paid. He also resold the property for $400,000 more than Garratt had agreed to pay for it. Despite his good fortune, Ikeda sued Garratt for the unpaid deposit balance of $130,000. One argument that Garratt raised in his defence was that s 8(3)(a) of the Contractual Remedies Act meant that his obligation to pay had been extinguished by Ikeda's cancellation.

On a literal reading of s 8(3)(a), one might be excused for thinking that Garratt's defence had substance. Section 8(3)(a) states:

> (3) Subject to this Act, when a contract is cancelled the following provisions shall apply:
>   (a) So far as the contract remains unperformed at the time of the cancellation, no party shall be obliged or entitled to perform it further: ...

However, Tipping J (for the Court if Appeal) held that, correctly interpreted, s 8(3)(a) did not have the effect of divesting rights that had unconditionally accrued before the event of cancellation. That was consistent with the pre-Act, general-law position,[130] and the Court stated that, 'the words of s 8(3)(a) are simply not strong enough to demonstrate a legislative intent to take away a right which already exists on an unconditional basis at the time of cancellation. ... [Section] 8(3)(a) should not readily be construed in such a way as to take away rights which would have existed prior to its enactment.'[131] Thus, s 8(3)(a) did not mean what it appears to say and Ikeda was free to recover the balance of the deposit from Garratt.[132]

It can thus be difficult to predict how the courts will respond to and interpret codal provision once they have been enacted, no matter how clear the drafting or apparent intentions of the original framers might be. This is, of course, a hazard with all legislation and not just codes in particular, but codes do seem to attract an extra element of controversy over just how far they ought to be seen as exclusive repositories of the authoritative law.[133] Perhaps, it might be suggested, all codes (in common-law legal systems, at least) are 'partial' in the sense that the prior law might inevitably require to be consulted in order to fill in gaps that

---

130 Reference was specifically made to the High Court of Australia case of *McDonald v Dennys Lascelles Ltd* (1933) 48 CLR 457.

131 [2002] 1 NZLR 577, 584–5 [22].

132 Garratt also claimed s 9 relief but lost on the basis that, by providing for a 'deposit', the parties had contracted out of s 9 (that is, forfeiture of a deposit was an 'express provision' for a remedy falling within s 5 of the Act), and otherwise 'justice' did not require s 9 relief, as Garratt, by signing an unconditional contract before securing his finance, had simply taken a business risk and lost. The merits of the case have been hotly debated between Professors McLauchlan and Watts: [2002] New Zealand Law Review 1–47.

133 See text to nn 36–48.

appear in the code (intentionally or otherwise) or to elucidate unclear or technical terms left undefined by the code (intentionally or otherwise). Even when those situations do not obtain, courts might, when interpreting a code, simply be unable to resist the allure of the pre-existing common law: 'old habits die hard'.[134] This has certainly been true of the New Zealand contract-law codes, especially the Contractual Remedies Act, which assumes rather than supplies the meaning of important legal concepts falling within the scheme of the Act. Hence, for example, it has been assumed that the common-law meaning, hence criteria, of actionable misrepresentation has not been affected by the Act,[135] and that that meaning and those criteria continue to govern the threshold 'liability' questions in this area. Presumably, too, the concept of 'affirmation' in s 7(5) of the Act[136] bears its common-law meaning, as it is not legislatively defined. This, however, does little to improve the accessibility, user-friendliness or predictability of the code, as every lawyer knows that the concepts of misrepresentation and affirmation can be highly normatively complex, and that they continue today to be attended by various practical and theoretical uncertainties or problems.[137]

At times the Contractual Remedies Act, while clearly intending to codify the common law in the field, nevertheless portrays a slightly modified meaning to fundamental terms or concepts used under the pre-Act law while still omitting to define those terms or concepts. This can make it very difficult to predict and advise the outcomes of disputes under the Act, especially when the courts have not

---

134 Burrows (n 108) 94 [1.109]. Burrows opines that such a practice by the courts is both 'inevitable' and, in the interests of consistency in the law, not 'undesirable' (ibid).

135 In other words, it has been assumed that the Act does not create legal sanctions for misrepresentation where none existed before. This is entirely consistent with the intention of the Committee that drafted the bill that became the Contractual Remedies Act; see Contracts and Commercial Law Reform Committee (n 96) 82 ('In this context [s 6 of the Act] the terms "representation" and "misrepresentation" are intended to have their common law meanings'). The courts have also taken this view. See *Ware v Johnson* [1984] 2 NZLR 518, 537 (Prichard J); *NZ Motor Bodies Ltd v Emslie* [1985] 2 NZLR 569, 593 (Barker J); *King v Wilkinson* (1994) 2 NZ Conv C 191,828, 191,832 (Holland J). The position is identical in relation to the Misrepresentation Act 1967 (UK), which also does not define 'misrepresentation' for its purposes; see *Andre & Cie SA v Ets Michel Blanc Fils* [1979] 2 Lloyd's Rep 427, 435 (Geoffrey Lane J). In his paper on the Act appended to the New Zealand Law Commercial 1993 Report, Professor Burrows opined that 'nothing is to be gained by codifying a definition of misrepresentation': Burrows (n 108) 66 [1.13].

136 Section 7(5) of the Contractual Remedies Act reads: 'A party shall not be entitled to cancel the contract if, with full knowledge of the repudiation or misrepresentation or breach, he has affirmed the contract.'

137 Essentially, the common law required proof of (a) a positively made statement of past or existing *fact* (a 'representation', express or implied), that (b) was *false* or *misleading*, and (c) *induced* entry into the contract in question. There are, of course, many 'contestables' underlying each of those criteria (such as materiality, intention to induce, the nature of 'fact', and so on). As for the difficulties surrounding the 'affirmation' concept, see Bigwood (n 10).

themselves assumed responsibility for amplifying the important term or concept at hand. An obvious example is the concept of 'substantiality', which is employed in both the Contractual Mistakes Act, s 6(1)(b) (in relation to the impact of a qualifying mistake upon the exchange values or the benefits or burdens relative to the associated consideration at the time of contract formation), and the Contractual Remedies Act, s 7(4)(b) (in relation to the need for substantial reduction of benefit or increase in burden with respect to the cancelling party as a precondition to cancellation). Despite being central to triggering key legal powers under each Act, neither Parliament nor the courts in their administration of the legislation have defined the concept of 'substantiality' or provided a precise test in relation to it. Although the idea of 'substantial reduction of benefit' under s 7(4)(b)(i) of the Contract Remedies Act, for example,[138] draws on the common law as set out in *Hongkong Fir Shipping v Kawasaki Kisen Kaisha*,[139] a less exacting standard is probably intended under the Act.[140] The courts, however, have refused to define the term 'substantially' with any greater precision than Parliament has.[141] So we are told, for example, that the question of whether a breach or misrepresentation is 'substantial' for the purposes of the Contractual Remedies Act 'is a matter of fact, degree and impression' and 'incapable of any kind of arithmetical analysis',[142] that it 'has the same flavour as "significantly" and "considerably"'[143] but is 'something more than trivial or minimal',[144] and that '[i]t calls for a robust value judgment which must in the end be somewhat arbitrary'.[145] Thank you for that. What remains is a lack of critical guidance to cancelling parties who, in the absence of agreement as to the essentiality of the misrepresentation or of the term breached, remain extremely vulnerable to misjudging the effects of a breach or misrepresentation on their material interests under the contract, and hence to being in repudiation if they in fact do so. Although the local textbook writers may well be right that 'it is not easy to see how any legislative solution could do much better [than the common law, which gave rise to precisely the same difficulty]',[146] this underscores the limitations of codes as a universal corrective for inaccessibility and uncertainty in the common law; for even under codal provisions rights-holders will often be

---

138 In *Realty Services Holdings Ltd v Slater* (2006) 6 NZCPR 657, the court applied to 'substantiality' under the Contractual Mistakes Act the observations of the court in *MacIndoe v Mainzeal Group Ltd* [1991] 3 NZLR 273 (CA) re 'substantiality' under the Contractual Remedies Act. See (n 142).

139 *Hongkong Fir Shipping v Kawasaki Kisen Kaisha* [1962] 2 QB 26.

140 See *Oxborough v North Harbour Builders Ltd* [2002] 1 NZLR 145 (CA), 153 (statutory criteria possibly 'a little less onerous' than those in *Hongkong Fir*).

141 See *Jolly v Palmer* [1985] 1 NZLR 685, 662 (Hardie Boys J).

142 *MacIndoe v Mainzeal Group Ltd* [1991] 3 NZLR 273, 284–5 (Richardson J).

143 ibid.

144 *Jolly v Palmer* [1985] 1 NZLR 685, 662 (Hardie Boys J).

145 *Betham v Margetts* [1996] 2 NZLR 708 (Fisher J). This is a sale of goods case that should not have had the statutory tests applied to it.

146 Burrows, Finn and Todd (n 69) 585.

heavily reliant on legal advisers who are sufficiently steeped in the (possibly very large) jurisprudence generated under the code as to be well placed to proffer sound guidance on the risks and decisional strategies relating to the exercise of rights and powers created by the code.

A Brief Excursus: The BCLI Report on Proposals for Unfair Contracts Relief

In September 2011 the British Columbia Law Institute (BCLI) published its *Report on Proposals for Unfair Contracts Relief*.[147] The Report recommends a 'Contract Fairness Act' for British Columbia, the main object of which is to 'guard against exploitation'.[148] The aim of the reform, however, is not to effectuate a 'radical overhaul or complete codification of all contract law's general rules dealing with fairness';[149] rather, it is to:

> ... clarif[y] vexing ambiguities in the application of unconscionability, duress, and undue influence, create [...] a framework to integrate those concepts, include [...] a definition of 'good faith,' provide [...] for a duty of good faith in the performance of contracts, and address [...] concerns about remedies for misrepresentation.[150]

Interestingly, the reform initiative is based largely on an explicitly tentative (and ultimately flawed[151]) model proposed by the New Zealand Law Commission in 1990,[152] which model was abandoned by that organisation in 1996.[153]

The relevance of the BCLI's Report to this chapter is twofold. First, the provincial Act would, if enacted, provide an additional example of the partial codification of fundamental aspects of domestic contract law, and one that is quite ambitious given the complexity and essential contestability of its subject matter. There is, however, no clear statement in the draft legislation that the Act is to function as a 'code'. Section 2 essentially provides that there can be no contracting out of the Act's provisions; and s 4 states that 'Nothing in this Act limits or affects the law relating to torts, unjust enrichment or breach of fiduciary duty'.

---

147 British Columbia Law Institute, Report No 60: *Report on Proposals for Unfair Contracts Relief* (2011). The Report was prepared for the BCLI by the Members of the Unfair Contracts Relief Project Committee. The proposed Contract Fairness Act is appended as Appendix B to the Report.
148 ibid 21.
149 ibid xi. See also ibid 15.
150 ibid.
151 David W McLauchlan, 'Unfair Contracts — The Law Commission's Draft Scheme' (1991) New Zealand Recent Law Review 311.
152 New Zealand Law Commission, *'Unfair' Contracts: A Discussion Paper* (NZLC PP11) (1990).
153 See New Zealand Law Commission, *Annual Report* (NZLC R36) (1996), Appendix G.

That last provision, though, highlights just how 'difficult [it can be] to engage with ambiguities and inconsistencies in the law of contract without trespassing into other core sub-fields of private law'.[154] The intention of the drafters[155] here is to follow the *Restatement (Third) of Restitution and Unjust Enrichment*,[156] but ironically that *Restatement* views at least two of the doctrines caught by the proposed Act (duress and undue influence) as independent bases of liability in *unjust enrichment*, rather than as belonging to the general law of restitution for wrongs.[157]

That point leads to the second way in which the Report is germane to this subject matter of this chapter. Much as the New Zealand contract-law codes have demonstrated, the BCLI's attempt to formulate a partial code in relation to the fairness-based doctrines of contract law underscores just how difficult it can be to avoid unintended (and potentially highly undesirable) consequences when reforming significant contract-law doctrines that are perceived to be deficient in some way. For although, according to the BCLI's Report, no 'radical reform' is intended, that would certainly be the consequence of the Act's implementation, especially in relation to the announced 'centrepiece'[158] of the proposed legislation: the general test of contractual unfairness in Part 2, which basically attempts to combine unconscionable dealing, duress and undue influence into a single test of 'contractual unfairness'. To be sure, even when the drafters are explicitly attempting merely to *restate* the law (for reasons of greater public accessibility) rather than reform it, they occasionally get the prior law wrong (or at least state it less accurately than it ought to be), with the consequence that, were such inaccuracies to be carried through to enactment, the law would be unintentionally altered.

Space permits of just a couple of examples of the above phenomena, although many more could be cited.[159] Section 5 of the proposed Act contains the general test for 'contractual unfairness', and it requires proof of *both* procedural unfairness *and* substantive unfairness before relief can be granted under the Act. This is true both for duress (s 6(c)) and undue influence (s 6(d)) situations, but neither of those general-law doctrines currently requires proof of substantive unfairness as an ingredient of the respective complaints.[160] Nor would it make sense that they

---

154 Doris (n 17) 25.
155 See (n 147) 23.
156 American Law Institute, *Restatement (3d) of Restitution and Unjust Enrichment* (2011).
157 ibid vol 1, ch 1, § 1, p 3.
158 See (n 147) 15.
159 For more, see Rick Bigwood, 'Fairness Awry? Reflections on the BCLI's Report on Proposals for Unfair Contracts Relief' (2012) 52 Canadian Business Law Journal 197.
160 I have never seen a case of duress turn on whether the impugned contract was substantively unfair to the victim (although that is usually empirically the case), and substantive unfairness is not an ingredient of undue influence either. The House of Lords in *CIBC Mortgages Plc v Pitt* [1994] 1 AC 200 (HL) held that it was not an element of actual (Class 1) undue influence, and the same court in *Royal Bank of Scotland Plc v Etridge (No 2)* [2002] 2 AC 773 (HL) made it clear that the presence of manifest disadvantage (or the now

did, as both doctrines respond to the lack of voluntariness implicit in the impugned transaction. They are concerned with the procedural injustice of a 'production by malign means of an intention to act',[161] rather than with the ostensible outcome of that intention's implementation when compared to similar transactions in the marketplace. What follows, then, if the proposed Act were to pass into law, is that relief may be denied where it ought to be allowed and, on the best view of the existing law in the field, *is* actually allowed. The regime thus does not represent the 'modest' reform proposal touted by the authors of the Report: a case, it seems, of unintended consequences caused by a basic failure on the part of the framers of the sponsored legislation to properly understand the prior law targeted by the reforms.

Another potential example of unintended reform, but this time where there is no actual intention on the part of the drafters to reform the law at all, can be seen in s 13 of the draft Contract Fairness Act. Section 13 is intended to capture all those legal situations where non-disclosure of a material fact during contract formation is tantamount to actionable misrepresentation. The Act's framers are explicit that their intention here is restatement rather than reform: 'this section presents a snapshot of the law as it currently exists, rather than a reformed statement of the law'.[162] But if this 'snapshot' of the law proves not to be accurate, and the Act were to be enacted in its current form, unintended reform would surely follow. Take, for instance, s 13(a), which is intended to capture cases of 'supervening falsification': situations where a continuing representation, though perfectly true when made, had become substantially false by the time it induced the representee to enter into the contract in question. The relevant provisions of the draft s 13 read:

Non-disclosure as misrepresentation
(13) In the following cases, non-disclosure by a person (the "first person") of a material fact known to him or her before or at the time the first person makes a contract with another person (the "second person") is deemed to be a misrepresentation that the material fact does not exist:
(a) if the first person knows that disclosure of the fact is necessary to prevent some previous assertion from being a misrepresentation; ...

The problem here is that s 13(a) seems to suggest that the first party must know not only of the subsequent falsification of his or her originally true statement, but also that she or he has come under a legal responsibility to correct it (because correction

---

preferred 'ordinary motives' test from *Allcard v Skinner* (1887) 36 Ch D 145, 185 (Lindley LJ)) serves in a forensic capacity only, as constituting part of the factual matrix that arouses a suspicion over the impugned transaction sufficient to generate a 'presumption' that undue influence actually occurred *inter se*, and is not an integrant of the 'wrong' of undue influence itself: [2002] 2 AC 773 [29] (Lord Nicholls), [104] (Lord Hobhouse), [220] (Lord Scott).

161 *Tanwar Enterprises Pty Ltd v Cauchi* (2003) 217 CLR 315 (HCA), 325 [23] (Gleeson CJ, McHugh, Gummow, Hayne and Heydon JJ).

162 See (n 147) 40.

is 'necessary' to prevent the second party from continuing under a false belief down to the time of contract formation). But although the drafters, quite rightly, cite *With v O'Flanagan*[163] as the 'classic example' of the targeted phenomenon and legal approach,[164] Lord Wright MR in that case explicitly acknowledges the possibility of a misrepresentation resulting from *purely innocent* non-disclosure of a known subsequent falsification:

> ... because the failure to disclose, though wrong and a breach of duty, may be due to inadvertence or a failure to realise that the duty rests upon the party who has made the representation not to leave the other party under an error when the representation has become falsified by a change of circumstances.[165]

The fact is that the law relating to misrepresentation by way of subsequent falsification is nuanced and normatively complex.[166] Such subtlety and complexity is certainly not captured by the current draft s 13(a), with the consequence that the law would become even more impoverished than it presently is if the Contract Fairness Act were to be enacted in its current form. Paragraph (a) of s 13 should be redrafted simply to read: '... (a) if disclosure of the fact would be necessary to prevent a continuing representation, which had previously been made, from becoming a misrepresentation.'

3 Lessons from New Zealand (and British Columbia)?

> [I]t is one thing for those who draft statutes to intend a particular result and quite another to achieve it.[167]

The problems affecting the partial codification of contract law in common-law legal systems are more or less identical to those perceived to plague the comprehensive codification of the same, except that the comparative modesty of the former makes it appear more manageable and attractive. And so it is, to a considerable extent. But virtually all of the problems that confront the drafters of wholesale (national) contract-law codes challenge the drafters of minor ones

---

163 *With v O'Flanagan* [1936] 1 Ch 575 (CA).
164 See (n 147) 41.
165 [1936] 1 Ch 575, 584. Possibilities are that the representor, when he came under the duty, may have honestly, but mistakenly, believed that the representee had also learned of the change of circumstances, or the representor may have forgotten the representation originally made by him. See, for example, *Jones v Dumbrell*, [1981] VR 199, 203 (Smith J).
166 Generally see Rick Bigwood, 'Pre-contractual Misrepresentation and the Limits of the Principle in *With v. O'Flanagan*' (2005) 64 Cambridge Law Journal 94.
167 Brian Coote, 'The Contractual Mistakes Act as a Code: Some Further Thoughts' (2002) 8 New Zealand Business Law Quarterly 223, 225.

as well. For even if a nation such as Australia could agree that codification (or similar) is a suitable methodological device for organising all or parts of its domestic contract law, it will inevitably be difficult to secure agreement on the *regulatory content* of the particular code (or similar) drafted – the more so when many minds and personalities are associated with the project.

The New Zealand contract-law codes are living examples of the challenges and successes of partial codifications of domestic contract law in a common-law legal system, and perhaps the BCLI-sponsored 'Contract Fairness Act' for British Columbia will be, too, if it is ever enacted as law in that province. The lessons that Australia can learn from those foreign experimentations with the partial codification of contract law are several.

First, effective new law cannot be drafted without an excellent (and non-idiosyncratic) working knowledge of the old law. The Contracts and Commercial Law Reform Committee behind the three contract-law partial codes in New Zealand was composed of senior scholars, lawyers and judges who clearly, judging by the quality of the reports produced in advance of the legislation, had an excellent comprehension of the prior law they were trying to reform. But they were a committee, the members of which did not necessarily share the same conceptual and policy starting points, and so compromises in settling the new law were inevitable from the start. Others were introduced during the legislative process as well. The end product, therefore, was never going to represent 'ideal law' (if that were even a measurable and attainable goal). Where the drafters of partial codes are less secure in their comprehension of the prior law being reformed or subsumed by the code, as I would argue the authors of the BCLI *Report on Proposals for Unfair Contracts Relief* were in the number of important areas, then all the compromises are built upon a foundation of a compromised version of the existing order, and suboptimal (albeit unintended) law reform must inevitably follow.[168]

Second, choices must be made as to the scope, detail and the level of exclusivity of the intended partial code. As for scope, one rather obvious precondition for partial codification is that the area being partially codified must be suitably 'discrete'. Reynolds has remarked that '[w]here the topic is not sufficiently discrete, statutes ... [of limited scope, cutting knots in which the law finds itself], as in New Zealand, turn out to have unexpectedly wide results. Experiments of this sort are easier in small countries or states of federations than in larger, unitary countries.'[169] Reynolds' last point strikes me as a fair one, especially for a large federation like Australia. Moreover, the less discrete the branch of contract law being codified, the greater the risk of trespass into other sub-fields of private law, as the BCLI-sponsored Contract Fairness Act perhaps illustrates, and as both the

---

168 This is not to suggest that unintended reform necessarily produces bad law, but as I have argued elsewhere in relation to the BCLI proposal (see Bigwood (n 159)), parts of the Contract Fairness Act, if it were to become law, would certainly produce a less just contractual order than the one that preceded it.

169 Reynolds (n 21) 27.

Contractual Mistakes Act and Contractual Remedies Act clearly do (the last Act intentionally so).

Trickier, perhaps, are the choices that relate to the detail and exclusivity of the intended partial code. The special challenge that confronts those entrusted with drafting a code, it has been said, is that

> ... the draftsman must not only find some passage or other between the Scylla of vague generalities and the Charybdis of mathematical precision. He must do more. He must steer the best course available by finding language that strikes an apt balance between certainty and flexibility and facilitates the orderly development of the law without unduly fettering judicial creativity.[170]

And there lies the rub. For once the decision has been made to codify, different levels of generality or particularisation are available to the draftsperson to effectuate the code's objectives.[171] The Attorney-General's Discussion Paper acknowledges this as well: 'One issue to consider would be the extent to which a restatement or codification should seek to go into detail (lessening its accessibility) or should confine itself to high-level principles (which might undermine predictability).'[172] Clearly, the New Zealand Parliament elected for codification that reflects the 'general-and-simple rules' end of the spectrum. One advantage of this approach has been the avoidance of risks sometimes associated with very detailed codes, namely, that they become rigid, stale and uncertain over time, and that they require continuous review by a suitable overseeing body. Also, as one commentator and former member of the Contracts and Commercial Law Reform Committee has suggested, 'a code is not usually designed to include every detail – so that if it is silent it is defective. Indeed, a mass of detailed rules is ... the antithesis of a practical code.'[173]

On top of its general-and-simple-rules approach to the partial codification of contract, the New Zealand legislature has also entrusted the judiciary with very broad leeways of choice in the administration of the codal provisions, essentially to allow for individualised justice as the case requires. Although this might be seen as an attempt 'to solve some of [the practical problems of codification] by

---

170 Kötz (n 28) 9.

171 Obviously the subject area being codified will dictate the outcome of the choice made in this connection. As Kötz (n 28) 10, has observed, 'tax law, industrial safety legislation, and building regulations must aim at a most precise enunciation of rights and duties, even at the expense of simplicity and clarity. In the law of contract and tort, on the other hand, and in commercial law and other more traditional areas of the common law, the statute, call it a code or not, can often do no more than lay down guiding principles lest the vitality and flexibility needed in these fields be lost.'

172 Discussion Paper (n 1) 19 [6.4].

173 BJ (Jim) Cameron, note to New Zealand Law Commission after March 1991 meeting, quoted Burrows (n 108) 95, fn 23.

not fully addressing them',[174] it might equally be thought that 'the most successful kind of reform is likely to be of the enabling variety, releasing the courts from self-imposed restrictions but leaving them as far as possible free to deal with unforeseen circumstances'.[175] There has been little in the way of enduring evidence that this approach has led to greater uncertainty or unpredictability than existed before the partial codes, at least since the legal profession has grown familiar with their workings and applications, but it really has done little to improve significantly on the coherence and harmonisation of contract law in New Zealand. Also, as private international lawyers will tell us, entrusting local judges with so much discretion can produce problems whenever a foreign court is required to exercise a discretion conferred by a domestic statute.[176]

Now, a rather obvious consequence of New Zealand's decision to elect for a general-and-simple-rules type of partial codification is that its codes can in no way be considered 'exclusive', despite 'exclusivity' sometimes being regarded as a core element of codification. As discussed above, the whole Contractual Remedies Act, for example, is premised on the unstated infrastructure of the common law. This is largely because key concepts within that Act, such as 'repudiation', 'breach', 'misrepresentation', 'affirmation' and 'substantiality', can only be understood against the backdrop of their common-law meaning and significance; hence, such concepts underlie and inform the code, rendering it necessarily 'partial'.[177] The same can be said for the objective '*Smith v Hughes*' principle at common law, which, after the initial hiccup in *Conlon v Ozolins*, now informs the process of screening mistakes for consideration under the Contractual Mistakes Act.[178]

There can be, I would suggest, no conceptual objection to using common-law concepts, rules or principles indirectly or analogically under a contract-law code, provided that such a use is within the purpose and spirit of the particular code.[179] However, it must be conceded that the simpler and more general the provisions of the code, the more room is left for judicial exegesis of a 'creative' variety, with the attendant possibility of unintended judicial reform. This is the third lesson

---

174 Swain (2012) (n 22) 54.
175 Waddams (n 17) 199. To be sure, the New Zealand contract statutes have been described as 'not an enduring code, so much as a liberating device': Richard Sutton, 'Commentary on "Codification, Law Reform and Judicial Development"' (1996) 9 Journal of Contract Law 200, 201.
176 See Dick Webb, 'Heaven Help the Overseas Contract Lawyers' [1979] New Zealand Law Journal 442; Reynolds (n 21) 24–5; David J Goddard, 'New Zealand's Contract Statutes: International Transactions' in New Zealand Law Commission, *Contracts Statutes Review* (NZLC: R 25) (1993) 239, 247–51.
177 Generally see Dawson (n 101) 106 [1.141]. The same is true for the Contractual Mistakes Act; see McLauchlan (n 65) 195, text accompanying fn 5.
178 See discussion in text to nn 77–93.
179 Obviously, if codes are not read with their purpose and spirit in mind, they fail to function as the central and dominant source of law, which *is* one of the core defining elements of codification.

that the New Zealand contract-law codes can offer Australia. For no matter how meticulous the drafters have tried to be in framing the codes, or no matter how clear the apparent 'spirit' of the codes or particular provisions within them, it is not always possible to foresee or control how the official administrators of the codes will eventually interpret and apply them, which has done little to advance the desiderata of predictability and public access to the law. Of course, this problem is exacerbated once the legal methodological decision is made not to define or flesh out key concepts within the governing code, not to mention conferring large amounts of discretion upon the courts, as is the case with both the Contractual Remedies Act and the Contractual Mistakes Act. So it can come as no surprise, then, that both statutes have produced the occasional 'rogue' decision from the courts – examples of the Acts leading to 'judicial reform by a sidewind'.[180]

A fourth lesson from the New Zealand contract-law codes experience is that it is sometimes nigh impossible, even via a code, to improve upon the common law or to make decisions any more predictable than they were under the previous law. But this difficulty is usually inherent in the subject matter itself (for example, 'mistake' or the tests in ss 7(3) and (4) of the Contractual Remedies Act), rather than in the legal methodology chosen for regulating it. Sometimes, however, it has not been; and the failure of Parliament to define key terms or concepts in both the Contractual Mistakes Act and the Contractual Remedies Act has produced litigation that might otherwise have been avoided.

A fifth lesson for Australia is that partial codification, because it is *ex necessitate* non-comprehensive, can leave the law in a fragmented, and hence very complex, state. This is especially true of the New Zealand partial codes, which, we have seen, are not only non-comprehensive, but also significantly non-exclusive in relation to pre-code concepts and terms. One obvious example in this regard is the cancellation regime under the Contract Remedies Act. Not only can parties contract out of the codal provisions by reason of s 5 of that Act, the cancellation rules under s 7 do not apply to significant types of contract that are widespread in our society, namely, contracts for the sale of goods and contracts for the supply of consumer goods and services. Contracting parties and their advisers must therefore consult discrete sources of law to discover the termination or rejection rules in relation to those other contract-types,[181] and this, of course, has done nothing to improve the simplicity and accessibility of New Zealand contract law.

Finally, if there is one overarching lesson that New Zealand's contract-law partial codes can teach other common-law countries that are, or might be, considering codifying all or part of their domestic contract law, it is that time and familiarity eventually breeds acceptance, or at least forbearance. For despite

---

180 Coote (n 123) 156. Examples in the text above include *Conlon v Ozolins* under the Contractual Mistakes Act, and *Newmans Tours Ltd v Ranier Investments Ltd* under the Contractual Remedies Act.

181 Respectively, the Sale of Goods Act 1908 (NZ) and the Consumer Guarantees Act 1993 (NZ).

trenchant criticism of the New Zealand contract statutes before and after their enactment, by 1993 the New Zealand Law Commission in its *Contracts Statutes Review*[182] was able confidently to conclude that all of the early fears, especially those surrounding the granting of so much discretion to the courts, had mostly proved unfounded. Clearly, not everyone would agree with that assessment, even today, although it is true that lawyers, academics and judges in New Zealand have largely gotten used to dealing with the statutes, warts and all, particularly as such lawyers, academics and judges are guided by a growing corpus of decisions rendered under the statutes. So, much like the massive accident compensation reforms in New Zealand of the same era,[183] a psychology of acceptance (or perhaps of resignation) eventually descended upon the end-users of the contract-law statutes (and, indeed, a whole generation of lawyers, but not yet of judges, has now grown up knowing nothing besides the statutes). Humans generally have a large capacity for coping with significant life-changing events beyond their control, and this must also be true for common lawyers who have codifications thrust upon them against their collective will. They just learn to live with, perhaps even grow eventually to value, the new situation, no matter how flawed they might personally have considered it initially to be. Unfortunately, Stockholm syndrome seems to work in a not-too-dissimilar way.

4 Conclusion

This chapter has not been offered as 'an *argumentum in terrorem* in the code debate';[184] for although history has shown that formidable challenges surround the successful enactment of codes, especially comprehensive codes, what it has not shown is that codification cannot work as a device for organising common-law legal systems.[185] It has largely been for political rather methodological reasons that attempts at codification in such legal systems have failed.[186]

As for Australia, I think it is beyond dispute that parts of its domestic contract law are in need of renewal, repair, reform or clarification. But the problematics identified by proponents of the wholesale reform (including codification or similar) of Australian contract law are, it seems to me, either not sufficiently evidence-based or else vulnerable to significant exaggeration. For dispassionate analysis

---

182 See (n 59).

183 The accident compensation scheme of the early-to-mid 1970s replaced the tort-based personal-injury liability regime with a no-fault statutory regime. The scheme was introduced by the Accident Compensation Act 1972 (NZ) and became effective in 1974 (after 1973 amendments to the legislation). It is now governed by the Accident Compensation Act 2001 (NZ).

184 To borrow Kötz's phrase (n 28) 10.

185 cf Weiss (n 22) 531.

186 Generally see Weiss (n 22).

of the current law, I believe, reveals the domestic contract law of Australia to be deficient in isolated and relatively minor ways only. And although there are well-documented advantages to the codification (or similar) of contract law, the costs and sheer magnitude of the task, relative to the tangible benefits likely to result from it, will, I believe, seal its rejection as a viable option for Australia, at least for now. Even assuming a political will to change,[187] the degree of present demonstrable difficulty with Australian contract law is neither persistent nor serious enough to merit substantial reform at this stage. In short, one does not need a codal sledgehammer to crack a common-law nut.

Still, given the notorious uncertainty, slowness, randomness and costliness of court-generated law-reform initiatives in private law, one cannot help but hope for a more direct and systematic approach to contract-law reform in Australia. Targeted reform, such as through the piecemeal codification (or similar) of distinct pockets of the law of contract in discrete statutes, might well be a viable near-future option, even in a federal system like Australia. The technique of 'partially codifying' sections of contract law has enjoyed success in New Zealand, Australia's nearest legal neighbour, although it is also fair to say that that success has been 'mixed'.[188] There are, therefore, a number of lessons for Australia in the New Zealand experience, which lessons have been noted in this chapter. But above all those lessons, perhaps, is the truism spoken by Aubrey Diamond in the conclusion to his inaugural lecture, in 1967, on the 'Codification of the Law of Contract': '[A] great deal depends on the quality of the code and the spirit in which it is administered by the courts.'[189] The success of the New Zealand contract-law codes, certainly, has depended on a legal culture that has grown to respect and treat each code as 'a code' of the particular type intended by Parliament. For that culture eventually came to discover that '"[c]odes ... are not monsters," ... and that, at any rate, "they can be trained."'[190]

---

187 This cannot be assumed. Both the departure of The Hon Nicola Roxon MP as Australian Attorney-General, and the departure of the Labor Government following the 2013 federal election, may sound the death knell for the Discussion Paper that has fuelled all the present interest.

188 Compare Farrar (n 21) 62.

189 Diamond (n 21) 384.

190 Kötz (n 28) 3–4, quoting, respectively, Harry Lawson, 'A Common Lawyer Looks at Codification' in *Selected Assays I: Many Laws* (1977) 48, and Denis Tallon, 'Codification and Consolidation of the Law at the Present Time' (1974) 14 Israel Law Review 1, 12.

Chapter 9
Codification and the American Discussion About How Judges Decide Cases

Richard Hyland

The question I would like to examine is this: What can be learned about the codification of contract law from American law, and in particular from the American discussion about how judges decide cases?

The question at first seems unpromising, since the opportunity to codify the law of contract in the United States, if such an opportunity ever existed, has passed long since and will never return. The closest thing we have to a code on these matters is the Restatement (Second) of Contracts,[1] which is not a code at all but an anti-code. And even that magnificent but largely fantastical experiment will never be repeated. Though most of the other volumes of the Restatement are now in a third edition, no one has proposed a third version of contract law. One reason is that there are now so many competing theories of contract in the American discussion that there is no dominant view on any of the interesting questions.

Working, as I do, in this field, in which doctrine is proliferating and consensus is disintegrating, I was surprised when I learned that Australia is currently considering codifying its contract law. I found it especially intriguing to examine the well-designed *Infolets* that the office of the Australian Attorney General has posted on its website and to learn that the government has received consultation on a number of topics, including the factors that are currently driving reform, the costs and difficulties of the current system of contract law, the legal needs of the digital economy, the comparative efficiencies of foreign contract laws, the perspective of internationalization, and the benefits of the different reform options—codification, restatement, simplification, and substantive reform.

Since I teach contracts in the United States, where I am never asked to reflect on how to codify our contract law, I was even more surprised to receive an invitation to participate in an international conference and to be offered the opportunity to discuss the Australian government's proposal. I was greatly affected by the abstracts submitted by the other participants and the chance to consider current concerns, including the urgency of adapting to globalization and the internationalization of contract law, the need for a duty of good faith to govern contract negotiation, the importance of adequate consumer protection, the meaning of national codification today, connected as the process has always been to the emerging nation state,

---

1 Restatement (Second) of Contracts (1981).

and concerns about whether, given today's legal complexity, codification is even possible, or whether perhaps a harmonization model might be preferable.

Despite the undisputed importance of these issues, they are not the concerns that would first come to the mind of many of those who participate in the American discussion. It is difficult to communicate the peculiar nature of our conversation to anyone who is not immersed in it. That is because it is based on a number of premises that are often accepted without question by those who work in this field—in fact accepted as though no one would think of questioning them—and yet, from the perspective of other legal systems, even including many in the common law, they are not only inaccurate but even outrageous. To present these ideas in the limited compass of this chapter, I will have to simplify, and that means, alas, to state them without the necessary nuance. Perhaps the way to engage with this chapter is not so much to disagree with my premises, which of course you will, but rather to ask what the meaning of contract law codification would be if these premises accurately described how the common law works.

1 Doing Things with Rules

As I mentioned, the common law long resisted private law codification in the United States. The nineteenth-century Field Civil Code was adopted in only five American jurisdictions.[2] Even in those jurisdictions, resistance of one type or another has continued. In Montana, jurists continue to debate whether it was a good idea to have adopted a codification that froze legal concepts as they were a century and a half ago.[3] The California Supreme Court solved the problem differently. In a remarkable decision, after reviewing the original justification for adopting the code—codification was the only real alternative in a new state—it then announced that the code was merely a continuation of the common law and therefore always open to judicial development.[4]

The antipathy to codification has been present from the beginning of the American common law. Blackstone's *Commentaries* were published in the Colonies in 1771, just before the Revolution. In the absence of a reporter system, the book served as the foundational text of American law. Blackstone began those lectures by warning his students against intemperate modification of the common law.[5] The common law, he noted, has always been based on the immemorial customs of the English people, customs, as he understood them, reaching back beyond the Norman

---

2 The Dakota Territory, California, Idaho, Montana, and Colorado. See Bartholomew Lee, 'The Civil Law and Field's Civil Code in Common-law California—a Note on What Might Have Been' (1992) 5 Western Legal History 13.

3 See Andrew P. Morriss, Scott J. Burnham, and Hon. James C. Nelson, 'Debating the Field Civil Code 105 Years Late' (2000) 61 Montana Law Review 372.

4 *Li v. Yellow Cab Co.*, 119 Cal.Rptr. 858 (Cal. 1975).

5 1 Bl Comm 10–11.

Conquest to the Anglo-Saxons and the Britons. In the context of established custom, legislative intervention usually does more harm than good. In fact, freedom is largely incompatible with norms mandated from above, which is why Blackstone suggested that the common law is the only legal system in the universe [Blackstone's phrase] in which liberty is the very end and scope of the constitution.[6] The role of the courts is to discover and apply the customs the people have developed for themselves.

Though Oliver Wendell Holmes despised the natural law implications of Blackstone's thought, Holmes agreed that the legislature does not alone provide the norms by which society is governed. While the form of the law tends to remain stable—by *form*, Holmes meant the linguistic formulation of the rules—the law's substance, the felt necessities of the time, continues to evolve and subvert those formulations.[7] The role of the judge is to grasp that evolving substance and apply it when deciding cases. Since the necessities are constantly reexamined, and since each judge will evaluate them differently, no codification will be able to fulfill the usual goals of such an exercise, namely predictability and uniformity.

In other words, from the perspective of this great tradition, a discussion of the possibility of contract codification would not begin with a consideration of its proper content and form. Instead, the initial task would be to ascertain the role and function of statutory rules. In the American common law, particularly as it has developed over the past century in the wake of the decisions of Justice Cardozo, many American jurists have come to believe that, though the rules play some role in the decisions, the internal resources of the law are virtually never capable of determining a unique legal result. There is in all cases a moment of judgment in which extra-legal considerations play a decisive role.

Arthur Corbin formulated Cardozo's insights into a brilliant Contracts treatise.[8] Karl Llewellyn, Corbin's student, developed these ideas into a theory that he called *realism*. In introductory lectures to first-year students at the Columbia Law School, Llewellyn explained that the rules do not decide the cases.[9] In fact, there are no rules at all in the sense in which they are often taught, namely pre-existing legal norms that play a preponderant role in deciding the legal questions that arise during adjudication. But if there are no rules, how then are cases decided? The best I can do is this: judges strive to decide each case appropriately, given all the facts and circumstances, circumstances that of course also include the resources of the law. In this view, there is no difference between the law and the facts, they are all inputs in the decision process. What we call the *holding* is not a rule but simply a summary of the result of one particular case. No case has precedential value—for the simple reason that cases are not decided by reference to other cases. Since the

---

6   Id. 5–6.

7   Mark De Wolfe Howe (Ed), Oliver Wendell Holmes, *The Common Law* (Little, Brown 1963) 5, 31–33.

8   Arthur Linton Corbin, *Corbin on Contracts* (West 1952). Grant Gilmore described this text as "the greatest law book ever written." Grant Gilmore, *The Death of Contract* (1974) 57.

9   Karl Llewellyn, *The Bramble Bush* (first published 1930, OUP 2008).

rules do not decide the cases, adjudication does not proceed by applying rules to the facts. Rather, each case is a case of first impression. As Llewellyn put it in one of his celebrated metaphors, this one based on an image from Plato's *Republic*, the rules are shadows cast on a screen stretched across the opening of the cave by the movement of the judges at the rear.[10]

Legal realism is now old hat, and its insights have become truisms. Yet one interesting thing about truisms is that they are true. Though the contemporary American debate on these questions is richer and more diverse than it was in the early days of realism, the major participants in the subsequent discussion have not fallen back behind Llewellyn's formulation of the problem. The major theorists today do not suggest that cases are decided by applying pre-existing rules to the facts of the cases. For example, Richard Posner has suggested that common law courts reach decisions based on considerations of marginal utility.[11] Roberto Unger, in contrast, has argued that legal decisions are based on the judge's political views.[12] Though these two scholars disagree about almost everything else, they agree that cases are not decided by applying the legal rules to the facts.

Thus, the American version of the common law involves not just a skepticism about whether cases can really be decided by applying the rules to the facts but also serious doubts about whether legal rules, in the conventional sense, exist at all. Instead it seems enough to agree that each case should be decided appropriately as required by its own merits. How do judges perform this task? No one knows. The common law tradition preserves case reports in one form or another going back 800 years. Judges may have decided these cases in more or less the same manner over this long period, and yet we know very little about how they reach their decisions.

An example, if one is needed, is the celebrated contracts case of *Webb v. McGowin*.[13] Webb, McGowin's employee, was permanently disabled as he risked his life and heroically saved the life of his employer. Following the incident, McGowin promised to pay Webb a bi-weekly pension of $15. The pension was paid regularly for a number of years until McGowin died, at which point the heirs refused to continue payment. When Webb sued, the heirs argued that the consideration doctrine barred enforcement of the promise. The traditional view, and apparently still today the majority position on the question, holds that the promise is unenforceable—no promise is enforceable at law unless it is part of a bargain. Nonetheless, the appellate court decided in Webb's favor, and the Alabama high court affirmed. The appellate court cited a number of cases, none of which compelled the result. Why did the court decide to make the effort to evade controlling precedent? As one of the judges, quoting Justice Marshall, wrote in concurrence, "'I do not think that law ought to be separate from justice, where it is at most doubtful.'"

---

10 Id 6.

11 Richard A. Posner, *Economic Analysis of Law* (7th edn, Wolters Kluwer 2007).

12 Roberto Mangabeira Unger, *The Critical Legal Studies Movement* (Harvard University Press 1986).

13 168 So. 196 (Ala. App 1935), aff'd 168 So. 199 (Ala. 1936).

Such a system seems at first to offer no assistance to a project that proposes to codify contract law. But, for two reasons, that is surprisingly not the case. First, the American system has produced in this field a highly instructive code, however idiosyncratic. Second, the American discussion itself offers suggestions that might prove helpful to contemporary codifiers. In the remainder of this chapter, I will briefly examine each of these ideas.

2 Using a Code

The Uniform Commercial Code (the UCC or the "Code") is a somewhat eccentric American product. In one version or another it has been adopted by all American states. Even abroad, the UCC is generally considered to be a useful codification of the private law. How can a code succeed in a common law environment?

The Code's chief architect was Karl Llewellyn, whom we just met as one of the founders of American legal realism. As noted, Llewellyn was convinced that rules do not decide cases, in fact, he believed that rules do not even exist in the traditional sense. Llewellyn sought a method for codifying the commercial law in a way consistent with his realist premises. Llewellyn was personally responsible for formulating Article 2, the UCC's Sales Article. He resolved the difficulties by a stroke of genius.

Llewellyn began by rethinking the nature of a code. Traditionally, a code is considered to be a comprehensive regulation of a particular area of the law, a source for answers to all legal questions that arise in the field. Llewellyn thought of the Code differently. For him, instead, the Code should offer a reservoir of new questions, questions the judge might wish to ask of the facts in order to assist in gathering relevant considerations before deciding the case.

Llewellyn's method is most helpfully examined by close reading. A good example is the Code's formulation of the obligations of a seller who has agreed to ship the goods. If the contract does not specify how the seller is to proceed, the seller will want to know what kind of carrier to choose, what kind of carriage contract to conclude, and how quickly the goods are to be shipped. In UCC § 2-504, the Code responds to those concerns:

> [The seller] must put the goods in the possession of such a carrier and make such a contract for their transportation as may be reasonable having regard to the nature of the goods and other circumstances of the case.

In other words, when the seller puts these questions to the Code, the Code looks back and asks "What do *you* think?" Figure out what is reasonable in the circumstances, the Code counsels, and then do that.[14]

---

14   See Richard Danzig, 'A Comment on the Jurisprudence of the Uniform Commercial Code' (1975) 621 Stanford Law Review 27.

This appears to be a joke, but it is not. As noted above, Llewellyn believed that the courts do not decide cases by applying the law to the facts. Instead, courts consider all of the facts and circumstances and attempt to come up with a result that is appropriate in the particular context. If the codifier insists on specifying factors and thereby preferring some considerations to others, strong judges will still find a way to decide the case properly, while weak judges may find themselves trapped into deciding the case against their inclination. Given this state of affairs, the best that a code can do is to clear out the underbrush and provide the courts with an open terrain where they can do their job.

Nonetheless, Llewellyn was not agnostic about technique. One of his principal goals was to eliminate abstractions. The more concrete and practical the considerations, Llewellyn believed, the better the decisions will be. He therefore replaced abstractions with concepts of a more practical bent, as he explained in one of my favorite passages in the Code.

> The legal consequences are stated as following directly from the contract and action taken under it without resorting to the idea of when property or title passed or was to pass as being the determining factor. The purpose is to avoid making practical issues between practical [people] turn upon the location of an intangible something, the passing of which no [one] can prove by evidence and to substitute for such abstractions proof of words and actions of a tangible character.[15]

In other words, no case should be decided purely on the basis of legal concepts. As a practical matter, and therefore as a legal one, the decision as to when risk passes has nothing to do with the very different question concerning when title passes. It may be tempting, even theoretically appealing, to employ the same criteria to resolve both questions, but doing so provides a purely aesthetic pleasure. Every legal question should be decided on the basis of its own criteria and not by relying on criteria elaborated for another purpose.

A code performs yet a third function, which is perhaps most essential—namely to provide a pathway to assist the judge in working through the complex thicket of considerations relevant in the private law. When a code is well-drafted, it provides a catalogue of remedies and provisions that list the elements the plaintiff must prove in order for a court to be able to award a particular remedy. In many cases, the individual elements of a cause of action contain cross-references to other code provisions, and they to yet others. In other words, a remedies provision is not really a rule. It is rather a piece of a complex structure. This insight of Llewellyn's, ultimately derived from German law, is incorporated in the Code's definitional sections and the intricate structure of sales remedies.

Because we already know this method from the civil law, it may seem irrelevant to discuss its appearance in the UCC. But that would be mistaken. The fact that this method is also applicable in the common law means that it is compatible with

---

15 UCC § 2-101 comment.

a system that does not require pre-existing rules. It is rather a general method for operationalizing the systematic nature of a legal system.

To understand how this can be done in a common law system, it is useful to examine how we use the UCC when we attempt to analyze a particular dispute. As mentioned above, the UCC does not dictate the final result. Rather the Code creates the framework by which the circumstances of a case should be analyzed and discussed.

Here a contrast is important. Code thinking differs from thinking in fields governed by the uncodified common law. In the common law, judges and common lawyers tend to solve cases by using a sophisticated version of the IRAC method that is taught in law school. They identify the *Issue*, find the applicable *Rule*, explain how the rule should be *Applied* to the facts, and then *Conclude*. Since purpose must be ascribed to an individual rule in order to interpret it, and since each side in the dispute will propose a different purpose, the discussion focuses on the goals the applicable norm is designed to achieve and how the norm should be constructed in the particular case. This type of discussion can be pursued with great subtlety, as exemplified by the great common law judges, particularly those whose names we remember. However, one feature of this approach is its programmatic lack of systematicity. Each norm floats on its own bottom. At every step, the focus is on the proper interpretation of the individual norm in the circumstances.

We approach a problem differently under the Code. We begin by locating the appropriate remedies provision. We then examine each of that provision's pre-requisites, a quest that usually requires us to review a number of other Code provisions and definitions. There is plenty of wiggle room and discussion, but when that discussion is completed, and all of the terms and cross-references have been examined, we have our answer. In other words, the Code encourages the logical consideration of a legal problem. An unstructured examination of all of the facts and circumstances of a case may produce a decision, but, from a code perspective, it would be difficult to call it law. The legal element enters when jurists are required to follow a specified pathway as they ask questions of the facts. The Code's structure guarantees that many of the essential issues are evaluated, and that they are examined in a rational order.

As mentioned above, when a seller asks about the shipment obligations, the UCC responds that the choice of carrier and the contract for carriage must be reasonable. Of course the concept of reasonableness decides nothing, since it is possible to be of different minds about what is reasonable in the circumstances. Nonetheless the Code's provisions provide the terms for the debate. The UCC similarly focuses the debate when it permits a court to refuse to enforce an unconscionable contract,[16] when it defines the obligation of good faith to mean the observance of reasonable commercial standards of fair dealing,[17] and when it

---

16   UCC § 2-302.
17   Id § 1-201 (b)(20).

requires goods to be fit for the ordinary purposes for which such goods are used.[18] The structure of the debate is posed, even though nothing in the norms requires any particular result.

Structuring the discussion is an essential aspect of the codification process. For each legal question, the drafters must assure themselves that they have indicated some of the relevant factors without excluding others. They will especially want to make sure that they have mentioned those factors that are most likely to be overlooked. The pathway must also be complete, allowing the user to move efficiently through the provisions, while touching on all of the necessary considerations.

In sum, a code drafted in a realist perspective attempts to fulfill a number of critical functions. First, for each question it provides a catalogue of useful considerations to assist the courts in taking the relevant factors into account. Second, it removes abstract or antiquated concepts that the law, particularly the common law, tends to drag along from one century to the next. Finally, a realist code provides a roadmap through the complexities of a field of law, a pathway that assists the judges in finding the relevant considerations and taking them into account. The one thing such a code does not do, in fact cannot do, is tell a court how to decide the cases. The goal instead is to create a statutory framework that empowers—and encourages—judges to reach the decisions they want to reach.

At this point it may be possible to respond to a frequent civilian challenge to Llewellyn's method. Civilian jurists often suggest that predictability and uniformity are the principal goals a system of private law should strive to achieve. Like cases should be decided alike. The reason is clear—freedom means that an individual is able to predict when and how the state will intervene in that individual's life. With all else equal, the more predictability, the greater a society's quotient of freedom. In his *Sociology of Law*, Max Weber demonstrated that the resolution of legal questions in the civil law does not depend on who is at work at the judge's bench. The civilian judge identifies the relevant legal norm, isolates the legally relevant facts, and then ascertains whether those facts are present in the case at bar. If they are, the rule is applied; if they are not, application is refused.[19] From Weber's point of view, the common law reduces freedom to the extent it reduces predictability. A system that attempts to take into account all of the facts and circumstances in order to produce a proper result in each case is necessarily less free.

Despite the Weberian critique, my sense is that adjudication in civilian systems is not significantly more predictable than it is in the American system. I have experimented with presenting a complex commercial case to a number of experienced American lawyers and asking how they think the case should be decided. Typically they agree on the outcome, though they often differ about how to explain the result. The congruity may be due to the fact that, with time, common

---

18 Id § 2-314 (2)(c).
19 Max Weber, *The Sociology of Law*, in *Economy and Society* (Guenther Roth and Claus Wittich tr, University of California Press 1978) vol. 2, 641–900.

lawyers develop similar intuitions about how to evaluate the facts of a case. The intuition is manifold and subtle, and I have never seen it stated clearly. If I were to try to state the idea boldly and without the necessary nuance, I would say that American law seeks to decide private law disputes fairly, with fairness understood not as a moral term but rather as an evaluation of many considerations, including the kind of society we prefer, the best way to prevent such losses in the future, and the proper role for courts in a legal dispute. To the extent these intuitions are shared, a well-trained observer can predict how a case will come out, or, at the least, indicate the best argument for each side. If this view is correct, then the American system may not be significantly less predictable than a system that attempts to disregard all those considerations that are not expressly stated in the statute.

3 Deciding Cases

As I mentioned, this is all old hat. The methodological brilliance of the UCC is well known. From our current perspective, however, it is very much an historical insight, an insight from the 1950s and 60s, and involves the high drama of twentieth-century American modernism. The question that the Australian project poses to us today is whether, in the past half century, the American discussion has produced anything new, whether we have anything additional to say about this process. As we have learned more about the dynamic of modern societies, we have recognized the importance of consumer protection and an expanded role for good faith, we understand the international stage on which contract law plays its part, as well as the critical role of information in the digital age. Because other participants in this symposium, much more qualified than I, explore these issues, I will ignore them here. I would instead like to continue to pursue the methodological questions. In this regard, the Australian project asks whether the last half century has produced further insights about the role of codification in a common law jurisdiction, particularly about how to integrate our understanding of the law as a system with our practice of case adjudication. The question, in other words, is whether we have gained insights beyond those taught by Llewellyn, beyond those incorporated into the UCC.

This question might be reformulated by restating the essence of Llewellyn's achievement. As we know from reading Cardozo, the American common law, by Llewellyn's day, had developed tremendous resources of self-understanding.[20] It had reached a mature grasp of adjudication as a process that, though distinctively legal, is nonetheless able to take into account all of the relevant facts and circumstances of a case. At the same time, the common law remains sufficiently aware of boundaries so as not to be overwhelmed by principles from other fields, whether from religion, morality, or marginal utility theory. Llewellyn's work

---

20 Benjamin N. Cardozo, *The Nature of the Judicial Process* (Yale University Press 1921).

expressed this newly-won sense of self-confidence, a belief that the law can open itself to the great reservoir of common sense and not be overwhelmed by extra-legal considerations.

Traditionalists have long argued that legal realism substitutes personal preference for law. This standard critique focuses on the fact that, in the realist view, rules no longer occupy center stage in the adjudication process. Since the internal resources of the law are insufficient to decide the cases, judges consider factors not explicitly sanctioned by the law. For that reason, we are told, if we do not understand a decision, we should ask about the judge's personal preferences, or even what the judge ate that morning for breakfast. But in fact realism, correctly understood, does not resemble the caricature. It represents instead the law's emerging ability to evaluate all of the facts and circumstances of a case without losing its specifically legal approach to reasonableness. To paraphrase Kant, realism is the law's emergence from its self-imposed immaturity, a celebration of its ability to use its understanding beyond the dictate of abstract rules.

4 Explaining What We Do

What then of relevance has happened over the past 50 years? Nothing short of another revolution. Based on the sense of self-confidence that legal realism achieved for the common law, several generations of scholars have attempted to systematize and theorize the insights of common sense and reasonableness that Llewellyn found at the root of common law adjudication. For these scholars, even those who have rejected the realist method, Llewellyn opened up useful theoretical elbowroom beyond the legal norms.

These theories too are well-known. The legal process school points to the importance of considerations of institutional competence, those which concern an institution's ability to evaluate the relevant facts and reach an appropriate decision.[21] Law and economics encourages the law to maximize utility.[22] Critical legal studies demonstrates that a case decision inevitably comes down on one side or the other of a political divide.[23] Postmodern legal feminism demonstrates that law both depends on and reinforces a gendered vision of reality.[24] Critical race theory reveals how inequality nests at the core of our conception of equality.[25] Deconstruction has revealed how metaphors can take control of our discourse.[26]

---

21 Henry M. Hart, Jr. and Albert M. Sacks, *The Legal Process* (William N. Eskridge, Jr. and Philip P. Frickey ed, Foundation Press 1994).
22 Posner (n 11).
23 Unger (n 12).
24 Mary Joe Frug, *Postmodern Legal Feminism* (Routledge 1992).
25 Richard Delgado and Jean Stefancic, *Critical Race Theory* (NYU Press 2012).
26 George Lakoff and Mark Johnson, *Metaphors We Live By* (University of Chicago Press 1980).

Public choice theory examines the constraints that limited information and self-interest impose on public decision making.[27] And comparative law has taught us that law is an element of a particular culture and that a legal system will prefer results that can most easily be integrated with other elements of the same culture.[28]

The challenge for codification today is to find a way to take advantage of these intellectual developments for purposes of case adjudication. Such a project could take root only in a legal system that is supremely self-confident, one no longer worried that the law might be overwhelmed by systematically elaborated viewpoints coming from outside the law, whether from economics, moral philosophy, game theory, or political science.

If we want to construct a code that is able to take advantage of these insights, what would that code look like? How might it encourage judges to benefit from this research without destroying the coherence of the legal system? This is the challenge the Australian project presents to us.

5 Doing Things with Theories

A first step might be to refocus the work of those legal scholars who draw insight from disciplines outside the law. Richard Posner's contribution to the theory of adjudication might serve as an example. As noted earlier, Posner argues that common law judges traditionally take concerns of efficiency into account when deciding cases. In fact, Posner argues that the common law often mirrors the marketplace.[29] Many legal scholars reject Posner's view, particularly since the courts almost never mention efficiency concerns. Moreover, Posner does not attempt to explain why common law courts would choose to follow economics rather than any of the multitude of other possible theories that are available.

However, Posner's thesis can be reformulated in a more meaningful way. We might read his theory as a model for how one set of considerations might be taken into account, namely how an economically rational judge would decide cases. Since all of us, judges included, are influenced to some degree by concerns of efficiency, this model represents one aspect of what the courts do when they decide cases. Among the numerous thoughts and theories that pass through their minds as they attempt to find an appropriate disposition for a case, they may properly ask what the market would do in such a case to reduce transaction costs and increase marginal utility. Restated in this way, Posner's argument is doubtless correct.

The same might be said of legal process theory. When judges decide cases, they do not rely exclusively on theories of institutional competence or an examination

---

27 Daniel A. Farber and Philip P. Frickey, *Law and Public Choice* (University of Chicago Press 1991).

28 James Q. Whitman, 'The Two Western Cultures of Privacy: Dignity versus Liberty' (2004) 113 Yale Law Journal 1151.

29 Posner (n 11) 24–26.

of the relevant institutional settlements. Yet it is also true that American courts are jealous of their jurisdiction. As Holmes was the first to make clear, the principal question before an American court is usually not which party acted properly in the circumstances. It is rather whether the court should intervene in the dispute at all. These prudential concerns are unquestionably central to many court decisions.[30]

The critical legal studies perspective also provides a useful insight, provided it is not exaggerated. The law, even the private law, is political, though of course the law is not simply politics by other means. A Republican judge sees the world differently from a Democrat, a judge who is a landlord may decide some cases differently from a judge who is a tenant, a white judge differently from a black judge, a woman differently from a man, a gay differently from a straight, a Mormon differently from a Buddhist, an Ivy League grad differently from an alum from a public university. The vast reservoir of individual experience and identity certainly plays a role in legal decision making. The point is not to program these extra-legal considerations into the decision process, but instead to make their impact apparent and thereby reduce their improper influence. The same use may be made of the other critical disciplines that have highlighted weaknesses in our reasoning, including deconstruction, legal feminism, and critical race theory.

In other words, post-realist American legal theorists have not rejected Llewellyn's insights; they have instead attempted to provide for them a systematic elaboration. They have examined many of the considerations that influence judicial thinking, and they have attempted to develop them, either to permit them to be used consciously or to allow judges to recognize them and eliminate undesirable influences. These theories are a triumph of insight into the infinitely complex process of case adjudication.

The question that the Australian codification project poses to us is whether anything can be made of these insights. We now know that these thoughts influence and determine the results of the cases, at least as much as—probably more than—the language of the statutes and precedents. And yet these extra-legal considerations are for some reason taboo. Though the internal resources of the law are insufficient to decide the cases, and though courts actually consider and rely on the kind of insights contemporary theorists have elaborated, the judges themselves are not permitted to discuss their decisions in this vocabulary.

At which point we may well ask the following: Are we well served by a system in which the actual sources of decision are hidden from view, in which the courts must cite to precedent or statute rather than attempting to explain the actual grounds for their decisions? And if we would like the courts to have the option of reproducing their actual decision tree for us—at least to the extent they are aware of it—is it possible to incorporate those considerations into a code without destroying the law's legitimacy and causing irreparable damage to the theoretical framework that a code provides? And if we wished to incorporate some of these ideas into a code, how might that be done?

---

30 See, for example, *Mills v. Wyman*, 3 Pick. 207 (Mass. 1825).

6 Building Theories into a Code

Since American law has confronted these questions for a century now, it is logical to think that some answers might be available in the American legal sources. In fact, this is not a new debate, and perhaps its most interesting product is the Restatement (Second) of Contracts. As the Restatement was being drafted, an argument arose between those advisors who insisted on preserving the consideration doctrine as an absolute requirement of contract formation and those who believed that the courts disregard the rule when necessary for an appropriate resolution of the dispute.[31] There were even radicals, like Arthur Corbin, who announced that there never was such a thing as the consideration doctrine.[32] The drafters developed a brilliant, though controversial, method to restate the issue—they included both positions. In one topic, the Restatement reaffirms the consideration doctrine—promises are enforceable at law only if they are part of a bargain.[33] The following topic is entitled "Contracts Without Consideration."[34] It collects cases in which the courts have found it wise to enforce promises that were not part of a bargain. The two alternative visions are there, still to this day, unmediated and without theoretical explanation. It is what Allen Ginsberg might have called a *reality sandwich*.

It is this aspect of the Restatement (Second) that, according to Gilmore, sealed its fate. With this kind of blatant, unreconciled—and irreconcilable—contradiction, the process of restating the law had advanced as far as is possible in the verbalization of legal norms. The contradictory impulses that motivate decisions had been uncovered. Nothing more could be said. That is why both Corbin and Gilmore refused to suggest how they thought the cases should be decided. The cases are primary objects, like works of art, available for examination and appreciation, but which retain their meaning despite conceptual criticism.

Since Gilmore's day, we have experienced an extraordinary dispersion in the culture of daily life. As a momentary glance at the newspaper confirms, it is no longer possible for Americans as a nation to agree on anything. This is of course all much regretted, and contrasted with a supposed Norman Rockwell universe in which all members of society can recognize themselves in the same images, an earlier time in which we all are said to have agreed on values and other important things—except, of course, for those who did not agree, including political opponents and minorities of all types. Whatever its history, this disintegration is here to stay and will accelerate. It will probably never again be possible to reach agreement on fundamental principles. The recent attempt to revise Article 2 of the UCC, Llewellyn's masterpiece, failed partially for that reason.

Is the world of law compatible with radical disagreement? In the end, that is the question we must answer. And if we answer in the affirmative, we must

---

31 Gilmore (n 8) 58–77.
32 Corbin (n 8) § 109 at 161.
33 Restatement (Second) of Contracts §§ 71–72.
34 Id §§ 82–94.

find a way to integrate contradictory premises into a working enterprise. The method used by the Restatement (Second) to restate the consideration doctrine is a reasonable possibility, so reasonable, in fact, that it had previously been used in the UCC[35] and was later followed by the drafters of the Vienna Sales Convention at those moments when agreement proved impossible. These are often considered the weakest provisions in the Sales Convention, but, given the world as it has become, they may be its most providential formulations. Everyone knows these contradictory provisions. Civilian jurists proposed that specific performance be recognized as the principal remedy for breach of the sales contract, while common lawyers responded that specific remedies must be subsidiary to money damages. No compromise was forthcoming, so the Sales Convention incorporates both solutions.[36] Jurists from the global north argued that notice of non-conformity must be speedily presented to the seller, while the representatives from the global south suggested that additional delay should be permitted when it is reasonable. Once again, a mechanism was found to adopt both solutions.[37] Socialist countries argued that international sales contracts should not be valid without a writing, while representatives from most other countries sought freedom from form requirements. Again a solution was envisaged that approved both solutions.[38] Other non-answers were found for the determination of interest rates,[39] the role of good faith,[40] and the validity of a contract with an open price term.[41]

The elements for the solution are present. Now only two things are needed before Australians are able to incorporate them into their codification. One is hard work. Lawyers are good at that, and it will not be lacking. The other element is genius. The Australians surely have that as well. It will be fascinating to watch as Australia attempts to rise to the challenge and formulate a contemporary vision of codification.

---

35 See, for example, UCC § 2-318 (third-party beneficiaries of sales warranties).
36 United Nations Convention on Contracts for the International Sale of Goods (CISG) arts 28, 46, 62.
37 Id art 39, 43, 44.
38 Id art 11, 12.
39 Id art 78.
40 Id art 7 (1).
41 Id art 14 (1), 55.

Index

Introductory Note

References such as '178–9' indicate (not necessarily continuous) discussion of a topic across a range of pages. Wherever possible in the case of topics with many references, these have either been divided into sub-topics or only the most significant discussions of the topic are listed. Because the entire work is about 'codification' and 'contract law', the use of these terms (and certain others which occur constantly throughout the book) as entry points has been restricted. Information will be found under the corresponding detailed topics.

abandonment 10, 121
abuse, of rights 67, 72, 123
academics 102–3, 107, 109, 112, 116–17, 165, 167, 202
acceptance 22, 35, 54, 70, 95–6, 129, 181, 201–2
accessibility 10, 12, 133, 136–7, 170, 192, 199, 201
   public 170, 195
ACL, see Australian Consumer Law
Acquis Group 81, 89–91, 94–5, 99
AGD, see Attorney-General's Department
ALI, see American Law Institute
ALRC, see Australian Law Reform Commission
ambiguities 136–7, 172, 194–5
American common law 206–7, 213
American Law Institute (ALI) 154–5, 158, 195
arbitration 3–5, 22, 25–6, 39, 41–2, 141, 156, 158
   agreements 25–6, 160
   clauses 25, 68
   international 6, 22, 53, 141, 162
      commercial 4, 26, 36, 141, 147, 150
Arbitration Act 1996 5
arbitrators 141, 147, 150, 176
assignment
   of contracts 45
   of rights 45, 47

Attorney-General's Department (AGD) 131–3, 138, 140–1, 145, 147–9, 152
Australia 3–8, 21–7, 131–9, 141–5, 147–54, 156–61, 166–70, 201–3
   Australian Consumer Law (ACL) 10, 20–1, 31–2, 133, 138–9, 146–7, 157–60, 189
   Australian Law Reform Commission (ALRC) 33, 133, 160–4
   choice of law 28–31
   common law 28, 59
   contract law 3–4, 7–8, 10–13, 57–61, 70–4, 133–5, 144–7, 167–70
   costs/benefits of internationalising contract law 149–53
   costs/benefits of restatement, simplification or substantial reform of contract law 153–7
   costs/difficulties for businesses arising from differences between Australian and foreign contract law 148–9
   costs/difficulties for businesses arising from domestic contract law 143–6
   courts 16, 20–1, 25–8, 30, 58–60, 139–41, 146–7, 152
   digital economy 146–7
   Government 32, 131–3, 138, 145, 152, 155, 163

High Court 16, 20, 60, 62, 132, 137, 187, 191
implementation of reforms 157–60
improving law 33–6
International Arbitration Act 4, 6, 25–6, 147
and international developments 32–3
internationalization 15–36
jurisdiction 24–7
Law Council of Australia (LCA) 136–7, 161
lawyers 19, 22–3, 70, 135, 142, 168
objective proper law 28, 31–2
private international law 22–4
problems and drivers of reform 133–43
Productivity Commission (PC) 145–6, 148, 161–2
review of contract law 10, 131–64
society 134–5, 139
Trade Practices Act 17, 20–1, 24, 138
Uniform Contract Code 3, 165, 168
Australian Law Reform Commission (ALRC) 33, 133, 160–4
autonomy
party 26, 29, 41, 139, 146
private 84–7, 103

b2b 42, 48, 52, 113, 120, 138, 146–7, 158–9
b2c 52, 156, 158–9
bad faith 65, 67–8
bargaining positions 63
bargaining power, unequal 7–8, 10, 62, 155
bargains 63, 71, 183, 208, 217
BC, see British Columbia
BCLI, see British Columbia Law Institute
BCLI Report on Proposals for Unfair Contracts Relief 194–6, 198
bifurcation 80–1, 89, 98, 100
bills of exchange 171–3
boilerplate clauses 188
Brazil 39, 41, 43–4, 97
breach of contract 43, 45, 47, 53, 183, 186, 188–90
British Columbia (BC) 11, 64, 69, 175, 194, 197–8

BCLI Report on Proposals for Unfair Contracts Relief 194–6, 198
lessons 197–202
British Columbia Law Institute (BCLI) 64, 69, 74, 161, 194–5
Brussels effect 80–1, 99
business operators 114, 116, 124–6, 128–9
business-to-business relationships 42, 95, 113, 138
business-to-consumer relationships 52, 95, 156
businesses 29, 81–2, 86, 88, 119, 129, 158, 165–8
buyers 32, 43, 135, 150

cancellation 116, 126, 183, 185–7, 190–1, 193
right 116
rules 186, 201
case law 10, 111, 113–14, 120–2, 138, 141, 143, 147
CCA, see Consumer Contracts Act
certainty 3, 5, 10–12, 33, 60, 64, 133, 140
CESL, see Common European Sales Law
characteristic performance presumption 33
China 19, 21, 32–4, 39, 59, 64–5, 149, 151–2
choice 25, 28, 30–3, 36, 41, 51, 146, 198–9
of court 23, 25, 27
forum 17, 29
of law 17, 23, 25, 41, 47, 61, 146, 151
Australia 28–31
clauses 41
rules 19, 27, 29–30, 35–6, 147
tort 23, 31
meaningful 63, 71
public choice theory 215
CISG (Convention on Contracts for the International Sale of Goods) 21–2, 29–30, 34–6, 43–50, 52–5, 111–12, 134–5, 149–52
Civil Code 9, 90, 95, 99, 163
European, see European Civil Code
German 42, 64, 66, 74, 94–5, 101
Japan 9–10, 107–29
Swiss 43

civil law 9, 41, 54, 64, 104, 206, 210, 212
   codes 8, 57, 73–4
   systems 8, 57, 72, 75, 107
civil lawyers 74, 98
civil obligations 17, 64, 110
codes 5–6, 12–13, 107–8, 171–5, 191–5, 197–203, 209–12, 215–17
   definition 4
codification
   see Introductory Note and detailed entries
   argument 79–83
   mania 9, 79–105
   partial 11–13, 165, 167, 169–71, 173, 175, 193–5, 197–201
commentaries 6, 11, 44–5, 47, 50, 53, 55, 57–8
commercial contracts 7–8, 13, 71, 144
commercial parties 20, 25, 32, 159
commercial transactions 6, 20–1, 36
   international 22, 50
Common European Sales Law (CESL) 48, 64, 69–70, 94–5, 97, 100–2, 148–9, 158–60
common law 5–7, 19–20, 184–5, 189–90, 192–3, 199–201, 206–8, 210–15
   American 206–7, 213
   countries 4, 29–30, 57–8, 64, 70, 107, 169, 201
   systems 6, 8, 17–18, 23–5, 71–3, 168–9, 171, 197–8
common mistake 178, 182
Commonwealth 157–8, 162, 168, 174
competences 20, 95, 101, 103
   institutional 214–15
comprehensive codification 10, 13, 170, 197, 202
comprehensiveness 5–6, 172
compromises 57, 119–20, 169, 198, 218
conclusive evaluations 116–17, 124, 128–9
conduct 20–1, 65, 67, 70–1, 142, 144, 161–2, 185–6
   deceptive 17, 19–20, 26, 147
   misleading 20–1, 24, 26, 32, 138
   unconscionable 71, 138–9
Conlon v Ozolins 179, 181–3, 200–1
consensualism 120–1

consensus 12, 80, 121, 179, 205
   international 17, 52
consent 21, 48, 53, 139, 158
consistency 30, 35, 67, 72, 192
constitutions 25, 85, 98, 107, 157–8, 207
consultation 137, 147–8, 150, 159, 162, 164, 205
consumer contracts 7, 10–11, 13, 58, 113, 117–21, 124–9, 150
   international 7, 11
Consumer Contracts Act (CCA) 10, 108, 111, 113–23, 128
   integration into Civil Code 116–19
consumer goods 44, 81, 186, 201
consumer law 9–10, 85–7, 89, 94–6, 98, 112–13, 117–18, 122
   Japan 107–29
consumer protection 52–3, 113, 118, 136, 140, 147, 205, 213
consumer transactions 96, 147
consumers 10, 31–3, 95–6, 112–16, 118–20, 124–9, 138–40, 158–9
   as norm 112–13
contract interpretation 19, 35, 134, 136, 156
contract law reform 108, 111, 131–2, 140, 142, 146, 161–4, 170
contract negotiations 58, 62, 66, 135, 152, 205
contract terms, see terms
contracts, commercial 7–8, 13, 71, 144
Contracts and Commercial Law Reform Committee 174–5, 177, 181, 183–5, 190, 192, 198–9
contractual mistake, see mistake
contractual obligations 33–4, 69, 144
contractual relationships 7, 138–9, 151, 177, 179
contractual remedies 11, 158, 161–2, 173–5, 183–93, 200–1
contractual unfairness 113, 155, 195
contractualism 120–1
control 45, 201–2, 214
   procedural 113, 115
Convention on Contracts for the International Sale of Goods, see CISG
Convention on the Limitation Period in the International Sale of Goods 45–6

cooperation 49, 84–5, 98
Coote, Brian 174, 190, 197, 201
Corbin, Arthur 207, 217
corporations 20, 112, 157
costs 42, 135–7, 143, 145, 148–50, 153–5, 161, 163
    transaction 50, 55, 143, 149, 152, 215
counterparties 142, 151–2
creditors 181–2
critical race theory 12, 214, 216
cross-border agreements 15, 35
cross-border transactions 7, 84, 134, 147, 159
cross-purposes mistakes 181

damages 20–1, 24, 70, 72, 121, 124–6, 184–5, 190
    liquidated 53, 114, 126
    total amount of 126
data protection 81, 99
DCFR, see Draft Common Frame of Reference
deceptive conduct 17, 19–20, 26, 147
deconstruction 214, 216
defects 43, 47–8, 126, 154
    latent 126
deference 12, 16
digital economy 166, 205
    Australia 146–7
disadvantage 60, 62–3, 71–2, 120, 140, 168
    excessive 10, 120
    manifest 195
disclosure 10, 72, 117–18, 120, 196–7
    duty 10, 117–18, 120
discretion 11–12, 25, 174–5, 182, 188–90, 200–2
discretionary justice 174
discretionary powers 11, 68, 174, 178
disparity 8, 114, 119, 124
distributive justice 132, 145, 149
domestic contract law 18–19, 34–5, 136–7, 150–1, 167, 170, 198, 201–3
domestic contracts 21, 34–5, 40, 52, 158
Draft Common Frame of Reference (DCFR) 44, 48, 81, 95, 111
drafters 32, 109, 150, 195–8, 201, 212, 217–18
duress 6, 45, 115–16, 123, 194–5

e-commerce 96, 133, 146, 156, 166
ECJ (European Court of Justice) 85, 102–4
economic efficiency 84, 163
economic law 84–5, 87
economic power 41–2
economic transactions 9, 85
economics 99, 163, 214–15
economy 84, 87, 99, 110, 145, 154, 212
    digital 146, 166, 205
efficiency 133, 148, 215
elasticity 133
elections 146, 159, 166
employees 8, 27, 31–3, 35, 125, 139
energy 9, 87–8, 90, 93, 96–9, 103–4
enforcement 22, 25–6, 66–7, 85–6, 88, 140, 144, 190
English law 4, 16, 25, 28–9, 32, 150–1
enrichment, unjust 108–9, 194–5
equity 17, 19, 61–2, 67, 166, 171, 175, 184
estoppel 6, 61, 72, 166, 189
EU (European Union) 9, 33, 79–85, 87–93, 95–9, 148–9, 152–5, 159–60
European Civil Code 47–8, 79, 81, 83, 98, 100, 153, 155
    failed project 89–92
European codification project 91, 94, 98–9, 101–2
European Commission 48, 79, 87–91, 99, 101–2, 148
European Court of Justice, see ECJ
European integration 83, 91–2, 100
European market state 83–4, 86
European perspective 9, 79–105
European private law 79, 81–2, 84–7, 91–3, 95, 99, 101–2, 104–5
European regulatory private law 79–80, 84–6, 88, 93–4, 99, 104–5
    and national regulatory private law 86–9
European Union, see EU
evaluations, conclusive 116–17, 124, 128–9
excessive disadvantage 10, 120
exclusive jurisdiction 158
exclusivity 172, 198–200
extra-legal considerations 207, 214, 216

fair dealing 64, 66–7, 69–70, 138, 211
falsification 196–7
fault 43, 121, 127–9, 185
    principles 121
fiduciary duty 175, 194
financial services 9, 87–8, 90, 93, 96–9, 103–4
flexibility 5, 52, 145, 199
food safety 81, 99
foreign courts 16, 25, 147, 200
foreign judgments, recognition 23, 34, 36
foreign jurisdiction 25, 32
    agreements 26–7
    clauses 25–6, 35
formal contracts 166, 180, 188
forum 16, 23–5, 27, 29–30, 35, 141, 147, 151
    law 24, 27, 30–1, 35
        application 28, 31, 35
    legislation/statutes 26, 28–30
    selection clauses 41
    shopping 28, 30
forum non conveniens 27
fragmentation 11, 13, 50, 93, 98
franchisees 31–2, 35
fraud 6, 45, 53, 115–16, 123, 128, 175, 184
    by silence 10, 117
fraudulent misrepresentation 185
freedom 85, 87, 207, 212, 218
    of contract 9, 52, 84–7, 103
frustration of contract 144, 158

general contract law 45–6, 48, 50, 52, 95, 111, 157
general rules 34, 113, 117–18, 173, 194
Germany 39–42, 86, 90, 94, 97, 111, 149, 151
    Civil Code 42, 64, 66, 74, 94–5, 101
    Constitutional Court 100–1
global contract law
    improvements by 54–5
    possible future work 51–4
global harmonization 10, 109, 111
global instruments on contract law 43–7
globalization 39, 42, 82, 121, 205
    and Japan 111–12
good conscience 8, 57, 62, 64, 74, 170

good faith 8, 35, 57–75, 115, 128, 137, 156, 166; see also fair dealing
    duty/obligation 57–61, 64–8, 70–2, 136, 145, 194, 205, 211
    performance 67, 72
    principles 63, 70–2, 74–5
    understandings of 64–71
goods 18–19, 21, 43–6, 53–4, 59–60, 124–5, 185–6, 209
    sale of 54, 135–6, 171–3, 186, 201
gross disparity 10, 45, 53, 114, 117–18, 120
gross negligence 125

harmonization 10–11, 15, 17, 34, 36, 39–40, 49–52, 133
    global 10, 109, 111
Herbert Smith Freehills 137, 142–3, 151, 163
honesty 65, 67, 70–1

ICC, see International Chamber of Commerce
identity, national 100–3
ignorance 177–8
illegality 19, 45, 47–8, 137
impossibility doctrine 121
in-house lawyers 41, 136
inflexibility 11–12
influence, undue 53, 175, 194–6
informal authority 83–4
injunctions 20, 28, 113–14, 124, 151, 186
innocent misrepresentation 184–5
innocent non-disclosure 197
innovation 20, 115, 133, 185
institutional competence 214–15
insularity 5, 7, 17
insurance contracts 7, 28–9, 31–2, 53, 138, 162
intention 72, 123–5, 127–9, 173–4, 180–2, 184, 190–2, 195–6
    manifestation of 123, 127–9
    mutual unexpressed intentions 31
inter-governmental agreements 138, 143, 158
inter-institutional interaction 93–4
intermediate terms 22, 187
internal market 80, 83, 85, 87–9, 96

international arbitration 6, 22, 53, 141, 162
International Arbitration Act 4, 6, 25–6, 147
International Chamber of Commerce (ICC) 50
international commercial arbitration 4, 26, 36, 141, 147, 150
international commercial transactions 22, 50
international consumer contracts 7, 11
international contracts 15–16, 18, 33–6, 42–3, 46, 52, 54–5, 156
international instruments 8, 23, 29, 36, 57, 70, 74, 149–52
international litigation 3, 19–20, 26–7, 36, 57, 61, 74
international sales 57, 59, 151, 156
　contracts 41, 44, 50, 59, 151, 218
international trade 7–8, 39–40, 46, 50–1, 55, 64, 67, 148
international transactions 15, 36, 41, 161, 200
internationalization 4–8, 13, 57–8, 133, 141, 161, 166, 205
　Australia 15–36
　as consideration in codification projects 58–61
internationalization imperatives 7–9, 37–75
internet 42, 55, 90, 137, 145
interpretation 6, 48–9, 52–4, 73–4, 172, 176–7, 181–3, 190
　contract 19, 35, 134, 136, 156
interpretative mistake 181–2
intuition 148, 150, 213
isolation 4, 17–18, 22–3, 58, 161, 166

Japan 32–3, 107–9, 112–15, 117, 134–5, 145–6, 149–50, 163–4
　assessment 120–9
　Civil Code 9–10, 107–29
　　current position 108–9
　　reasons for reform 109–10
　　reform 108–12
　　transparency 110–11
　Consumer Contracts Act (CCA) 10, 108, 111, 113–23, 128
　　integration into Civil Code 116–19

consumer law 107–29
　integration 113
　remnants 119–20
　consumers as norm 112–13
　and globalization 111–12
　Interim Proposal 119
　Legislative Council (LC) 108–10, 113, 117, 119
　procedural policing 115–16
　re-codification attempt 107–29
JCC, see Japan, Civil Code
judges/judiciary 12, 107, 141–2, 173, 198–9, 202, 207–12, 214–16
jurisdiction 7, 19–21, 23–7, 31–5, 69–70, 143, 155, 161–2
　agreements 26–7
　Australia 24–7
　exclusive 158
　foreign 25, 32
jurisdictional rules 28, 31, 35
justice 74, 85, 108–9, 137, 139, 164, 167, 176
　discretionary 174
　distributive 132, 145, 149

knowledge 18, 23, 120, 123, 125, 127–9, 140, 192
Korea 32–3, 41, 49, 149, 152

land 110, 180
Lando Commission 91, 94
latent defects 126
Law Council of Australia (LCA) 136–7, 161
law of obligations 107, 112, 117, 127, 149
lawyers 21, 23, 57, 59, 142, 145, 172, 202
　civil 74, 98
　in-house 41, 136
LC, see Legislative Council
LCA (Law Council of Australia) 136–7, 161
legal realism, see realism
legal services 142, 145
Legislative Council (LC) 108–10, 113, 117, 119
legislatures 4, 18, 30, 35, 107, 111, 114, 207
lessees 63, 115

lessors 63
lex mercatoria 92, 160
liability 70, 124–6, 155, 184–5, 188, 195
   limitation of liability clauses 42, 53, 114
   strict 150, 185
limitation of liability clauses 42
liquidated damages 53, 114, 126
litigation 16, 20, 22–3, 36, 41–2, 104, 139, 189
   international 3, 19–20, 26–7, 36, 57, 61, 74
Llewellyn, Karl 12, 207–10, 213–14

McLauchlan, D.W. 173–9, 181, 183, 185, 188, 191, 194, 200
major trading partners 132, 148–9, 151, 166
mandatory effect 30, 32, 35
mandatory rules 34, 52, 159
manifest disadvantage 195
manifestation of intention 123, 127–9
market states 9, 79–86, 88–9, 91–2, 104–5
markets 79, 83, 85, 87–8, 96, 142, 163, 166
   internal 80, 83, 85, 87–9, 96
   national 87–8
   regulated 93–4, 96–9
   services 89, 103–4
minimum standards of protection 138, 140
misleading or deceptive conduct 19–22, 24, 26, 32, 138, 147
misrepresentation 20–1, 116–18, 124, 127–8, 183–9, 192–4, 196–7, 200
   actionable 192, 196
   fraudulent 185
   innocent 184–5
   non-disclosure as 196–7
   pre-contractual 184, 197
   tortious 184
mistake 123, 128, 173, 175–84, 189, 193, 197, 200–1
   cross-purposes 181
   mutual 178, 180, 182
   unilateral 178, 180
modernization 10, 13, 17, 36, 94, 104, 109, 112
mutual mistake 178, 180, 182
mutual unexpressed intentions 31

NAFTA (North American Free Trade Agreement) 50
nation-building 79, 132, 163
nation states 9, 79–84, 86–92, 94, 100–1, 104
   building 94, 105
   and private law building 100–4
national identity 100–3
national laws 13, 17, 36, 64, 66, 82, 148
national private law 79, 90, 94, 96, 102–4
national private legal orders 84–5, 92, 94, 96, 98–9, 102
national regulatory private law, and European regulatory private law 86–9
nationalism 100–1, 103, 153
negotiations 65, 67–8, 116, 120, 135, 140, 180, 188
   contract 58, 62, 66, 135, 152, 205
   pre-contractual 8, 64–6, 68–9, 71–2
new regulatory private law 9, 13, 89, 98
New South Wales, see NSW
New Zealand 10–11, 133–4, 154–5, 157–8, 161–2, 173–6, 183, 198–203
   contract-law codes 173–97
   Contractual Remedies Act 1979 11, 158, 173, 183–94
   Law Commission 161, 174–6, 185, 187, 189, 194, 199–200, 202
   lessons 197–202
   partial codification 165–203
non-business purposes 138, 147
non-disclosure 116; see also disclosure
   innocent 197
   as misrepresentation 196–7
non-state law 22, 30, 36
NSW (New South Wales) 5, 19–21, 24, 136, 143, 171, 173

OAS (Organization of American States) 147
objective approach 179, 181
objective proper law 28, 31–2
obligations 52–3, 57, 64–6, 68–9, 96–7, 107–9, 117, 121
   civil 17, 64, 110
   contractual 33–4, 69, 144

law of 107, 112, 117, 127, 149
  transfer of 45, 47
obligees 45, 47, 53
obligors 53, 66, 121
  plurality of 45, 47
offer 95–6, 124–5, 128–9, 181, 209
OI (optional instrument) 100, 159
opt-in 11, 48, 69, 147–8, 159
optional instrument (OI) 100, 159
Organization of American States (OAS) 147
overseas suppliers 147, 159

PACL (Principles of Asian Contract Law) 49, 111, 154, 158–9
palm tree justice 174
partial codes 11, 171, 173–4, 195, 198, 200–1
  intended 198–9
partial codification 5, 11–13
  New Zealand 165–203
party autonomy 26, 29, 41, 139, 146
PC, see Productivity Commission
PECL (Principles of European Contract Law) 40, 44, 47–8, 64, 69, 91, 94, 111
People's Republic of China, see China
performance 45–6, 48–9, 64–6, 68–9, 71–2, 144, 186, 188
  good faith 67, 72
PICC, see Principles of International Commercial Contracts
plurality of obligors 45, 47
Posner, R.A. 208, 214–15
post-Nation State era 80–1, 83, 91–2, 94, 98, 105
postal services 90, 96–8
powers 80, 107, 157, 162, 173, 177–8, 187, 194
  discretionary 11, 68, 174, 178
  economic 41–2
pre-contractual misrepresentation 184, 197
pre-contractual negotiations 8, 64–6, 68–9, 71–2
precedent 6, 143, 157, 208, 216
preconditions 172, 184, 186, 193, 198
predictability 11–12, 50–1, 54–5, 189, 192, 199, 201, 212

preliminary reference procedures 103–4
Principles of Asian Contract Law, see PACL
Principles of European Contract Law, see PECL
Principles of International Commercial Contracts (PICC) 44, 46–9, 54
prior law 172–3, 183, 187, 191, 195–6, 198
private autonomy 84–7, 103
private international law 7, 15, 17, 19, 22–3, 26, 29, 33–6
  Australia 22–4
private law 7, 9, 39–40, 79–93, 97–100, 102–4, 153–4, 209–10
  as economic law 84
  systems 94–5, 100, 102, 212
  traditional 9, 13, 80, 85, 88–9, 94–6, 98–100, 103–5
private law building, and nation state building 100–4
private legal orders, national 84–5, 92, 94, 96, 98–9, 102
private regulation 13, 81, 84
privity 137, 156, 167, 173–4
procedural policing, Japan 115–16
Productivity Commission (PC) 145–6, 148, 161–2
promissory estoppel 139
proper law 28, 30, 32, 146
  objective 28, 31–2
property 109–10, 179, 186, 191, 210
proportionality principle 95, 104
protection 10, 87, 90, 94, 101, 110, 118, 159
public accessibility 170, 195
public choice theory 215
public policy 25, 35, 114, 123
public services 87, 89–90
public Submissions 132, 142–3, 154

rationality 9, 92–3, 95–6, 105
  single 92
rationalization 9, 92–8
re-codification 9, 107–29
realism 12, 207–9, 214
reasonableness 60, 67, 211, 214

reform 107–10, 112, 137–8, 140–1, 153–4, 160–2, 168–70, 194–6
    contract law 108, 111, 131–2, 140, 142, 146, 161–4, 170
    initiatives 132, 148, 152, 173, 175, 194
    radical 169, 195
    unintended 196, 198
regional instruments on contract law 47–50
regional perspectives 9–12, 77–218
regulated markets 93–4, 96–9
regulatory private law 80–1, 83, 85, 87–9, 91, 93–4, 98, 103
    new 9, 13, 89, 98
relational contracts 133, 166
reliance 10, 20, 62, 72, 142, 181
relief 26, 138, 144, 175–9, 183, 186–7, 190–1, 195–6
remedies, contractual 11, 158, 161–2, 173–5, 183–93, 200–1
repudiation 157–8, 183–7, 192–3, 200
rescission 47, 72, 116, 118, 123–5, 127–9, 185, 187
reservations 51, 53, 102
residential property 134, 190
resources 54, 162, 207, 213
responsibility 100, 118–19, 127–8, 166, 184–5, 193, 196
restatements 58, 66, 71–2, 153–60, 165, 195–6, 205, 217–18
    US 63, 155, 158, 161
restitution 19, 48, 179, 190, 195
rights 43, 45, 47, 65–6, 68, 123–5, 127–8, 191
    abuse of 67, 72, 123
    contractual 134, 140
    strict legal 62, 64, 67, 72
    third party 45, 53
rigidity 11–12
risks 45, 58, 63, 150, 168, 178, 194, 198–9
Rome I Regulation 8, 33–4

sales law 43–4, 48, 100, 164
    Common European Sales Law (CESL) 48, 64, 69–70, 94–5, 97, 100–2, 148–9, 158–60
scope of application 29–30, 34, 53, 113
secured transactions 109–10
self-regulation 81

sellers 32, 135, 150, 209, 211, 218
service, out of the jurisdiction 23–4, 35
services 71, 85, 90–1, 93, 96–7, 99–100, 103, 124–5
    contracts 96–7
    legal 142, 145
    postal 90, 96–8
    public 87, 89–90
services markets 89, 103–4
set-off 45–6, 48, 53
shrinking ambition 113, 116, 120, 122
silence, fraud by 10, 117
simplification 133, 137, 140, 153, 155, 158, 161, 169
SMEs 42, 133, 135, 138, 140, 145, 154, 159–60
social order 9, 85
soliciting 124–5, 129
sources 4, 6, 12, 16, 18, 70, 107, 171–2
    primary 172
standard-form contracts 139, 150, 160
standard-form terms 146, 160
standard terms 10, 42, 53, 114, 118, 120
standardization 81, 97
standards 42, 133, 153, 170
    of conduct 133, 153
    of protection, minimum 138, 140
statutory interpretation 5, 30, 179
statutory interventions 87, 140, 156, 161
strict legal rights 62, 64, 67, 72
strict liability 150, 185
sub-agents 129
submissions 3, 131, 133–41, 143–4, 146, 150–8, 160–4
substance 62, 72, 74, 86, 110–11, 113, 134, 207
substantiality 193, 200
substantive unconscionability 63
suppliers 68, 71, 97, 146–7, 159
    overseas 147, 159
Swiss Civil Code 43
Switzerland 39, 42–3, 51, 97–8
    Supreme Court 42–3
systematization 9, 13, 92–8, 214
systems 7–8, 73–5, 86, 92–4, 96, 173, 209, 211–13
    commonalities, differences and problems 71–4

telecommunications 9, 87–8, 90, 93, 96–9, 103–4
terms 58–61, 63, 86, 135–6, 142, 178, 186–90, 192–3
　intermediate 22, 187
　standard 10, 42, 53, 114, 118, 120
　standard-form 146, 160
　unfair 45, 48, 63–4, 113–14, 118, 136, 150, 156
territorial diversity 82
　and unification of contract law 98–100
territorial integrity 100–1
Teubner, Gunther 8, 73, 92–4
third parties 46, 65, 123, 125, 127–9, 134, 143–4
third party rights 45, 53
time of contract formation 178, 193, 197
tort 17, 19, 23–4, 84, 86, 108–9, 125, 184–5
　choice of law 23, 31
tortious misrepresentation 184
trade 20, 32, 58, 67, 72, 157
　international 7–8, 39–40, 46, 50–1, 55, 64, 67, 148
Trade Practices Act 17, 20–1, 24, 138
trading partners 8, 32, 36, 59, 61, 148–9, 169
　major 132, 148–9, 151, 166
traditional private law 9, 13, 80, 85, 88–9, 94–6, 98–100, 103–5
transaction costs 50, 55, 143, 149, 152, 215
transactions 62–3, 67, 70–1, 110, 120, 138, 158–9, 179
　consumer 96, 147
　economic 9, 85
　international 15, 36, 41, 161, 200
　secured 109–10
transfer of obligations 45, 47
transparency 10, 109–11
transplants 8, 72–3
transport 87–8, 90, 96–9

UCC (Uniform Commercial Code) 6, 11–12, 63–4, 66–7, 107, 209–11, 213, 217–18
UK, see United Kingdom
uncertainties 8, 10, 134, 136–7, 145, 159, 193, 200
UNCITRAL (United Nations Commission on International Trade Law) 43, 46–7, 51–2, 54, 150, 159, 164
unconscientious assertions 72, 74
unconscionability 10, 16, 35, 58–64, 71, 137, 159, 194
　understandings of 61–3
unconscionable conduct 71, 138–9
undue influence 53, 175, 194–6
unfair contract terms, see unfair terms
unfair contracts 113, 116, 161, 194
unfair terms 45, 48, 63–4, 113–14, 118, 136, 150, 156
unfairness, contractual 113, 155, 195
UNIDROIT 46–7, 49, 54, 154, 164
UNIDROIT Principles of International Commercial Contracts 18, 22, 34–6, 44, 46–7, 64, 66–7, 111
unification of contract law 36, 39–55, 107
　and territorial diversity 98–100
Uniform Commercial Code, see UCC
uniform contract law 40–1
　need for 40–3
uniformity 28, 52–3, 55, 68, 112, 136, 207, 212
unilateral mistakes 178, 180
United Kingdom 40, 44, 97, 101, 149–50, 152, 172, 176
United Nations Commission on International Trade Law, see UNCITRAL
United States 6, 40, 42, 132, 134, 149, 154–6, 205–6
　American Law Institute (ALI) 154–5, 158, 195
　building theories into a Code 217–18
　codification and discussion about how judges decide cases 205–18
　common law 206–7, 213
　deciding cases 213–14
　doing things with rules 206–9
　doing things with theories 215–16

explaining adjudication 214–15
Restatements 63, 155, 158, 161
UCC (Uniform Commercial Code) 6, 11–12, 63–4, 66–7, 107, 209–11, 213, 217–18
using a Code 209–13
unjust enrichment 108–9, 194–5
US, see United States

validity 7, 41, 48–9, 53, 108, 115, 135, 159–60

Vienna Sales Convention 21–2, 54, 59, 135, 150, 166, 218
von Gierke, Otto 86–7
vulnerable groups 139, 153

weaker parties 8, 41, 63, 90, 94
  Australia 31–2
Webb v. McGowin 208–9
Western Australia 136, 143
World Bank 98–9
World Trade Organization (WTO) 39, 43–4